D0899461

Beyond the Realms of Morning

a circumnavigation that reveals my personal journey

Joanna + Tony . . .
meeting nice friends is a
bonus to this sailing business, .

Mary Lou Miller
port canaveral April '02

Beyond the Realms of Morning

a circumnavigation that reveals my personal journey

Mary Lois Miller

Old Mountain Press

Published by:
Old Mountain Press, Inc.
2542 S. Edgewater Dr.
Fayetteville, NC 28303

www.oldmountainpress.com

© 2001 Mary Lois Miller

ISBN: 1-884778-98-4
Library of Congress Control Number: 2001092009

Beyond the Realms of Morning: a circumnavigation that   reveals my personal journey
Printed and bound in the United States of America. All rights reserved. Except for brief excerpts used in reviews, no portion of this work may be reproduced or published without expressed written permission from the author or the author's agent.

First Edition
Manufactured in the United States of America
1 2 3 4 5 6 7 8 9 10

CONTENTS

*And I have felt a presence
that disturbs me with joy
of elevated thoughts;
A sense sublime of something
far more deeply interfused,
Whose dwelling is the light of setting suns,
And the round ocean and the living air,
And the blue sky, and the mind of man:
A motion and a spirit,
that impels all thinking things,
All objects of thought,
And rolls through all things.*

-Wordsworth *'Tintern Abby'*

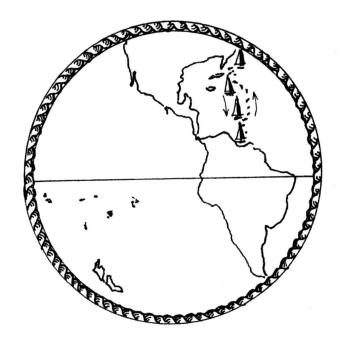

Maine to Venezuela to Annapolis

CHAPTER 1
BUTTERFLY SAILS

A narrow passage, twelve feet long, with the ceiling just above my fingertips and a floor that rarely stays level, is defining the surroundings that will now shelter our lives as we move into a world of discovery. 'So confining,' friends say, 'You must be mad'. . 'You'll have to be exceptionally good friends'. . 'It'll never work'. . 'We'll see you again in six months' - and so on. This chatter from the naysayers continues as we doggedly move into this narrow space. We plan to prove them wrong. This confining passage they see is hiding the possibilities we see.

The days and years ahead will reveal not only possibilities but breathtaking moments that hadn't been imagined in early dreams: the reality of being stranded on a remote island with our own initiative the only help available - my personal struggle with doubts about such a voyage as the blue depths of the Pacific stretches in a circumscribed horizon around me - to the exhilaration of first seeing the peaks of Fatu Hiva after thirty-seven days at sea giving a sense of accomplishment new to me - even my transport to a realm beyond reality during the night watch near Tahiti where cradled by *Horizon* while suspended inside a delicate crystal globe somewhere between heaven and earth, a calm sea mirrors the stars - to the awesome vagaries of wind and water that will gently nurture us along a path or like Greek Furies rage at us until exhausted, we heave-to for respite. Finally, feeling the depth of brotherhood we share with companions dwelling on this globe as each brings a unique quality and expression to the vibrant tapestry unfolding. These are possibilities that become reality beyond my wildest dreams. It is their presence that 'disturbs me with joy of elevated thoughts.'

The cocoon sheltering us is our 37-foot cutter rigged sailboat with its twelve-foot passage in the cabin below. A cutter sailboat carries two sails, the jib sail and the smaller staysail, forward of a single mast whereas a sloop carries one sail here. Attached aft of the mast is the boom (a rigid extension) to which the foot of the main sail is secured. Sheltered in this cocoon we will emerge to find the freedom a butterfly must feel as it shakes loose those twig constraining boundaries. Each day we experience the freedom these wings release as our sails swell with the exuberance of the wind. We're exhilarated to attain some new accomplishment or perceive a new vision of this complex world stretching before us. Our wings have become the sails, straining as they catch those winds that will carry us along the equator for three hundred and sixty degrees with some digressions to higher latitudes along the way.

It is 1987. Searching local newspapers will be to no avail for news concerning two grandparents planning to use sailing skills they've earned by the seat of their sail-pants as they embark on this journey of a lifetime, a sailing safari to circumnavigate our planet. Nevertheless it is a headliner day for us as we leave the Ft. Lauderdale dock on this cool, rainy morning, the first week of the New Year.

These skills are a result of many years sailing aboard a 23 foot sailing sloop. Ten years ago when we lived at Elkhart, Indiana, this became our vacation home as we explored the reaches of Lakes Michigan and Huron with our four children. Back and forth across those lakes we sailed, at times beating against the wind. We followed the compass north along the coast of Michigan, past Sleeping Bear Dunes to gaze at that grand cathedral of Mackinac Bridge as we sailed beneath its splendor into fall sailing on Lake Huron. We knew we had found unrivaled possibilities for retirement. To discover the knowledge of the wind's effect on sails and hull would become a new language of life for us.

These last decades of the twentieth century we've looked in awe at views of our planet taken from space. It is beautiful beyond description. Now, in our small craft we will circle that same glorious globe. We are especially thinking of our great, great grandchildren. We will never know you, yet we'd like for you to glimpse our world and to know us. Perhaps these will be strange tales to you, but we want you to know they were accomplished by the same heart, body and soul which you share a part. To you we dedicate these words. You will know us as Mary Lois and Don, mates to your lineage. All these words would be meaningless had not our four children, Dale, Linda, Tom, Steven and their families given us their support and encouragement.

Years before when we were raising our family in Elkhart, Don's interest in sailing grew from a weekend crew member racing small boats with his friend, Bob Barkley, to dreams of some day sailing long distance. By 1980 with our children grown and setting their own agendas and goals, we decided to buy a larger sailboat and become serious about sailing the ocean. We purchased a 37-foot sailboat in Florida. It was built in Taiwan and fulfilled my idea of a classic and a 'classy' look and Don's idea of a fine sailing craft - a Tayana 37` sailboat.

For two years we kept this boat in Florida flying there from Indiana those weeks Don had off from his Emergency Room medical practice. Our first nighttime sail originated here. We crossed the Gulf Stream from Ft. Lauderdale to Gun Cay in the Bahamas. Dodging the abundant freighter traffic as we crossed the Gulf Stream was a rather frightening first step into sailing offshore.

We purchased a satellite navigating instrument called a sat-nav. This personal navigating marvel triangulates fixes from satellites making it possible to keep a position fix on our progress. However, there were times when periods of four or more hours elapsed between up-to-date fixes. Because of this we thought it prudent to use dead reckoning to accompany these latitude and longitude positions. Dead reckoning basically uses compass course, speed and elapsed time to determine position, considering as well, currents and tides. All of this was easier than using the sextant, the navigational tool used for centuries. However, as additional insurance, Don spent many hours using this tool to sight the noon sun as it reached its zenith. At his call of 'mark', I noted the time to determine our position. This valuable information we used years later off the coast of Madagascar when there was a blackout of all satellite information for six days while the U.S. military reprogrammed updates.

In the Bahamas those early years, we discovered a new world of sailing- knowledge waiting. Weather and water challenged our experience. We needed to learn more. The water in the islands is crystal clear, giving an impression the boat is floating on air. Part of the knowledge we gained among the islands was our ability to 'read the water'. As we approached shallow water, the yellow of the sand became apparent through the blue sheen of the water. Those occasional dark patches might be a coral head or a grassy spot. When the sun sent shafts of light into twenty feet of water, the whorls of striated shadows accented with swirls of light took on the rich hues of malachite. The gemstone lending shades of its splendid green to this luminous, liquid dimension. The deeper water was signaled with a rich cobalt blue. The more time we spent in these waters, the easier it was to recognize the differences. We realized the importance of this knowledge thousands of miles later in the Pacific atolls where navigation among the coral reefs relied on this valued and useful tool.

With Don's license to fly a small airplane we discovered an airstrip stretching down the back of a lovely Bahamian Island, Staniel Cay, centered among the Exuma chain of islands. This gave us an idea to extend our range of sailing experience. With the good care of Birkie Rolle, who consented to monitor *Horizon* while moored at Staniel Cay, we flew there with food supplies for a two week sail around the Exumas without having to sail across the Gulf Stream each trip. We did this for two years until Don's retirement in 1984 at age 57.

That July, with our family together at a rented vacation house on the New Jersey coast, we made our farewells to a land-oriented life style and extended invitations for the family to join us as we sailed the East Coast. Our home was sold. We were ready to move aboard *Horizon*. Knowing warm weather would still be with us for several months, we set the autopilot to a heading of 055 degrees that brought us face to face with our first experience sailing through dense fog. To hear the buoy clanging off the Cape Cod coast assured me that Don's reliance on the sat-nav to find this spot, with foggy curtains drawn round the boat, was warranted.

We recognized manning a watch on long passages would become another safety requirement for us. As nightfall descends I begin my watch. Sitting alone in the cockpit with Don asleep below, I question my ability to distinguish weather changes that demand my response. The first night out is always my hardest. As darkness encloses me, I feel isolated. The points of reference are lost. There's no horizon - lights vanish offshore. I pray for clear skies that place me under stars' guidance. Subsequent evenings I follow a routine that allows me to relax and enjoy the stars or the luminescent trail we make through the water. I develop a schedule to check the sails, log the compass, sat-nav, the wind and cloud formations, that allows more peace of mind. The clouds at night lose their buoyant, fluffy daytime quality. They pose a threat to me with their dark heavy shapes. I try to determine whether theirs is a non-threatening appearance or cause for me to reduce sail. For my watch, Don usually rigs the sails with the smaller staysail and a reefed mainsail. Reefing a sail reduces the size of the sail. This gives me an easily handled configuration for wind speeds of 15 to 20 knots. If the wind lessens I can add muscle to this equation by increasing the size of the jib, the sail furled on the forward stay. Stays and shrouds are cables from the hull of the boat supporting the mast. I can handle this large sail from the cockpit. Early on, as we sailed the East Coast, the Bahamas, and the following year continuing down the Leeward and Windward Islands of the Caribbean, we used a six-hour watch schedule for the night watches. During the day, we were both up and about to share the watch.

Recalling those early years, we found our sailing skills improving enough that we pushed on south beyond the Bahamas into the Caribbean Sea. By November of 1985 we sailed south to the Virgin Islands, adding one more page to our book of knowledge - the page of paperwork that's required to be a guest of another country. The unique beauty of a landscape and its people compensates the mounting frustration when completing our clearance into a country. How exhilarating to add new flags to our growing collection: St.Thomas, St.Martin, Guadeloupe, Martinique, Bequia, Mustique, Granada and Venezuela, all contributing their colorful signatures to our flag locker. With each new stop, we realized it was time to really get serious about a circumnavigation.

We left Venezuela in late spring of '86 and beat a path north to New York where we joined our families in July to celebrate the refurbished Statue of Liberty festivities. Partying aboard *Horizon* in New York harbor with Don's niece, Cheryl, and her family, my sis, Anne with her family and son, Dale, his wife Linda and eleven month old Amanda, just back from London - it was a fireworks affair. Catching our breath, we decided it's time to get to work.

For three years we logged many miles on the nuts and bolts, canvas and fiberglass of *Horizon* prompting us to sail to Annapolis where our knowledgeable friend, John Potter would help us prepare for the voyage. So with redo, repair and refurbish, we spent the fall of '86 working until we were seaworthy again. I read in Shakespeare's Tempest - 'Our ship is tyte and yare'- translated this means, *"Our ship is seaworthy, manageable and answers readily to the helm."* This seemed to summarize our readiness to begin this dream of a lifetime.

With boat parts of every description filling the bunks, on the counters and under the table, Don reminded me of a watchmaker those days in Annapolis while he fitted each to its proper site. We stored replacement parts in lockers. Items we planned to use for barter along the way found their place in the remaining nooks and crannies. In reality, we were carrying a second boat under the covers in bits and pieces. The last challenging chore became stowing food staples. A nearby supermarket filled our order for cases of canned tomatoes, mushroom soup, green beans, spinach, pears, peaches, coffee, tea, toilet paper and towels, twelve dozen eggs (they needed no fridge if rubbed with shortening), sugar, flour, cereal and other delights we hoped to enjoy for the next six months. As we unloaded cases of canned goods into the dinghy, load after load, it was amazing that *Horizon* seemed to have no problem grasping all of this into her remaining bins and lockers. With some evening courses studying French to fuel the fantasy we'd be ready to greet new friends in French Polynesia, preparations seemed complete.

With so many good people helping us while we struggled to make our water world safe and comfortable, we threw a party for all on shore at John Potters' Ocean Outfitters boatyard. The next morning, heralding an icy, gray November day, the lines tying us to shore were thrown aboard. We hoisted the sails as a stiff breeze blew across Annapolis. Sailing down the Chesapeake Bay, we tried not to slip on the icy decks. Both of us were wrapped in layers of sweaters, down-vests, caps and mittens. We even carried this warm accompaniment to bed when our watch was complete. The North Pole seemed a likely destination instead of our planned voyage across the South Seas.

Since earlier trips usually found us sailing the Atlantic Ocean, just offshore, we planned this trip to explore the Intracoastal Waterway south to Florida. It's really a lovely journey through the salt marshes. Here we saw the cormorants, their outstretched wings drying as they perched on the waterway markers, while near shore the beautiful white egrets, standing on one leg, were poised to catch a fish. The white sails of other boats seemed to be making impossible passages through grass as the waterway coursed a wandering path through the marshes. Careful sailing is required along the narrow course of the waterway with many boats traveling north and south. Because the northern boats known as 'snowbirds' were heading for that warm weather south this time of year, most of the traffic was joining our path for temperate climes.

By Christmas we anchored off Rodriquez Cay just offshore from Key Largo with all our North Pole clothing packed as deep in the locker as possible. We were tidying up and hanging decorations in anticipation of a last family celebration with my sis, Anne, her husband Lynn, and daughter Dana. They were here from Denver on vacation from their teaching. With good fun snorkeling on the reef, frustrating fishing results and great restaurant finds, the week passed quickly. The visit was filled with their enthusiasm for our watery lifestyle. They agreed what fun it would be to join us somewhere out there in the world. They would work on planning such a visit. We hugged, shed a few tears and waved goodbye as they dinghied to shore.

With one last stop in Ft. Lauderdale before heading for the Bahamas we met good friends from Indiana, Bob and Marilyn Barkley with daughter, Julie, to join in a toast celebrating the New Year 1987. We took advantage of their car to stock up with fresh food that completed our larder. On a rainy day that first week in January we turned and waved farewell to our friends, then boarded *Horizon*.

Ready to begin this dream of a lifetime.

Don shooting the sun to determine our position.

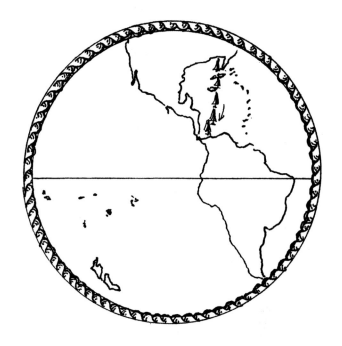

Florida to Jamaica to San Blas

CHAPTER 2
TO REACH BEYOND

Enough dreaming and remembering, the time has arrived, the world beckons and *Horizon* stretches her sails to leave the familiar and predictable lives we have enjoyed, to a world of discovery and new challenges. Reading about the Portuguese Prince of Explorers, Henry the Navigator, who encouraged his country's mariners in 1432 to chart unknown passages, to reach beyond their known world and expand their knowledge of the seas resonates a theme we are feeling. We have been handed the knowledge. Ours is the choice to use it and reach beyond the established patterns of our lives - beyond the expected - *'beyond the realms of morning'* - Prince Henry's challenge to his seamen.

This first leg through the Bahamas will ease us into this new world. We have frequently sailed these waters with their familiar anchorages now ready to welcome us once more. Holding the new video camera, I take a picture of the moon rising ahead of us then turn to catch the last glimpse of an outstanding sunset behind us. Our path leads us southeasterly through the Turks and Caicos Islands.

A rendezvous in Jamaica arranged to meet our daughter and her friend, Paul early in February, has us hurrying to Port Antonio on the northeast corner of this country. Relishing the exotic greenery including orchids hanging in exquisite hues over our heads, we are poled on bamboo rafts down the rippling rapids of Jamaican rivers. We watch the clean butchering of pigs along the road and enjoy eating the barbecued jerk-pork with its traditional spicy flavor. Dr. Bob and Mary Ellis from Elkhart, where he was a part of the medical staff with Don, are visiting their birthplace. They extend an invitation to join them at their home here on the island. With fascinating stories they share their love of this country as we enjoy a wonderful Jamaican dinner by candlelight.

By the end of February we continue sailing southwest to discover a culture unlike any we have known before. We drop our anchor beside *Sloop du Jour* and her crew, David and Susan, who wave us welcome. With their good information to navigate around the San Blas Islands, we drop our anchor at a spot just off the small island, Nargana, where we see thatch huts and hammocks under swaying palm trees. San Blas is home to the Kuna Indians, a self-governing indigenous tribe under the protection of Panama. The Indians are short and with my five-foot height I can look over their heads crowned in shiny black hair. Seeing their dancing dark eyes and their broad smiles, we do feel welcome. They are generous as they share their islands in the visits we make with them. A great grandmother, Carolina 72 years old, chuckles at and tries to help my faltering Spanish each time we come ashore. We become good friends. I am sure of getting a hug with her greeting 'mi amiga Maria Luisa' when I come ashore. The handwork the women are sewing with a kind of reverse appliqué, is vibrant in designs depicting animals and flowers. These 'molas' are created with the tiniest stitches into squares suitable for framing. We purchase several of them. I am delighted when Carolina's daughter agrees to sell me a sundress she is hand sewing. It boldly displays parrots amid blossoms appliqued down the front with an intricate Grecian key design along the bottom.

We share the anchorage with four other sailboats, one each from England, Germany, Greece and *Sloopy*. Don caught a 2-foot grouper today while fishing with Tomas, a native father of twins. This evening we dinghy ashore for a cookout around the campfire. Over plates of grilled fish we share sailing information. We realize that yachtsmen are a pretty independent bunch that rarely sail in groups, preferring to determine their own pace, whether it is time spent at an anchorage or the time of departure. Since we had already established this lifestyle as our own sailing pattern, it is reassuring to know there are others who have similar ideas about passage making. Before we leave these islands we embark on friendships with two more couples aboard *Sunshine* and *Rhinoceros.* Friendships that continue to flourish as we make our way around the world together.

It's time to move on to Panama to meet the challenge of maneuvering through the locks awaiting us. Somewhere in my thinking, I consider the Panama Canal a western wall containing to its east, the familiar waters of the Caribbean and, if we can clamber over it, waiting to the west is a whole new world. A world unknown but I keep reminding myself, a world of water that shouldn't be that different from the world of water we have already experienced. Can it be Eden ahead?

We anchor in the large anchorage at the east end of the canal with the large rather threatening city of Colon on shore. Recently teenagers have targeted visitors, robbing them at knifepoint. However, the helpfulness of taxi drivers, who escort you into the building at a destination, makes up for their mischief. Knowing this is our last access to easy phone calls to the family before departure, we spend considerable time talking with each of our children, my mother now 85 years old and siblings. Farewells are always hard, but especially troublesome is the news that Anne, my sister, has been diagnosed with breast cancer. Our conversation is interlaced with tears. She declares she will conquer this battle, insisting she and Lynn still plan to spend time with us in Fiji next year. I assure her we look forward to it. Our two families have enjoyed so many great times together skiing and hiking the Rockies. The news, however, really takes the wind out of my sails.

The anchorage is full of sailboats from around the world. Boats of every description and size are waiting to pass through those enormous gates to that world beyond. One evening we are invited aboard *Mah-Jong*, a Danish ferro-cement sailboat made by the couple, Kaj and Monika, now aboard. Their profession as restaurateurs is obvious as we enjoy a delicious dinner. Afterwards, Kaj with his haunting accompaniment on the guitar sings Danish folksongs that resonate with his wonderful baritone voice. We see among the dozens of boats anchored, our friends, Jim and Jimmie aboard *Sunshine* and Charles and Cornelia on *Rhinoceros.*

News is circulating through the fleet of sailboats that the canal will be closed to all traffic for two weeks of routine maintenance. Not only is the small boat anchorage full, the large tankers and cruise ships are filling their anchorage as well. This gives us time to meet other sailors and sort out information that is spinning through the anchorage. It seems everyone is buying the cheap seven-gallon vegetable oil jugs from the marina restaurant to store extra fuel for the long Pacific passage.

In order to make the canal passage our sailboat has to be measured and processed before we make arrangements for line handlers to help with the tying of our lines to the sides of the locks. Since each lock holds nine sailboats, three rafts of three boats each, this makes it possible to help each other through the canal and gain experience on the whole process. Before your transit, you can acquire this skill by signing on as a line-handler for friends as they take their vessel through the canal. A train ride will bring you back to this anchorage to ready your passage.

Finally, April 2nd arrives. We motor forward to the immense doors of the first lock. As we wait outside with each boat now having aboard a Panamanian adviser and three line handlers, three sailboats are tied together as one broad raft. The large doors slowly swing open. Just as slowly a cumbersome raft ahead of us is awkwardly making its way into the lock ahead. We pay attention to their maneuvers as we start our move in behind them. Then the last of our three rafts enters. Those enormous doors gradually close once more. Here we sit isolated in this huge tank with walls reaching, what seem like a mile above us; a tiny blue rectangle of sky trying to find us huddled in this watery nest.

Now we watch as our own line handlers show their stuff. We are fortunate to find a lady, DJ, living for several years near the canal, who often hires on to help boats through. Could she ever sling that line! With a large knot tied on one end, she tosses this to the dockworker standing up there a mile away! With her trim body attired to show its beauty, we receive prompt attention. We also hire two brothers, Tom and Joe from England, good handlers as well, earning their way back home. When all three rafts are tied securely, the water begins swirling into the lock. It really is turbulent. With the water roiling like a boiling cauldron, one of the boats in the raft behind us tears loose from its lines then is flung against the sidewall. The churning water immediately stops. There doesn't seem to be major damage to the yacht. That raft again ties its lines more securely. We surge once more to reach the high-water mark. With the lock full of water, the front doors open ahead of us. With a short, clumsy ride the three rafts slowly make their way along the waterway and into the second lock. Following this, there is one more lock to surmount. Finally we are in Lake Gatun, high in the mountains of interior Panama.

We enter this mountaintop lake just after lunch. The rafts are disassembled. Knowing we still have quite a distance to go, sails are hauled and we are underway. During the day, as we make our way across Lake Gatun, we follow in the wake of the large ships and tankers, reminding us just how small we are. The locks holding these giants ran parallel to ours. Following the channel markers across the lake we arrive close to the descending locks that will be our journey tomorrow.

Our Panamanian adviser points out a small anchorage where we anchor for the night. We are now anchored in the famous Galliard Cut. Laborers in 1910 blasted away eight miles of rock through the mountains to construct the locks on the western slope. Water from Lake Gatun is used to operate the locks toward the Pacific Ocean. This marvel of engineering has often been called the eighth wonder of the world.

Our adviser goes ashore for the night assuring us he will return tomorrow. Here we are in fresh water, a pleasure we haven't enjoyed since leaving Elkhart all those years ago. While there is still daylight, everyone, including our happy bunch of line handlers, dives overboard to swim and splash with crews of other boats anchored nearby.

This evening, as we sit in the cockpit enjoying our spaghetti supper, we recall the day's events. Each of the three boats in each raft has a Panamanian adviser aboard. The directives they give to the owners who stand at the helm are, many times, contradictory. *Horizon* is tied as an outside boat of the raft. The two outside boats with motors running, remain in gear to help maintain the raft's position in the lock. Several times our adviser would tell Don to put the boat in forward gear while the adviser in the center boat instructed Don to engage reverse. It became a contest among these three advisers just who held the most authority. Frustrated, the owners finally told them to coordinate their commands. At this time, Panama is in the beginning process to administer the canal and, no doubt we are early in their learning curve. As I recall this trip, I rank it low on the scale of pleasurable experiences logged on my entire world voyage.

The next morning with the Panamanian advisers aboard the sailboats, we again tie together in raft formations. Slowly we motor into the first of the three locks that will drop us to sea level. Now we sit high in the water of the lock. The surrounding landscape, its bare cliffs in stark relief with opuntia cactus thrusting through crevices, presents a distinctive silhouette of bold outlines, in contrast to the jungley shores of Lake Gatun. The lines tying us to the bollards along the edge of the lock again need to be adjusted as the water gently lowers in the tank. Through the first lock, we are separated to cross the smaller Millaflores Lake, then rafted again to bob as corks in the remaining two locks. Not knowing what to expect, the gentle descent of the water is a surprise. The whole crew relaxes as we enjoy the three locks down. Out of the last lock, our raft is separated as we form a line to motor a short distance down the waterway then round a curve. Suddenly, Panama City glistens in the afternoon sun as it climbs over hillsides stretching ahead. We drop our adviser and the three handlers off at the Balboa dock, pay their fees and express our thanks for helping bring us safely to the Pacific Ocean. They wish us farewell and good luck.

Again it is late in the afternoon. Rather than anchor in the very full anchorage, we continue along the waterway to a quiet spot offering protection from strong winds. We drop the anchor here for the night. It's been an exhausting day - sleep comes easily. The next morning with the sun shining, our spirits are revived. Since Don received a favorable weather report over the ham radio, we decide to leave. The Perles Islands, about 75 miles south of us, will be our next stop.

The following day as we pass one of the islands of this group, our noses twitch with the strong odor in the air. Using binoculars, we see hundreds of birds perched on the rocks and cliffs that define this island. Checking our chart we see it's a bird sanctuary. The barren island is covered with their droppings called guano, giving the appearance of snow covered rocks. The air is heavy with its distinctive pungent aroma. We move on. A small bay at a nearby island offers protection and fresh breezes. We spend the night at anchor here before our last leap from the sight of any land.

Today these islands harbor a bad reputation. Reports of thefts aboard boats continue to be a constant threat. We pick the one island known to be friendly. The ham radio license Don received while we were in Annapolis is already reflecting the benefits it offers. We keep in touch with other boats on our same trek where information like the Pearl Islands keeps us abreast of valuable data.

Across Pacific Ocean to Fatu Hiva

CHAPTER 3
INTRO to the PACIFIC - 101

We haul the anchor before dawn. Unlike any college course I've ever taken, I am about to embark on a curriculum that doesn't allow auditing or dropout. My education is about to unfold with 'learn as you go' experiences. In anticipation, the credits I receive will fulfill more than the usual requirements.

Contemplating this circumnavigation as I sit here on the bow of our sailboat we've christened *Horizon* and look ahead, I see no horizon. The blue of the Pacific Ocean has merged with the azure sky - there is no visible line, it's truly a study in shades of blue. Stretching back I look overhead. The brilliant blue sky holds a translucent dimension that expands to that invisible horizon where it reaches to grasp a cobalt blue plunging to depths beyond my comprehension. As I recall our decision process to engage in such an adventure, to circumnavigate, it too, seems to have been a smooth transition. Remembering the events and thoughts that composed the beginnings of our voyage, I find they are much like this view with no horizon visible. Don and I grew into the possibility of a life at sea gradually . . . a smooth passage.

The dreams Don had of such a journey were more defined than those I held. I could sense the determination and excitement he had, to realize a move away from the demands on him as an Emergency Room physician at two hospitals, to that of a simpler life. Perhaps I can muster the same enthusiasm, but somehow the expanse of water offering little protection or help from any neighbor, makes me reluctant to hoist my sail on his dream.

With the western lock of the Panama Canal closed behind us, I am surprised to see a calm ocean stretching ahead. Then looking over my shoulder at the last rim of the Pearl Islands growing faint, a big cloud of doubt rises to shake the conviction that we have chosen the right path. It is big out here. This cocoon of a boat suddenly seems tiny on the vast horizon I see stretching ahead. This shell has been our home for three years. I have felt safe in its ability to provide safety and comfort. Such experience will need to be my security blanket while I adjust to this new voyage. The sailing that we did these last years was charted along or near coastlines from Maine to Venezuela and offered a safety quotient that I'm not easily feeling, estimating our next landfall will be thirty-some days away.

Nurturing these doubts as I sit on the bowsprit, I turn to look longingly over my shoulder at the receding haze of land. I am reminded of our first child, Dale, as he left the house, turning to wave as he walked to his first day of school. Such anxiety was in those blue eyes. His whole body language expressed his fear of the unknown. Today I identify with that fear. Looking at Don I see only his exhilaration. He doesn't identify with such thoughts. To him, it's a challenge worth exploring. He doesn't realize he's carrying my hesitancy on his shoulders. Although the same blue sky stretches over us both, I am doubtful we share the same horizon. However, I am determined this baggage of mine shall not spoil the experience.

For the next two weeks we arrange the schedule that will afford a comfortable routine to live by. About 7:30 a.m. Don is talking on the ham radio, sharing positions, weather and jokes with other boats, boats that could be hundreds of miles away. There are times that his medical expertise is sought over this public forum. After a breakfast of fried potatoes and eggs or omelets or pancakes or sometimes oatmeal, maybe just toast and jam, we set about this small environment to maintain or clean.

The sailing is behaving very well, perhaps for my benefit. The winds of ten to fifteen knots keep us moving along with speeds of five to six knots. As a unit of speed, a knot is slightly faster than a mile - five knots are approximately equal to six miles an hour. We installed an Aries autopilot that is geared to the helm; with its wind-vane off the stern it will automatically steer the boat in a fixed position to the wind. Days may pass when the helm or the sails need no adjustment or with just a tweak or two to its gears, the Aries will have us back on course. In addition to this steering apparatus, we also have an electric automatic steering device available when the wind dies or becomes very light. With these two automatic resources for guiding the boat, the fatigue factor is greatly reduced. We are free to read, study our French or Don tunes the guitar to practice 'Will you Still Love Me When I am Old and Gray?' It's prudent on a voyage of this kind - in this limited space - to foster congeniality. We have years ahead to love, honor and obey. And to answer some of the questions of finance that Uncle Wilbur raised before we left, we'll be able to assure him that cash out of pocket for these thirty-seven days was zero.

As our course takes us closer to the equator we begin to sail into the trade wind belt where the southeasterly flow of wind becomes a steady ten to fifteen knots. These winds carry us with such steady assurance. I try to imagine what might be the source of their strength. Have they tumbled down the slopes of the Andes in Peru, perhaps bringing zephyrs from Machu Picchu with ancient rhythms of Inca glory? Or have they swept thru the treacheries of Tierra del Fuego to thrust north along the South American coast, tamed to spin a circle of trade winds along the equator that send us on this buoyant journey?

On the morning of April 12 with the last glimpse of the Perles Islands now ten days past we see a smudge along the horizon hinting of land once again. Recognizing this outline with its ever-so-faint presence reminds me of the mark I make while sketching. Using my finger to create a smudge along a pencil line seems to suggest far away land. There on the distant horizon is this growing blur, gradually emerging into its distinctive shape. A shape that defines the low lying hills of Isla Pinta, one of the smaller northern islands of the Galapagos Archipelago.

For the next four days we average only fifty miles each day. The previous ten days we enjoyed good winds pushing us at least one hundred twenty miles each twenty-four hour period. Now this fifty miles breaks down to about two miles an hour. Before long we are putting up with the sails slapping and slating against themselves in an ever-bothersome staccato cadence as they search for a breeze. Although we had tied along the lifelines on both sides of the boat, those eight jerry jugs of extra fuel purchased in Panama, we now hesitate to run the engine beyond the necessary time needed to maintain the fridge and freezer. Not knowing what demands for fuel we might need when navigating close to land, we decide to keep this a sailing experience here on the open sea. The winds become so light and erratic that Don decides to dive overboard into the calm sea and scrape off some of the barnacles beginning to accumulate along the waterline. I try to dismiss images of the ocean's depth where he is casually swimming.

Drifting across my thoughts are those vivid words from Coleridge's 'Rime of the Ancient Mariner' - "*Day after day - day after day, We stuck - no breath - nor motion; As idle as a painted ship Upon a painted ocean.*" By April 14, still flopping around on a flat sea, a radio message comes through from our ham contact, Jake Swartzendruber in Indiana, that Lindsey Betts Miller has made her tiny presence known on this earth. The day is suddenly aglow. We celebrate life's continuity. With a fitting display, the evening sky applauds as it bursts forth with a double rainbow, ablaze in its mirror image against a deep purple evening background. It becomes a delicate and beautiful cord stretching from our tiny place on the planet to that promising point where family is blooming. Knowing there will be celebration in Seattle with the proud parents, Dale and Linda and sister Amanda, we too, make our special ceremony. With the balloons somewhere aboard, we find them and blow them up to dance buoyantly from the flag pole while we sing 'happy birthday' to our fourth grandchild - all grand daughters. Natasha, the oldest was born three years before, as we waited in Beaufort, NC before taking off on the sail south to Venezuela. It becomes obvious to me there will be a lot of catching up to do before we learn to know these very special girls, Natasha, Amanda, Michelle and now Lindsey.

By April 19, Easter Sunday, we are crossing the equator with good wind again, making one hundred and forty-five miles one day. We are rolling now with the birds from nearby Galapagos circling the boat as they try to figure out this strangely moving tree. Finally gaining courage, one hovers over the rail on the bowsprit to make a shaky landing. Encouraged by their leader, four more birds perform the same precarious landing. Since there is room for only four large blue-footed boobies at one time, the one left flying dives in to push a buddy off. This continues for half an hour as they play musical chairs on the bow of the boat. Meanwhile alongside, dolphin are diving and displaying their awesome gymnastics with leaps and cartwheels as they play tag with the boat and our bow wave. All this entertainment prompts us to lay aside the books we've been reading and watch the wildlife darting around us. Such a front row seat as this fills us with awe. We become aware that we are not alone on this vast global expanse.

After two weeks, our towels and bedding need a washing machine. *Horizon* lacks such luxury. Because I'd been warned about large thirsty turkish towels and the difficulties they present at laundry time, I purchased large hand towel sizes for our bathing. Pondering the task at hand, we are presented with the ideal solution. As the wind is diminishing, a quiet and steady rainfall starts to fall. Where the deck joins the hull on *Horizon* there is an eight inch wall called a bulwark. This outlines the gunwale, a walkway on the deck where the rain is streaming. We quickly dam the scuppers (drains) along the bulwark with foam rubber, then bring out the sheets and towels along with the few clothes we've been wearing. Tossing this pile inside the gunwale now filling with water, we proceed to shake soap powder over all as we join each other in the *Horizon* two-step. It is a first rate washing machine even to the last rinse. Just as we finish the rain dance, right on schedule, the sun begins to shine. There's still no wind so we drape the sheets over the boom and pin towels and t-shirts along the lifelines. By bedtime there is fresh linen on the bed and the bath, or nautically speaking, the 'head' is now sweet with fluffy towels. Our spirits soar. We are beginning to recognize that in this new lifestyle, it is these small episodes that bring great joy - the gift of simplicity.

Another joy out here on this vast expanse is the occasional fish we catch. Our success at fishing never matches that of other sailboats, but we are able to have all the fish we need. With our 200-lb.test line dragging behind the boat we catch tuna, mackerel and dorado fish. Don cleans it in the gunwale then I package the fillets into meal sized servings. That first meal always includes slender slices of sushi we cut from the tenderloin to dip in a soy or horseradish sauce . . a delicate, delicious sunset appetizer. While in Panama, we bought fifty pounds of potatoes. These are an appealing addition to our diet, but now after twenty days with the temperature in the nineties day in and day out, it's important to sort through these and heave the bad ones. There is no stronger odor than a rotten potato - except, perhaps, that island in the Perles.

The sailing is going well with all sails flying. We continue to log from one hundred-twenty to our fastest, one hundred-sixty miles a day. An added safety quotient that we religiously adhere to is wearing a safety harness when we step from the cockpit to the deck. We clip onto a line (called a jack-line) that is stretched from the cockpit to the bow. This insures we are attached to the boat should a sudden wave cause us to lose our balance. There is one nightmare that continues to disturb our thinking. To come topsides when your watch begins and realize the boat is sailing along with your mate nowhere on-board is a lingering, haunting fear.

We have observed only two other sailboats on the distant horizon. The sky stays clear of airplanes or their contrails as we chart our course across the longitudes. The Pacific Ocean has lived up to its name. My doubts about such an adventure are tumbling overboard as each mile passes under the hull. We continue to chart our progress across the Pacific with this path slowly taking us ten degrees south of the equator.

Because the wind continues to push us along with its fifteen to twenty knots, we have the spinnaker flying for several days. This balloon of a sail, billowing at the bow, pulls us along with its flashes of brilliant sunset colors. It is constructed of light but strong parachute-like fabric. The only constraints to its energy are the sheets (lines) tied to the corners of the sail. These give the appearance of a team of horses, straining as they prance smartly across the waves driven with dexterity by the yaw of these reins. Suddenly, one afternoon, crashing into the sea beside us, this enormous sail begins sinking. With its sheets still attached to the boat, we struggle to pull it aboard as we try to spill the water trapped in its enormous envelope. With great effort, we finally pull it aboard. The seam across the top triangle has split. The sewing box comes out as I hand- sew this seam as sturdily as possible. With only a few days remaining, we decide to continue with the mainsail and jib as the energy source and stuff the spinnaker in its bag.

All is going well when one of the aluminum struts that secures the Aries wind-vane to our boat, breaks. This whole steering apparatus is swinging wildly off the stern. Don tries to rig a broom handle as a support but with the strain inherent in this equipment, it too, soon breaks. To continue our path, the Aries is disengaged and the backup electric autopilot is connected with its little motor making grinding noises while it holds our course.

Over the ham radio, the morning of May 12, comes a shout from *Cool Change* excitedly announcing they've just anchored in a tiny bay of Fatu Hiva, the southern island of the Marquesas. Our two boats have never met but we've become acquainted over the ham radio. We sailed along similar paths, never seeing each other the entire trip. Binoculars in hand, we scan the western horizon, thinking we are getting close enough for a visual confirmation. Trusting the accuracy of our navigation these past thirty-seven days will provide an occasion to celebrate. Sure enough, there it is, just that wisp on the horizon. We pan back and forth with the binoculars to make sure it hasn't been an illusion. Our elation leaves us speechless until Don lets out one celebratory 'Yahoo' as he lowers the sails. With a new sense of accomplishment we motor around the magnificent tall peaks that are Fatu Hiva.

Hoisting sail as the Pacific stretches ahead.

Looking forward to good meals from this dorado fish.

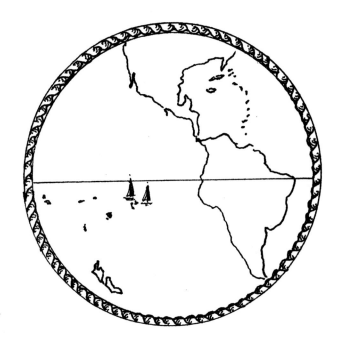

French Polynesia–Marquesas and Tuomotos

CHAPTER 4
QU'EST-CE QUI SE DIT?

With a short motor ride along the western shore of this steep island we gaze transfixed as the bay at Hanavave unfolds before us. What a sight! This v-shaped bay draws our attention into a deep valley guarded by majestic rocky pinnacles like magnificent carved gods standing in regal splendor along its sheer slopes. Ahead, along the floor of the valley a village is nestled under tall palm trees, their fronds dancing in a sweeping motion as the wind funnels through this garden-like setting. A small shore of black pebbles lies ahead where steep waves are constantly breaking with a foamy remnant spilling and rattling the shingled beach. Getting ashore is going to be a real challenge. Getting ashore is a big reason we have made this journey.

Talking by radio to the four boats anchored here confirms our depth sounder datum - the bay is ninety feet deep. Being familiar with ten to twenty foot anchorages in the Caribbean we hadn't bargained on an anchorage this deep. It's not bad lowering the anchor with enough scope to insure safe anchoring, it's the challenge of raising all that line and chain when ready to move on. At this time we have a hand operated anchor windlass that brings the anchor up one slow chain-link at a time while we crank the long handle back and forth. There's no other choice, the anchor and all the line and chain we have, three hundred feet, goes overboard. In previous anchorages, Don was quick to point out the female crewmember hauling in the anchor at the bow of a neighboring boat. This puzzle concerning a crewmember's responsibility stayed with him the entire voyage. His duties as anchor person had been established early in our sailing curriculum. I assured him it had not been a requirement to complete my mariner's course.

Making its way toward us is a dinghy being rowed by a pretty young girl. Sitting with her is a towheaded boy and their father. Dad, with a red bandana tied around his head and a black beard flowing across his chest presents an attention-getting presence. Waving and smiling as they approach, this is the crew from *Cool Change*. Brian is about six years old, his sister, Shannon rowing, is about nine and their dad, Gary all exclaim about the harvest of long-neck barnacles we are carrying on our hull. It's great to put faces to these voices. We conversed for weeks as we crossed the ocean together. They are a young family from the Chicago area. Gary worked with several companies in Elkhart as a 'headhunter', finding positions there for executives. His first mate Karen will pay a visit later. She had been one of the patients on whom Don had done a verbal, medical physical. With the help of Gary, carrying out Don's directives to him, her medical history was broadcast over the ham radio with all those boats in the Pacific listening.

Knowing there is no need to keep a watch our first night at anchor, we sleep like babies on bunks that gently cradle us. Up early the next morning, we unroll the rubber dinghy that's been stored on the foredeck. Gary told us of the precarious procedure they had used to get ashore. Now we are about to try.

I gather some of the barter items we had gathered from sailors' recommendations while in Panama: paint brushes, t-shirts, fishhooks and line, vegetable seeds and bright colored cloth. Instead of attaching the outboard motor to the dinghy, we use the oars to move in close to the huge breaking waves. Poised, with the oars ready to pull fast and strong and our plastic wrapped purchasing power clutched tightly, we gradually ease to the top of a huge wave where we are swept headlong, with breathtaking speed, onto the steep beach. We scramble out quickly, pull the dinghy high on the embankment. Our beginners' luck prevails - there's no damage to the dink or us.

We climb to the top of the bank. Looking down the path leading into the small village, we desperately try to remember the meager French we've been working on daily these last thirty-seven days. Gathering courage we stroll under the palm trees as we nod and try out 'bon jour' to these new faces. Their golden complexion and the graceful manner they carry themselves display a bearing of confidence and self-reliance. They seem friendly and are patient with our halting French. We learned later that their preferred language was a Polynesian vernacular. Hungry for fresh fruit we see growing along the path, we start the bargaining process. It's a process we have never handled very well. For a T-shirt we barter for a half dozen pamplamousse, a greenish yellow thick-skinned grapefruit that we find very sweet. A large papaya is ours for some fishhooks and for some plastic shoes, a whole stem of green bananas. We discover the information we had gotten in Panama is already out-dated. The preference now is for fingernail polish, earrings and perfume, none of which we have. This sounds like the needs of the men have been taken care of, now the women are demanding their due.

We watch one of the women making poi. She kneads this gray mass on a large flat stone with a concave basin in its center. Poi is made from taro root that has been buried in deep pits and left to rot for a year. The thoroughly rotten mass is now sticky and will be kneaded into one of the favorite dishes of these islands. This taste is one we never share with any enthusiasm.

Since Fatu Hiva is not an official port of entry, we only remain a few days. But it is at this island that we become acquainted with Joao and Ligia, a young couple from South Africa also on their circumnavigation. Don and I have been trying to barter a watch for some tapas, the artwork made by the island women. We are having no luck. Either we are asking for something unknown to her in the French we are using or she doesn't want to sell this black warrior painted on bark. This bark, from the mulberry tree, is pulled across a log as it is hammered into a pliable sheet ready to be painted with ancestor inspired designs, called tapas. Joao and Ligia happen by, sense our problem, and offer to translate for us. Que'est-ce qui se dit? 'Is this how you say it?' They smile at us, then using their fluent French soon have our artist smiling and nodding. Before we know what happened we have two tapas for the price of the watch.

Taking the dinghy from the beach back to the anchorage involves a different strategy. We tow the dinghy along the beach then walk onto a narrow dock along the side of the boathouse where canoes are stacked. We pull the dinghy along over large breakers rolling in. With a fast jump aboard, we row like mad to get clear of the waves surging to shore. It's just a few strokes back to *Horizon,* resting quietly with her hull scraped clean of barnacles. Although Don removed the shell with a paint scraper, each barnacle has left its circle of cement still attached to the hull. Not a tidy sight as we row towards our pride and joy.

With our long stem of bananas now tied to the mast, we leave this beautiful gem - a jewel that will always hold a special place in our memories as a magnificent landmark to celebrate completion of our first ocean passage.

We set sail for Nuka Hiva, an island on the northern boundary of the Marquesas. Sailing past Hiva Oa, the largest island in the center of the archipelago, we continue on to the small island of Ua Po as dusk approaches. We drop the anchor in a little bay on its west side. Here in this quiet spot is one other boat appropriately called *Solitude*. We share the evening with Tom, a handsome young man sailing alone. He sailed to these islands from his home in California. All these sailors we are meeting become good friends as we continue to meet each other in anchorages along a route heading in the general direction of New Zealand. Next morning *Solitude* and *Horizon* sail the last miles to anchor in the large bay at Taiohae on the southern coast of Nuka Hiva, the larger island to the north.

The islands of the Marquesas are all volcanic in origin. Their formations are easily recognized. We realize the bays where we've been anchoring are a result of craters having tipped while the volcano sank, leaving jagged peaks still exposed as reminders of the volcano rim. The villages are built along the shores. They depend more on water commerce than on any roads that would need to cross the high jagged peaks dividing the bays.

Our first order of business is to gather our passports and pertinent papers such as boat documentation and, in the case of French Polynesia, of which the Marquesas are a part, our checkbook! This is the only country we encounter that insists on each foreign boat posting a bond equivalent to the cost of a one-way airfare to its home country. The 'une caution' remains in a bank in Papeete while we visit their country. It will be refunded on our departure at one of the ports of entry/exit. We pay $2400 for the two of us this year. The French see it as insurance to rid themselves of misbehaving tourists. Some boats feel cheated because the government has the use of their money for three months, keeping any interest accrued during that time. As a rule we never become too bothered about the foibles and variances employed by a country. Our reason for choosing this life style of simple denominators is to remain as hassle free as possible. We feel we are seeing all of these countries on a modest outlay of funds. With our lodging traveling with us at no extra cost, beyond maintenance, and choosing local foods at the markets, we are able to keep our expenses low. Paying fees that sometimes make little sense doesn't cause us to lose sleep.

We go ashore to the 'aduana' (customs office) to have our passports stamped, walk on to the port captain for more paper work, then finally to the bank where we post our bond. The French tri-color will now be raised on the starboard shroud of *Horizon* indicating our clearance. These tasks finished we take a walk along the shoreline, following the road where there are occasional small shops. Only one store is selling groceries and propane. We are happy to find propane because our second tank is getting low. With the different adapter we purchased in Panama, we find a new process is used here to fill the tank. Their tank is hung upside down on a tree limb with the hose attached to ours. 'Voila', gravity does the filling. Just as simple as that. *Cool Change* ran out of propane mid-Pacific and ate cold meals for many days. They'll find this spot a cause for celebration.

Robert Louis Stevenson and Paul Gauguin spent time in these beautiful islands. The magnificent beauty of these bays surrounded by this green fringe of waving palms and hazy purple peaks gazing over all, might inspire creative ideas even in common folk like us. It truly is one of the most beautiful places in the world. Wood carvers are expressing the local creative talents. On one of our daily walks we find a church nestled away from the road where this talent is displayed. Standing as pillars along the porch of the Sunday School rooms are life-size carvings of Biblical characters. Represented is the Apostle Paul, fisher of men, holding a net intricately carved holding the catch of fish. Nearby stands a life-size carving of Moses, looking a great deal like the Moses in the Sistine Chapel. As we open the large carved doors into the church, a quiet subdued light filters along the walls to highlight carved Stations of the Cross. The sunlight softly lends its rays through the high windows onto the altar, again beautifully carved. We don't know if all of this has been the creation of one carver or the gift of many. We passed the little shop along the bay with carvings for sale that held prices beyond our budget.

There are several dozen sailboats in the anchorage now. About ten of us decide to explore the northern shore of the island. It is an easy day sail to discover a bay within a bay. As we enter the deep bay, we encounter another hidden bay offering great protection at right angles to the obvious one. With a nice sandy bottom and not too deep, it's a perfect anchorage as our base for exploration. With Tom, we hike along trails through thick tropical forests, never finding the stone platform called a marae. These are sacred sites where ancient ceremonies have been performed.

This is to be the first of what becomes an expected ritual whenever more than three yachts arrive together at an anchorage - the beach party. A large catamaran from Canada, *Canowie* with Peter, Joyce and their son Paul aboard making all the arrangements, it turns out to be an evening of shared stories over a potluck supper. *Canowie* has a printer and copier aboard. At each beach party from this one until Fiji Joyce passes a clipboard for the crews to sign. The next day, with a knock on the hull, Joyce or Paul delivers a printed copy of the partygoers' names, addresses and boat name. Included will be some pertinent item about the anchorage or country, or 'overheard on the beach' gossip. By the time we arrived at New Zealand, Joyce gave us an alphabetical list with pertinent information of every boat they met or talked to on the beach or via ham radio.

We return to the south shore of the island to anchor in a different bay. Here are Joao and Ligia on their boat, *Solmar*. They are excited about a wonderful vegetable garden they discovered on one of their walks ashore. A local man who moved here from Tonga, is growing a great selection of vegetables. He is more than happy to sell from his abundant crop. Since there have been no markets to buy fresh veggies, we engage the man in conversation and are surprised to hear English spoken. A few years earlier, he met a pretty Polynesian lady and before marrying her, had to promise her family they would live together on the family island. So with love in his heart and a suitcase in his hand, he left Tonga to settle with his bride in this bay. His skin is a darker color than the native population. Being energetic, working from dawn till dusk in this garden, he says he is teased and called a 'nigger' by his neighbors. He grins while saying this because, he says 'I can make a living by selling my vegetables and it's work I enjoy'. It is true, we found several men from Tonga marrying outside their country who become enterprising businessmen in their adopted country.

Solmar's engine has failed to start. No matter how hard Joao coaxed and threatened it with his large hammer there is not a cough or a sputter out of the monster. There's no wind so we tow them around the headland to our original anchorage. Here they hope to find help from the knowledge that surely will be available among all these sailors. Repeatedly, we discover among our fellow sailors, answers to problems that are always arising. These can be problems ranging from diesel engines, electrical and batteries, plumbing or rigging to good cleaning solutions for mildew, perhaps new recipes for taro. There are many times Don's medical experience is also called upon. This collection of *Encyclopedia Britannica Brains* and *Service Manuals* moves around the world beside us. It's all free for the asking.

Before leaving these magnificent peaks and valleys of the Marquesas, there is one more tiny bay we want to see. The entrance is hidden and narrow. Other boats that have been in the small anchorage assure us it's worth the hunt. The morning is clear. We set off around the western headland, searching with binoculars for the described landmarks. It's very hard to visualize indentations along a coast. We have found either a morning or afternoon slant of the sun's rays helps to create shadows indicating a recess or bay. Using this tool before the noon sun, we see a shadow that looks like a possible entrance. We ease closer to shore and soon realize our mistake as the water depth continues getting shallower. There doesn't seem to be an opening. We quickly turn away. With more care we continue searching along the forbidding rocks. Finally, looking over our shoulder, there is the opening to the sun sparkled little bay lying behind us through an obtuse cut. The water is crystal clear, making the passage through the entrance and around coral heads much easier. The anchor is dropped. We feel Lilliputian as we look straight up to peaks hundreds of feet above us. There really isn't much of a valley floor or a walking beach along the bay. But it's just as well. Both of us are nursing nasty infected sores on our feet. We have been soaking them in hot salt-water baths and taking antibiotic medicine hoping these remedies soon will show results.

A week ago we had hiked the mountains rising above the bay where we met the vegetable farmer. It was a misty day with the steep trail tracing a course through thick underbrush as it pushed straight up muddy, slippery slopes. We didn't consider turning back. We were eager to see the *marae,* a ceremonial stone platform, surrounded by its sentinels of tiki gods carved in stone. These sites are sacred places, still used and treasured by the Polynesians. There are some that are forbidden to visitors. I struggled up the muddy slope with my sandals falling apart. Much of the way I was barefoot in the mud. Finally pulling aside the long leaves of the banana plants hiding them, we saw several squat carvings in stone. The heads were enormous with large eyes and a grin skillfully carved; the arms folded across the chest balanced the round belly resting on squat legs. Each tiki, etched with tracings of black, ancient mold, seemed to be protecting a section of the *marae.* Vines and grasses overgrowing the whole area made it hard to find the raised stone platform. We tried to envision the rituals that would have taken place on this ceremonial platform. The sun began to push aside the clouds as we finished taking pictures. Feeling centuries of ancient traditions embodied at this place, we then turned to make our way down the curves and slopes. We were covered with mud when we returned to the boat. A dip in the bay, clothes and all, remedied most of the problem. The next day we realized what bad sores we had gotten while on our little expedition.

With our feet in buckets of salt water and reading the guidebook about the remaining islands of French Polynesia outlined on our chart, our attention is drawn to the behavior of two natives standing on the rocks along the shore. With their arms outstretched above their heads, they are flinging something against the rocks over and over again. Getting out the binoculars, it's hard to make out exactly what's being flung so severely. Surely it wouldn't be clothes; they would be in tatters with such force. Don gets in the dinghy and rows over to talk to them. This is the way, they say, to prepare octopus to insure the tough muscle is tender enough to eat. Later, when Don had success catching octopus, he too, got into the flinging mode to bring to the cooking pot a delicacy we savored.

We have enjoyed the Marquesas for a month but with so many new places to visit before our planned arrival in New Zealand by Christmas, we must heed the loose schedule we've set ourselves. Looking at the chart, our next stop will bring us to the Tuomotos Archipelago about four hundred-fifty miles to the southwest. These islands are also a part of French Polynesia. We are certainly learning geography in a real way. When you are trying to either find a place or miss it on a dark night, you start paying attention to the latitude and longitude of an area. As we study the charts covering our path, we are surprised to see islands scattered widely across the waters we are about to explore.

This next group of islands, the Tuomotos, defines a contrast to the splendor of the peaks we are now leaving behind. The mostly circular atolls, low lying with just enough coral and meager soil to support a few palm trees are scattered across a thousand miles. They are the remains of volcanic mountains that have sunk beneath the sea leaving a lagoon surrounded by a reef of coral that marks the remnant of the volcano rim with small islands called motus dotting the perimeter. In order to see these atolls from the boat, we have to sail within eight miles of one before we can see the top of a palm tree. Because of this, the time of arrival becomes crucial. Arriving at nighttime is out of the question. This is also true for most lagoon entrances.

By the end of our fourth day as we sail towards the Tuomotos, we heed the good information from the sat-nav about the distance and the set of currents around these islands. We decide to sail towards Manihi. We are twenty miles off - time to heave-to in the darkness. It is 3 a.m. We'll wait for daylight before entering the pass into the lagoon.

The heave-to process we use is a procedure of setting the sails in combination with the locked helm that keeps the boat heading into the wind and reduces forward speed. If there is a current, the boat will drift in that direction. So with some mathematics and information from the sat-nav, we can determine how fast and in what direction we will drift. Considering these factors, twenty miles gives us a good margin to work with for arrival at the pass after daybreak.

Searching as daylight dawns, we soon see the faint line etched along the rosy horizon. It takes us another hour of sailing to approach this unique landscape. The shoreline is a sandy beach with casuarinas and palm trees gently swaying behind it. Just offshore coral heads are visible in the water. There are no mountains or valleys, just this narrow strip of meager vegetation. We find the pass, a break in the coral where the water swirls through at each change of the tide. With a chart of the tides at these atolls, we realize we are too early to enter. This is evident as we look at the pass. We see the force of the water rushing through the narrow cut. So we anchor outside the pass to wait for slack tide before we enter. This gives us a chance to look at the village built along both sides of the pass. Small wooden frame houses, many with corrugated tin roofs, look well maintained. Some are painted in light pastel colors, blue, pink or yellow, reminding us of the homes in the Bahamas. As we look through the pass and into the lagoon we see scaffolding type structures in the water. Sitting at anchor to wait for slack tide, we try to guess the reason for these strange structures. Another sailboat arrives, drops their anchor and we wait together.

Finally, according to the chart, slack tide should be starting. This will give us about an hour before the reverse tide will slowly begin. Don hauls the anchor. We begin motoring into the pass. As we get close to the lagoon, there are markers indicating the channel by-passing some coral heads. With eddies swirling as we approach the markers, we are swept to one side, then manage to motor into deep water safely. As we turn along the inside of the narrow strip of land, a sudden change in the depth-sounder readings indicates we are in sixty feet of water. This is a developing pattern that we add to our expanding log of knowledge. So down goes all of the anchor rode (line) once more.

This lagoon is thirty miles long and about fifteen miles wide. We see more of these stick structures dotted around the lagoon. A few have a small shed on stilts built beside them. Next to us is a sailboat the same size as *Horizon*. Their transom has the name *Dolfin* printed across the stern and California as their homeport. We invite them over for supper and enjoy the evening together with Bill and Patty and seven year old Kelly, who that evening wanted to be called Janie. They haven't a clue either about the purpose of the sticks nearby.

The next morning we dinghy a short distance to the village where we are welcomed with friendly smiles and tests again to our halting French. The stores offer only meager supplies but we really don't need any at this time. Across the pass we come to a resort where tourists are already sunbathing and walking the beach. The inside of the atoll has no beach just a stony shoreline of scrubby bushes that doesn't offer easy access to the outer beach.

While visiting the village, we ask about the poles that we see in the lagoon. Traditionally, we are told, the Polynesians had made their living raising coconuts and fishing, but in the last ten years a lively pearl industry has developed. This is one of the few places in the world where black pearls can be cultivated. The individual natives apply for a section of the lagoon that is then registered to them in Papeete. They pay an annual fee of twenty cents per square meter on which they are permitted to farm for pearls. This requires trapping the baby oysters in a mesh and later selecting the ones that will be 'seeded'. These oysters hang by strings suspended in the water on these scaffolds that we have been seeing. The 'seed' is prepared from mussel shells found only in our own Mississippi River. This mussel shell is sent to Japan to be cut and processed into different sizes. A Japanese specialist comes to these atolls with these 'seeds' to implant them into the mantle of individual oysters. The oyster is scrubbed underwater every two months to ensure good growth. It will then be harvested at the end of two or three years. The pearls are checked for quality and form then x-rayed for thickness. They grow approximately 2mm. a year. Every October they are sold at auctions. A farmer can make from $2,000 to $20,000 a year, depending on the quality of his pearls.

Another atoll, Ahi, lies just an overnight sail from this one. The entrance through the pass is more straightforward and broad than the pass at Manihi. It's only after we are inside the lagoon that we see the different challenge this one presents. The depth is not a problem but there are coral heads scattered everywhere. The village is at the far end of the lagoon, quite a distance from the pass. The clear water makes it easier to read the water and steer around the heads. We anchor in front of the village with about six other boats. *Solmar* and *Solitude* are here as is *Pegaso*, a beautiful sixty-foot sailboat from Mexico with Herta, Jorge and son Luis aboard. This village seems larger than the one at Manihi, perhaps because the width of the land is broad here at the tip of the atoll. Along the dirt streets wooden homes are neatly spaced. A church, a school and the telephone building present a busy quality to life here. And in the little bay off the town is the shed on stilts that is the sorting house for their pearl industry.

A grandmother living here has been asking each boat arriving at her place in the Pacific to create a page in her scrapbook. She is now on her third, thick scrapbook. It makes fascinating reading to review the boats that have crossed her path. I try to be original with my painting of an oyster with the pearl, Ahi, in its center, as I add the page from *Horizon* to this unusual visitors log.

The next evening we are invited aboard *Pegaso* to enjoy dinner and after-dinner music. Joining us for dinner are several local young men. Two of these men will be the troubadours of the evening. To their own accompaniment, one on a guitar the other on a homemade ukulele made from a wood plank and a leather drum sounding board, their beautiful voices blend in duets of Polynesian folksongs for a two-hour concert under the stars. They invite us all to their home for dinner tomorrow.

The seventy-four year old grandfather greets us at the door and welcomes us to his home. Don had given some medical advice to one of his sons earlier in the day and Grandpa, who speaks only French is enjoying talking to the 'doktor'. He tells us stories of his early years as a pearl diver before the use of snorkels or fins. Holding a rock to help him dive deep to the oyster beds, he would dive over a hundred feet deep while holding his breath. After collecting shells into a basket he would return to the surface. His eyes are bloodshot but his sense of humor and joy of life still sparkle in those eyes. It is obvious his family treasures him and their lives center around his comfort. He presents all five of the guests with palm hats made by his children and shell necklaces created by the women of the family. We are seated as guests around the dining table to be served first by all the family members. When we finish eating, the family eats their meal from the food remaining. The meal consists of fried fish and poisson cru, a delicious combination of raw fish marinated in limejuice then mixed with tomato, onion and peppers, and another new and pleasing dish, papaya cooked in coconut milk. It is an evening of warm hospitality and a generous gift to us from this family. Hiti and Dufty, the two musicians of the evening before, entertain us once more before we return to our boats

The next morning we move *Horizon* from the village end of the lagoon to the middle. Here we anchor at a small cove just inside the pass. Following us is *Solitude* and *Pegaso*. There now are restrictions concerning anchoring in their lagoon. Several weeks before we arrived, over one hundred oyster shells had been stolen, a serious offense. As a result they have assigned specific areas for anchoring. Although this new spot is protected, the area is a bed of coral heads. It's deep enough but means the anchor will surely be caught among the heads.

Don and Tom agree about the promising prospect of great spear fishing this pass appears to offer. At slack tide while we float current free through the pass, we are surrounded with fish of every size and color swimming among beautiful soft coral of sea fans and sponges. In twenty minutes Don is able to spear six grouper, five to ten pounds, in fifteen to twenty feet of water. Another morning, before daybreak, Don, Tom and Luis venture outside the pass in the *Pegaso* dinghy to seek the rewards of deep sea trolling. Returning about 8 a.m. with a forty-pound tuna aboard, it is one crowded dinghy.

When we decide to leave the anchorage and make our way to Tahiti, we discover the anchor has tangled among the coral. Looking over the bow into the clear water, we can see the chain disappearing between the coral heads.

With Tom on *Solitude* anchored nearby, we both spent the previous night awake. The winds shifted and picked up velocity during the night. The rocky shore behind us threatened to do us harm. The sterns of both our boats swung to just a few yards from this shore. Forbidding as it looked, we felt the anchor was secure in all that coral. With no rope overboard, just chain to the anchor, chafing should not be a problem. We were concerned, however, the yanking on the chain might do damage to the bow.

Beginning the process of raising the anchor, we find it doesn't budge. Tom is also having trouble with his anchor. He's diving overboard to get a closer look at both our situations. Popping out of the water beside *Horizon*, he yells he can unwrap and free the chain to our anchor. He proceeds to free-dive sixty feet in pursuit of the coiling anchor chain. Splashing out of the water to catch his breath, he shortly dives again and then again and still again until exhausted and breathing hard he yells 'start pulling, it's free'. And so it is.

As we get ready to leave the anchorage, a speeding motor boat pulls along side. Aboard is the mayor of Ahi. Sitting on his lap is a small girl who has a deep cut on her palm inflicted three days before. Don examines the injury and feels the delay has made stitching the cut inadvisable. With medications we have aboard, he tends it then bandages her hand as she bites her lips, trying to be a brave little five-year-old. As they prepare to leave with instructions for caring for her wound, the mayor expressing their thanks, drops into Don's lap a plastic bag with at least a dozen shell necklaces.

There's still a favorable tide to leave. Hoisting the sails we slip through the pass to continue sailing towards the most beautiful and memorable night voyage that I'll ever experience of the hundreds of midnight watches I log.

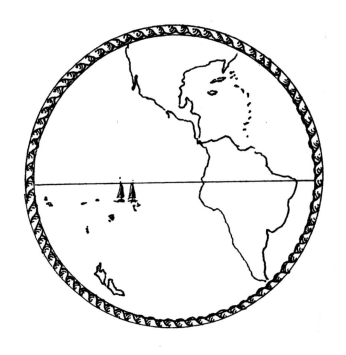

Tahiti to BoraBora to Mopelia

CHAPTER 5
TO PEER INTO A CRYSTAL BALL

The sky is a deep cobalt blue, with boundless clarity and an inner radiance that seems to stretch into infinity - each star is twinkling. The constellations I have memorized display familiar outlines among this vast carpet of sparkling gems. Venus, with its bright guiding light is just ahead to the West. As I look for a horizon, again I see none. However, this is completely different from those hazy daylight horizons that had disappeared before me weeks ago. Where I supposed there to be one, I find no hint of a horizon. Instead I see stars staring up at me from a mirrored sea. There are stars above. There are stars below - not a whisper of a breeze. I have the sensation that I am floating, suspended in the center of a glass ball completely surrounded with stars. There is no up. There is no down. I am weightless in time, space and movement. A crystal clarity has me holding my breath. There is no wind. It is completely calm - a stillness that invites reverence. The broad expanse of the sea stretches a circumscribed circle of mirrored smoothness about my center. For long moments I feel our barque has taken wings as we glide across a star-studded sky, free to soar as far and as high as our wings will take us through the constellations. And then, as I peer over the side of this noble mobile, I am plunging to depths of starry majesty with no bottom visible to confuse my sense of earthly boundaries. Soaring and diving, I have been granted a rare gift. The verse of a Blake poem comes to mind as I contemplate such majesty:

> *To see a world in a grain of sand,*
> *And a heaven in a wild flower,*
> *Hold infinity in the palm of your hand,*
> *And eternity in an hour.*

Holding this infinity and eternity in my grasp, I realize with a throb of mortality that moving through the Tuomotos with currents curling around each island I cannot drift aimlessly, *Horizon* must hold its course. It is the throb of the engine that imparts the only distraction to an otherwise enchanted evening. Remembering this night months and years later continues to arouse memories of a transcendent world that stands apart from any experience of this, my earth bound existence.

Our second day towards Tahiti the wind regains its claim to dominance and the spellbinding fascination of that glorious night is never, during any turn of my watch, to display such wonder again. By July 1st we see clouds on the distant horizon providing a familiar indicator that we are approaching land. Just before noon, the tall peaks of Tahiti, green as emeralds glistening in the sunlight, rise as twin peaks from a turquoise sea. The two peaks wear a necklace of ethereal clouds; just wisps of mist settling on the shoulder of the mountains. For a background setting, we listen to the tape we made of Dufty and Hiti harmonizing Polynesian melodies as this South Seas panorama enfolds us.

Again it is a search along the coast to find the harbor. We had been told of large water tanks nearby that aid in locating the harbor breakwater. By 4:30 in the afternoon we make our way through the wide entrance towards a long line of sailboats, their bows pointed away from shore. As we get closer, two dinghies from these boats come along side to help tie us into this necklace of sailboats. Using the procedure known as a Mediterranean Mooring, we drop the anchor ahead of this line of boats and with the help of these new friends, have two stern lines taken ashore to be tied to trees or cement bollards placed there. A quick estimate suggests thirty sailboats are anchored in this fashion. Flags flying off the stern herald as many different countries. We could be an international conference on 'How to see the world on a shoestring'. What a visit this will be! Getting to hear and share experiences with such a varied group of sailors will be a bonus beyond our expected joy of absorbing this part of French Polynesia. By watching our neighbors, we soon learn the easy way to shore. Sitting in the dinghy off the stern, we pull ourselves, hand over hand along the stern lines, to shore.

In this South Seas setting, we enjoy breakfast next morning while we sit in the cockpit. Cradling mugs of steaming coffee and enjoying freshly baked flaky croissants touched with orange marmalade, we settle down to view the bay bustling with canoes. Most of these canoes have outriggers attached. There are some, very long and sleek, that display fine woodworking skills in the smooth contours of the varnished hull. These carry twenty bronze skinned Tahitian men stroking in an easy cadence - their glistening paddles throwing arches of rainbow touched spray across the sparkling bay. In their midst just ahead of our bow, are simple canoes that youngsters are smoothly paddling through the water.

For the month of July, the natives of all the archipelagos of French Polynesia come to Papeete to celebrate Bastille Day in a month long festival. For the remainder of the week we enjoy a front row seat on the bow of *Horizon* as we watch these canoe races. As part of all these festivities, there are races for women as well as the men. The races are exciting with competitive vibrations resounding across the lagoon. Many times a chantey will drift across the water as the men intone a mantra to accompany the cadence of their strokes.

Adding to the excitement a race arouses, we become aware of the beautiful designs in the clothing worn by the racers. Both the women and men have adapted costumes using the pareu in a practical way for this sport. This rectangle of soft cloth, six feet by four feet, with beautifully dyed patterns, becomes high fashion. These French Polynesians take this simple dimension and adeptly transform it into a practical design for clothing with stylish French flair. The vibrant colors enhance the many ways these pareus are worn. The men wear them as a large diaper affair with an attractive flap in front completed with a simple tuck at the waist. With appropriately placed twists and knots the women construct theirs as a bodice with a short sarong that shows off their bronze shoulders and legs. Taking the abundance of flowers - frangipani, orchids, hibiscus and others that grow along the by-ways, they weave garlands, headbands and armbands into exquisite designs. Many are composed of flowers and palm fronds. Some use only fronds incorporating varied greenery textures to create still another artistic dimension. Using the natural beauty growing around them, they add a colorful ingredient to the sweat of the race. Each team, men or women, wear similar colors and designs in their pareus and garlands.

While we were in Baie Taiohae in the Marquesas last month, we spent an evening enjoying the singing and dances of the villagers as they prepared for this competition in Tahiti. We hadn't realized it then, but now as we attend the performances in the large stadium here in Papeete, we see some of these dances and songs of that earlier evening. The accomplishment of the performers impresses us with the exceptional costuming and very professional quality of their performances as they compete against each other. It equals any Las Vegas performance.

We walk the palm-lined streets of Papeete looking in the shop windows at items beyond our budget. It seems to be an expensive port. There is an extensive display of the pearls grown in these waters. Not only are we seeing black pearls but pearls in a rainbow of hues. There are green and pink ones, the more familiar pearly white ones, and those with a yellow or a gray cast as well. How amazing that this kind of beauty can grow in a distorted body housed in such a misshapen shell.

We discover a simple coffee break with a croissant cost close to 5 dollars, while the flaky buttery croissant practically melts in your mouth, the hole in your pocket scratches all the way to the boat. Our supply of food is sufficient enough that we have no need to purchase the expensive groceries we see in the markets. However, one day as we purchase our daily bargain of a baguette for thirty cents, we discover frozen chicken with a familiar American label and Stateside price. We buy fifteen pounds of frozen chicken. After I process it in the pressure cooker, we have a dozen pint jars of canned chicken. By using original recipes, we can make one jar last for two meals.

There is a young couple who sailed from their home in New Zealand. Their small boat is anchored beside us here in Papeete. They married before leaving on their voyage to Canada, where they plan to attend Bible School. Since they came this distance with only twenty gallons of water, we purchased two ten-gallon jerry jugs as a wedding present for them. Because the chicken is such a bargain, they also want to learn the canning process. My experience has been recently acquired but I am happy to share my success. Our stove becomes a busy piece of equipment for several days. Later, when we arrived in New Zealand, we were told the young man had been a worker in the boatyard where we had a great deal of work done. We were glad to hear they had arrived safely in Canada.

Before our daughter, Linda, arrives here in Papeete, we plan to see more of the coastline of Tahiti. The island is shaped like the figure eight with its easterly section smaller than the western circle that cradles Papeete. This smaller circle is called Tahiti Iti. Surrounding the entire island is a reef of coral that poses challenges to the boat that dares to pass through its many passes. As we sail outside this reef, the huge breakers roar a challenge with enormous waves tossing high the spray as they surge along the coral walls that protect calm water inside. The first pass we enter really has our adrenaline pumping. There are good charts for each pass with descriptions of the hazards we might encounter. Closely following these directions, we make our move into this obtuse cut. By motoring along the outside of the reef holding a straight course, we pass inside the opposite side of the opening. As soon as we are beyond the breaking waves, we quickly change heading to starboard and steer a course between two coral walls into the quiet bay. We drop the anchor in calm water. I am usually at the helm steering while Don stands on the rail at the bow keeping a sharp lookout to direct me with hand signals for the clear passage. My mouth is dry. I breathe hard. Every pass brings to focus, with sharp intensity, all the senses as we aim for a safe passage through its limited boundaries.

There is only one other boat nestled quietly here with us. *Onrust* is a steel boat from Tasmania. We had noticed this boat anchored nearby in Papeete harbor. My first impression as I watched them doing the shuffle to get in and out of their dinghy was - this is a couple early in their sailing experience. They seemed awkward and a bit clumsy getting in and out of their dink. We are invited to enjoy sundowners aboard their boat in this calm bay. During our delightful visit we learn of the challenges Tasmania throws at sailors. It harbors awesome seas. Much to my chagrin, both of these two have worked harvesting lobster off the wild coasts of Tasmania. They know considerably more than we do about sailing. Judge not . . . .

The next morning with hearts in our mouths again we retrace the course through the pass and continue south along the outside of the reef towards Iti. The next pass, Rautirare Pass, is straightforward with markers guiding us straight through the wide break between the coral. We sigh with relief. It's known as the best pass in Tahiti. Once inside with calm water we turn to starboard then follow the channel close to shore. We find the anchorage near the Gauguin Museum. Along the way are the botanical gardens where we plan to stroll after visiting the museum. The gardens are testament to a Harvard professor who made extensive searches throughout the South Pacific for plants native to the islands. He established this magnificent setting that displays their beauty. It surrounds the museum dedicated to the life of Paul Gauguin. The seventeen original paintings have long since been moved to galleries throughout the world, but artifacts are displayed that speak to his twenty years spent in the Society Islands. Here is a careful description of the tortured path that led him from a successful stockbroker in Paris to these charmed islands. Here he expressed an inner passion using his vibrant colors to portray the beauty he found in the islands and their inhabitants. Had he remained a stockbroker, our awareness to the beauty of this world would be diminished. We learn that he had done considerable sailing himself, including a circumnavigation. But his life is a sad one of loneliness. Penniless, he died of syphilis with few friends to mourn him. He is buried on Hiva Oa in the Marquesas.

Learning from experience, we wear comfortable hiking shoes and put band-aides in our pockets before starting off on hiking expeditions. Following the many streams that flow from the mountain peaks to these bays, we find shaded glens beside small rapids that course over rocks. We splash along pebble beaches to find a pleasant spot to enjoy our packed lunch. Palm trees, mango and breadfruit trees grow beside large stands of bamboo and ferns that thrive on the floor of the forest. With the moist air creating the humidity and the warm equatorial temperatures surrounding us, we walk through a greenhouse setting of lovely, lush vegetation. Caves with mosses and ferns clinging to the walls open dark entrances with forbidding rocky depths yawning before us. Not a challenge we care to explore. We spend several days at this beautiful anchorage. It is here that we edit and finish the first videotape of our trip since leaving the Bahamas. Linda Joy will be flying to Papeete in a few days; we will send this tape home with her.

There is an easy pass into Phaeton, the town on the smaller Tahiti Iti. We spend a few more days anchored here before making the sail back to Maeva Beach, an anchorage close to our first stop in Papeete. It will be a bit closer to the airport to welcome Linda.

For land travel of any distance, we take 'Le Truck'. These small vans comprise the bus system for transport around the island. One of the more interesting trips we take is to a fire walking performance. Cornelia and Charles from *Rhinoceros* join us to watch a ten-foot path of coals being fanned with palm fronds till there is a fierce glow in the evening dusk. With ceremony and the throb of drumbeats, a priest intones a chant as he waves a feather-embellished staff over the richly garbed performers. The barefoot procession then moves across the coals in an unhurried gait. This is repeated several times before they invite audience participation. Quite a few members of the audience put their 'best foot forward'. With more chants and some instruction, they, too, walk the ten foot burning path. Some are leaping. Some run as fast as they can. Still others demonstrate astonishing calm as they proceed over the coals.

We arrive at the airport with a fragrant frangipani lei to welcome Linda on her midnight arrival. Even at this hour, musicians and dancers with traditional songs and dances greet travelers to Tahiti. Her flight is four hours late but she still looks fresh. She's still just a little kid as she runs to greet us. Many of the other sailors have been entertaining family here. We are delighted that it's our turn to join in that special joy - to hug family once again. Only a few hours of darkness remain when we return to the boat. A need for sleep never crosses our minds as we share news and exclaim about the photos she's brought from the family. A picture of three month old Lindsey joins the stack of family memories. We will add these to the collection of family pictures framed above the table on the boat.

Saturday we join Jim and Jimmie from *Sunshine* and Charles and Cornelia to attend a Polynesian Luau at the large hotel here in Maeva Bay. We gather with guests standing around a pit dug in the ground. Here hot coals under rocks support a large wire basket that is roasting two pigs. Placed alongside are kettles, one with chicken and taro leaves, another with taro pudding in a coconut cream sauce, still others hold sweet potatoes roasting and fish wrapped in banana leaves - all baking together. This taro plant resembles the elephant ear plant my grandmother grew as a houseplant. The root is cooked much like a potato or rotted to produce poi cuisine. It is the leaves we found to be a nice addition to our menu. The leaves, tasting much like spinach, need to be cooked at least a half-hour to diminish the oxalic acid present in the leaves. The kettles are being covered with sheets of metal where more hot coals are placed. At noon, with native drums beating a now familiar cadence, the hot coals are raked off the sheets of tin. Long poles are threaded through the baskets of roasted pig then carried with the other dishes into the pavilion to be presented on banana leaves and blossoms. Whatever the occasion in this country, flowers highlight each affair with a profusion of colors and fragrance. Displays of exotic centerpieces decorate the tables and flowers adorn the supporting posts of the thatch-covered pavilion.

We find a table close to the open floor in the center of the pavilion then join the line of guests at the buffet. As if this array of new tastes isn't sufficient, a large table is rolled out displaying an outstanding variety of French pastries for the final course . . .oh my, oh my. .

After enjoying this island cuisine, we sit back to be entertained by a Polynesian extravaganza. There are native dances with the exceptionally beautiful women attired in grass skirts and necklaces of frangipani leis as they perform their fluid, hula type dance. The men show their warrior stance in dances, threatening and bold. For a light-hearted portion of the program, the audience is encouraged to join in the dances. Gregarious Jim offers to show his agile balance - gained, no doubt, sailing the Pacific - as he dances from our table. He is bedecked in a grass skirt and shimmies and shakes in response to the movements of his partner, a lovely Polynesian beauty. When, alas, his skirt swings off his hips, he acknowledges his humorous part in the entertainment of the crowd and dancers alike. Jim, captain of *Sunshine,* maintains a sunny disposition. He continues to be a source of hugs and generous goodwill as we move around the globe together.

Another part of the afternoon show is a display of the difficult process to open a coconut as a performer successfully completes the job using only his teeth. Performers demonstrate the many ways to wear the pareu. As we leave this taste of island charm, we agree unique beauty has been offered us from the pits to the pareus.

The next day we sail across the fifteen-mile channel to the island of Moorea. It is just a short trip with the tall peaks of the island looking close enough to touch. So when we encounter strong winds and really turbulent waves, we are taken by surprise. It is one of the more challenging legs we have sailed to date. A steep wave suddenly tosses the boat on its side. Linda is helping her Dad tie down the mainsail to the boom. With the doused sail stretched along its length, the boom careens across the deck. Linda, still hanging on to this swinging mass is swept across the deck until her feet dangle over the side of the boat. The sheets (lines) that secure the boom had not been made fast. I jump to the cleat and haul the sheets tight. Don pulls the boom back to settle on the boom-gallows, its point of rest. Her feet once again touch the deck. The winds funnel between these two islands making this patch of water heave with confused seas - a test to our sailing skills. The return trip to Papeete several days later, was likewise a gusty one.

We anchor in a tight anchorage in Cook's Bay with quite a few of the crews that are becoming familiar friends. At the beach party we organize here, quite a few introduce a friend or family member from home to the group. Linda and I hike along the beach to spend some time and money in the shops along the way. Both of us find attractive pareus to buy. We wear them on the boat and enjoy this comfortable way to stay cool while looking cool.

We are here in Cook's Bay on our 36th wedding anniversary. When there's a knock on the hull we are surprised to see six year-old Brian from *Cool Change* beaming as he gives us a key-lime pie he's baked. And later in the day, when we return from a hike to Bellevue Mountain with its view of the entire fringe of reefs around Moorea, a bouquet of wild flowers nestles in the cockpit to greet us with its abandoned beauty. What good fortune is ours to share the joy of such friendships.

After the roaring sail back to Tahiti in time for Linda's plane departure, we do some house cleaning and take stock of supplies.

Although we had purchased fuel in Nuka Hiva, we realize it might be a while until access to fuel would again be this easy. It certainly wasn't an easy process in Nuka Hiva. There we attached a hose to our electric drill to which a small pump was connected. Then with one end of the hose in a fifty-gallon drum on the dock and the other end in a filter placed into the access outlet on the boat, we ran the drill to pump the fuel into our tank. Since the drill ran on batteries that needed recharging quite often, it became an all day greasy process. Here in Papeete, it's a simple matter of a regular diesel pump at the dock with a straightforward fill. As soon as the tanks are filled we leave for the overnight sail to Raiatea. We anchor here overnight and sail the following day between the two islands to find the pass through the long continuous reef that encircles them.

We continue sailing northwest. These Society Islands are defined with islands each sketching their own distinctive silhouette. Once again we see peaks wearing that delicate necklace of clouds in the afternoon - this time on Bora Bora. This diaphanous necklace is becoming a signature of the beauty of French Polynesia. Mt. Pahia with its twin peak outline, rises from this small island only five miles in length. Surrounding these lush green peaks the crystal clear lagoon is shimmering with sunlit diamonds tossed across its turquoise water. Somehow this spectacular sight seems familiar. Reading in our guidebook, we realize this panorama is one of the most photographed spots in the world. It is used by airlines, hotels and travel brochures to advertise a place you will never forget, a place that lingers in your memory.

Sailing through the wide and hazard free pass, we turn south to anchor off a tiny motu. The snorkeling here reveals the sand trails of many shells. I find many auger shells here as well as many varieties of the cone shell. I am particularly careful as I dive to pick up the cone shell. I'm aware of the deadly barb that will inflict a poison that can be fatal. While I lazy around snorkeling, Don is searching for the evening meal. It will be either grouper or yellow snapper that seem to be hiding in the coral heads.

We enjoy an evening at the Hotel OaOa with all the yachts that have anchored off their beach. The young couple owning this hotel continues to have their welcome mat out to the fleet. We each bring a plate of hors d'oevers to supplement the main course provided by the hotel hosts. *Canowie* is here - again their clipboard is passing around the group to provide a nice reminder of friends sharing this place.

We spend the rest of August, about two weeks, exploring the lagoon that surrounds Bora Bora. It's charted well, making navigation through the crystal clear water an easy passage to interesting anchorages. One little motu that we find nestled in the lagoon far from the village, Viatape, is home to a family of goats with a billy that is very aggressive. We stumble and trip over the rocky hills to stay clear of his belligerent moves. Every spot we anchor has interesting marine life flourishing when we dive around the coral heads. It's in this lagoon we find very large mussel shells, some measuring twelve inches long.

Before leaving Bora Bora we reverse the process we pursued in Nuka Hiva, now receiving the papers we will need to enter our next port. Along with these we pick up the bond refund we posted those months ago. A quick stop in the village to find yeast for our bread-making only yields tins of baking powder instead. Sandwiches will now take the shape of biscuits. Variety might be a pleasant change. At the wharf, ready to jump in the dinghy one last time, our attention is drawn to hand carved ukuleles on sale. As a reminder of the enjoyable evenings when Hiti and Dufty serenaded us, we purchase an attractively designed one.

Taking one last look at the peaks we join *Solmar*, also leaving Bora Bora, for an overnight sail to a tiny atoll on the western edge of The Society Islands. Mopelia is a ring of coral with motus, or tiny islets, scattered on the reef. The atoll measures about four miles across. The only way to visit it is by sailboat. *Solmar* is waiting for us outside the pass where we wait together for slack tide. This is another pass that sends Don climbing the mast steps to the spreaders. These spreaders are cross pieces high on the mast that contribute to its strength as shrouds (cables) from their fixed position at the top of the mast are stretched over these spreaders then attached to the hull. Sitting high on the spreaders he has a better vantage point to read the water as we navigate the intricate passage around coral heads.

We make our way to an area near the two stilt houses on shore where we drop the anchor in crystal clear water. Behind the thatch houses is a copra plantation with the rustle of palm branches stirring in the breeze. On the trunk of the coconut trees a metal collar about eight inches wide is nailed six feet above the ground. We are told this is to discourage rats from climbing the trees to make their nests and eating the crop.

The number of plantation workers may vary. There have been as many as seventeen persons working on this tiny atoll. But at the time of our arrival there is only one Polynesian man living here with his dog. A dog whose talent of hunting sharks did attract the attention of Jacques Cousteau. This canine talent prompted him to come to Mopelia and feature the dog in one of his nature films. Although we learned there were two more men working the crop, they had now returned to Tahiti, leaving behind Michelle.

Michelle, whom we designate Commodore of the Mopelia Yacht Club, is a generous host. He takes great pleasure in sharing his island with the six yachts that have anchored at his front door. Among the many talents he demonstrates is his ability to catch lobster. One night he invites Joao and Don to join him for a walk on the reef. Using flashlights and a coal-oil lantern, they search for lobster. Michelle uses as his spear, a wooden trident he has made from flotsam found on the beach. He is deft at thrusting the prongs over a lobster as it makes its way across the reef. Sometimes these crustaceans are seen walking across the top of the coral. Others are caught as they emerge from a hole or crevice in the coral. The trio returns with two gunny sacks full of lobster.

This heralds the *raison d'être* for a beach party the next night. Michelle once more has surprises in store for us. After we enjoy the lobster feast around a blazing campfire, he asks if anyone has a guitar. Don rows out to *Horizon* to fulfill this request. To our delight, Michelle accompanies himself as he sings Polynesian and familiar tunes. He tells of plans to sing professionally when his contract is finished here on Mopelia. We all agree his career will be a headliner. His rich baritone voice blending with his inventive guitar harmonies is accompanied with the whisper of ripples along the quiet, moonlit beach. Harboring no distractions of that sometimes noisy civilization we've left behind, we have discovered a truly special place of quiet serenity. Under a moonlit sky the last glowing embers evoke a closing reverie.

Michelle is a fine French cook. He shows us where to collect a certain kind of seaweed for tender and crisp salty salads. He sautés tenderized octopus with fresh ginger and garlic then simmering all in coconut cream creates a delicious dish. We keep discovering new possibilities for recipes.

The men on these six anchored yachts, with Michelle as guide, do a lot of 'aquarium diving'. They coin this phrase to describe the unique diving configurations at the outer edge of this reef. There's a steep drop-off to cobalt depths at the edge of these coral walls. Here the edge is replete with irregularities and deep indentations that house somewhat enclosed aquariums or underwater caves where fish swim in great numbers. With their spear guns, it is like shooting fish in a barrel. Since our freezer capabilities are limited, Don brings to our table only the 'the catch of the day' plus two. Our menus have never enjoyed such freshness until this voyage.

These ports of call become small wonders scattered around the world. They could charm our desire to remain indefinitely, but we know we have to push on. Continuing to sail closer to the equator, we soon realize that yet another jewel of the Pacific awaits us. We are leaving The Society Islands. French Polynesia, with its emerald peaks thrusting from the sea or its low hazy line of atolls stretching along the horizon where friends like Michelle will spend their lives, now outline a faint silhouette behind us.

Don is always ready to catch our supper.

Don's world.

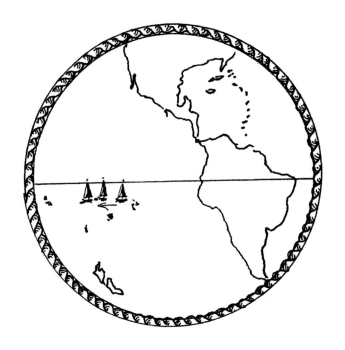

Suvarov to Samoa

CHAPTER 6
FINDING ROBINSON CRUSOE

Lying ahead of us, we sail into the territory of the Cook Islands to discover another of these special places. Suvarow is one of the northern islands of the Cook Islands chain. Again there is the pass to locate and navigate safely. Each of these arouses a keen sense. We keep learning with each pass we make, to maintain a good lookout. If we can, we time our passage with the sun behind us, insuring that we can read the water ahead. This makes it possible to see any heads that may pose a threat. That possibility, and the currents and tides can make some passes a bit dicey. This pass at Suvarow is another broad one but opens up only as we sail close to the outer shore of the main island. After passing the tip of this motu called Anchorage Island, we turn a sharp corner to starboard keeping an eye on a line of coral heads stretching to the tiny anchorage. We see three boats anchored very close to another bank of heads. There isn't a great deal of space for many boats to anchor and enjoy the hospitality of Suvarow.

Recently this atoll has been designated a National Park of the Cook Islands. It has a history sailors have envisaged as a fascinating quest. A kind of Robinson Crusoe story has teased the dreams of many armchair sailors as they contemplated such an adventure. In 1952 Tom Neale, a loner and a dreamer, having enough of the noisy world, began spending periods exploring a new life sailing to and from this tiny atoll some two thousand miles northeast of his home in New Zealand. Finally he dropped his anchor permanently in this little harbor where we now sit. He lived here until 1977 all alone, glad to welcome any sailor who could navigate to his little paradise. Using the wrecks remaining from buildings left here after World War II when New Zealand coast watchers were stationed here, he built his home. These modest buildings remain and now are home for the Kora family. Tom lived a simple life while writing about his unique lifestyle. The few possessions remaining after his death of cancer in '77 still are displayed in one of the rooms. The logbook he kept as a diary with a list of all the sailors that spent time with him, is missing. This in spite of his entry placing a curse on anyone that removed his possessions from the island.

Although we are at this remote atoll, we soon discover there are procedures and formalities to be carried out just like any other port. No sooner has the anchor dropped, than a small canoe is coming along side with a smiling, robust Polynesian man reaching out to shake our hands with a welcome to Suvarow. He hands us a typewritten legal paper introducing him as Petuela Kora, Administrator of these islands as designated by the government of the Cook Islands. We invite him aboard. After casual conversation he asks us to come ashore to finalize the stamping of our passports and other papers. He, with his wife Jane and their four children have turned Tom's island into patches of cleared paths lined with seashells. A taro pit flourishes with tall taro plants growing beside a vegetable garden and papaya and banana trees. Composting palm fronds and scraps from the vegetable patch has produced enough fertile soil to maintain themselves.

Their children range in ages from eight to sixteen and are anxious to converse after some first shy moments. We are speaking English again with these folks. When Petuela learns Don is a physician, he asks to have physicals given to each member of his family. Jane and I walk around the park-like setting they have created. Before long she is expressing some of the disadvantages she is feeling with their isolation. Especially worrisome for her is the depression she is noticing in her older children. They yearn to have companionship with friends their own age. They have been here three years with only a few trips back to their home island where they try to maintain their former relationships. She feels alone with this concern because her husband, a dominant figure, demands certain behavior from the children. Being an attentive listener as she shares her concerns is really the only support I feel able to give her.

With the sun setting we are invited ashore with *Canowie, Belair* from Bermuda and *Marimba* from Israel, to enjoy a meal around the fire. The evening is spent singing a happy variety of songs under the hilarious leadership of two crewmembers aboard *Belair.* Mr. Kora describes the many fish living in the lagoon and warns there are a fair number of sharks cruising through these schools of fish.

The next day Don joins Serge from *Marimba* to explore some of the coral reefs and spear fish for dinner. In a short while Don has speared three large grouper, each weighs about ten pounds. Serge is having success as well but the reef sharks are beginning to circle in ever increasing numbers. Don has been used to having an occasional shark lurking in the background while he is spear fishing but the numbers here are becoming alarming and he chooses to end the fishing foray for the day. Serge isn't about to let such a good fishing opportunity elude him. He continues his pursuit of good meals a while longer.

Next morning we say farewell to the Kora family and thank them for their warm hospitality. Meanwhile we make preparations for the next leg of our voyage. American Samoa will be about a five day sail due west from Suvarow.

After spending time at anchor, we make sure any loose items are once again restored to their secure place before sailing again. On top of the desk at the navigation station is a large shelf where I've arranged several baskets we've collected from different countries. In these I have arranged shells and live plants. A Christmas cactus that is doing very well offers its green presence to our sea-borne home. It already has buds that look like they will favor us with blossoms at Christmas. To date none of these treasures have tumbled to the floor, even though the boat, on some passages, is heeled on its side at a twenty-five degree angle. Books and kitchen tools are stowed once more. We look ship-shape again.

We chuckle as we see *Canowie* leaving the harbor. They continue to be a warm and generous shipload of folk. Captain Peter, a former pilot with Air Canada, likes to travel fast (as on jetliners). Perhaps this is why he is subtle in the manner he leaves a port. Their large catamaran leaves with all the sails flying. As he chats on the radio to the rest of us still in the harbor, he assures us his *Canowie* is moving 'right along'. But what is not commonly shared is, once he feels he's out of sight of the rest of the fleet, the stalwart engine is engaged to throw a wake churning behind that 'cat'.

So, of course, when we arrive in the fjord-like entrance to American Samoa and sail into the wide anchorage at PagoPago (pronounced PangoPango), there is *Canowie* already swinging on her anchor. And the host of friends we have met so far are here also. We all have been looking forward to this port because of access to U.S. products in the stores. Our first impression of this deep, well-protected harbor is how dirty it is. There is an odor in the air that denies you a deep breath. This, we discover is caused by the two large tuna fish canneries across the bay from the town of PagoPago.

This group of islands is the only U.S. territory south of the equator. Our government has poured enormous sums of money into this little country. We question the effect these sums must make to the cultural heritage of these natives and their response to such prosperity. The streets are dirty and the ambition noted in other countries seems lacking here in PagoPago. At the small bazaar where crafts are sold, there are no tables. With her wares displayed on the ground, the plump saleslady lies prostrate beside them; her bent elbow supporting her head as she casually beckons your attention with a staff in the other hand - a laid-back approach to marketing.

However, when a group of us rent a van with a local driver as guide, we see more energy and pride among the folks living in the more remote tiny villages scattered over this large and mountainous island of Tutuila. Once again we are back to mountainous islands that are the vestiges of extinct volcanoes. The harbor here is the result again of a crater that has been opened to the sea as the volcano sank.

We take advantage of the facilities at the American hospital here to have our teeth checked and cleaned. We need no medical attention, but we purchase a good supply of vitamins to supplement our somewhat lopsided diet. Equatorial Samoa harbors a tiny shop that beckons Charles and I to frequently linger and satisfy our longing for ice cream - that sublime concoction of mid-ocean dreams.

The process of checking in and out of this country is straightforward and reasonably fast. We are ready to leave. Charles and Cornelia on *Rhinoceros* also plan to set sail for Western Samoa. It will be just an overnight sail to the west. We travel within sight of each other and watch as their night navigation lights gain, then pass us. Charles was a racing sailor back in New England and was to be part of an Olympic racing team at one point in his life. So again little ol' Horizon is last to the finish line. There is one advantage to this strategy, however; we gain information from those early arrivals about the entrance we are about to navigate and learn of any problems we might encounter getting to the anchorage. We satisfy ourselves these tardy arrivals fit our casual approach to this new lifestyle.

At the broad entrance between the menacing reefs, we look into the open bay lying at the foot of the capitol, Apia. A large Catholic Church with white- washed walls has been the landmark for many years to sailors offshore. Since it is late in the day, Cornelia informs us customs is closed. We anchor nearby. Tomorrow morning we will join them to tie up beside a barge at the dock and formalize our stay in Western Samoa.

This is an independent country. The Western Samoans have worked hard to resist interference from any nation that tries to impose standards contrary to their ancient customs. Where a lot of the countries we visit encourage some commerce, either commercially or in ideas, Western Samoa seems content with its own identity. We become aware, as we extend our stay that a complex set of rules and accommodations exist here. Our response as guests must be measured and respectful to these dynamics. To help us in the process, we are fortunate to know the young couple from Goshen, Indiana, who are here on their two-year assignment as Peace Corps workers. Doug Minter works in the agriculture project and Jill, his wife is trying to work with the women in food and nutrition projects. She faces more problems than Doug because the authority of a woman is questioned, not seriously considered valid.

It is a country of tribes with chiefs whose authority is paramount. The governance of a village is one of communal ownership where wealth and success is measured in terms of the group rather than the individual. Care must be taken when accepting an invitation to visit a home so not to create jealousy among neighbors. Jill and Doug were presented with a problem when they accepted an invitation that included us. It was to the home of a family with whom they had been working. However, a family that felt they too were included in the Minter's circle of friends was distraught when the invitation did not include them. The occasion was then canceled.

At this time, Western Samoa has one of the highest suicide rates in the world. A lot of this is due, Doug feels, because of the quick temper displayed by so many. Suicide, many times, is a hasty response to an argument without much, if any, forethought.

Because of their cultural pride, we are privileged to see a landscape unlike any we have seen up to this time. On a bus trip around this island Savai'i, we drive through palm shaded villages. We stop at a remote forest to try the chocolate taste of the white pulpy texture of the cocoa nut. The dirt road takes us through small villages. A home is called a 'fale'. It is an oval platform of sand covered stones around which poles support the thatch roof. The dirt yards have been swept clean. Some display hedges or bright flowered borders. The open sides of the fale forthrightly express their idea that privacy is not a desired attribute. When we stop for lunch of barbequed chicken, corn on the cob and coleslaw, we notice we are sharing the beach with pigs. There must be ten pigs snuffling along the surf's edge as they dig with their snouts for clams and crabs. How does a pig open a clam or handle the claws of a crab? The explanations are vague, yet there has to be some success as we witness the perseverance of those pigs.

The men we pass seem huge to Don and me, perhaps because both of us are short. We look at their commanding stature, never thinking to question the fact that all the men are wearing skirts called a lavalava. The women also carry abundant weight and bear this with a kind of majestic grace. It is the children who look thin. According to the Minters, this is a result of the hierarchy where a child is placed at the bottom of the 'being cared for' list. They are fed last and are passed over when favors are shared.

Because individual ownership is not really a part of their experience, it is possible that a native may consider something of mine, an item he could use. When I take a lovely book of poetry with photos describing the beauty of Western Samoa to the post office for mailing, the shadow of a doubt crosses my mind as I hand the package to the postal clerk. She casually slides the package under the counter. Anne never received the book. One other aspect of this culture catching us by surprise is the behavior of the children. A band of them shouting with threatening gestures will surround us. It is a culture that has attracted many anthropologists, with varying and sometimes contradictory analysis and insights. This was the culture that attracted Margaret Meade as she traced their origins to assess the cause and effects molding this unique people.

We enjoy an evening at Aggie Gray's restaurant with its origins dating back to WW II. After enjoying new tastes at a large buffet, a performance begins with elaborate dances by men and women. The men are huge and sport tattoos covering their bodies. Their muscled torsos gleam above the loincloth bound hips as their dances emphasize an aggressive and warrior-like attitude. There is a lot of stomping and lunging with loud grunts and shouts. At one point, as I look through my video camera to record this raucous demonstration, I jump with surprise when a dancer leaps off the stage to glare directly into the camera. I had been granted permission to video the performance and this display was, no doubt, part of their act to impress the 'palagi' (foreigner) of a fierce demeanor. The dances of the women, in contrast, display a graceful character - using fluid gestures of swaying arms and wrist movements that accompany a slow shuffle of the feet. These motions speak eloquently to the melodies they are singing. At the Friday evening marketplace, under a blanket of stars, many of the church choirs offer melodic background to the bustle of the buying and selling atmosphere - a mesmerizing experience.

Robert Louis Stevenson spent the last five years of his life on this island, on bush-land he had purchased here. He called his spot high above the sea near a quiet stream 'Vailima'. He was known and loved among the tribes. They lovingly called him 'tusitala', teller of tales. We hoped to see the inside of his home, now a Government House, but were only allowed a glimpse of the outside as the bus drove through the grounds. His grave is here with a verse he wrote inscribed on the tombstone.

It reads in part:
> *'This be the verse you grave for me:*
> *Here he lies where he longed to be;*
> *Home is the sailor, home from the sea,*
> *And the hunter home from the hill.'*

In the morning, as we make preparations to leave, we hear one last time the music of the policemen's band performing as they raise their national flag above the parade grounds. With these strains drifting across the harbor, we raise our anchor, hoist the sails and take our leave from this fascinating country.

It is the seventh of October. Tonga is about three hundred miles south of Samoa. This takes us three days to sail. However, instead of arriving in Tonga on the tenth, the calendar says we have arrived on the ninth. We've lost an entire day as we crossed the international dateline, 180 degrees longitude. It is possible to celebrate October ten all over again. I don't know that we can improve the tenth's path. It sped us along on one of the more comfortable points of sail, a broad reach. The wind crosses the boat just aft of amid-ship, pushing us along with only a slight heel. It's what I like to call a 'peach of a reach'!

Before leaving Elkhart, I had spent many hours transferring to tape the music from the LP records in our library before donating our collection to a retirement home. On passages such as these 'peach of a reach' days we enjoy custom designed concerts of Brahms, Chopin, Puccini, Dave Brubeck, Streisand or others from our catalogue of favorites. Very special moments are these as we drift under blue Pacific skies, the waves rippling along the hull make a background accompaniment of quiet energy to the strains of favorite composers. This is the sum of all things beautiful.

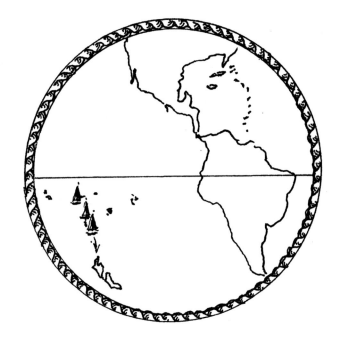

Tonga

CHAPTER 7
LEAPING A GALE

As we make our way around the Vava'u group of islands in the northern portion of Tonga, it seems almost familiar. At first we can't put our finger on the similarity until we realize the islands here remind us of the islands of northern Lakes Michigan and Huron that we explored all those years ago on *Horizon 1*. We are looking at granite like, rocky islands that, with a substitution of tall pine trees for the tall palm trees, we might envision ourselves back with the cool breezes across the northern lakes of Michigan. As we continue along the serpentine route around islands then navigate a narrow pass, we arrive at one of the best-protected anchorages in this part of the world.

The main village, Neiafu, is stretched along high banks that surround this inland lake. It is the center of administration for this northern group of islands called the Vava'u group. Tonga consists of three distinct groups. This Vava'u group of islands displays high rocky shores with plateaus stretching inland, a contrast to the mountainous peaks or low-lying motus of French Polynesia. The central group of islands is low lying and resembles the atolls with motus that we visited the previous months. This middle group is known as the Ha'apai group.

The southern group some two hundred-fifty miles from Vava'u, called the Tongatapu group, is the home of the king, King Taufa'ahau Tupou IV. He is the direct descendant of the first king, King George Tupou I, who was first converted to Christianity by a British group of Methodist missionaries. He was able to overcome the traditional tribal leaders and proclaim the throne as his sovereignty. Under his guidance, slaves were freed. He established an appointed legislature to represent all classes of his citizens. Eventually, by decree, he gave parcels of land to each family. A kind of benevolent dictatorship became the standard of governing. Now as the population expands there isn't enough land to award to eligible native born Tongans. As a result there are large numbers of people unemployed. Many have left their home shores to look for work in New Zealand and the United States. Tonga is the oldest kingdom in Polynesia and the only Pacific realm to have never known foreign rule.

We drop our anchor in thirty feet of water beside *Sunshine*. Nearby we see *Cool Change* with the catamaran *Canowie* close as well. The new names on boat transoms are now familiar after listening on the ham radio to this fleet making passages together. Knowing the congeniality we've been enjoying to this point assures us there will be new friends added to our roster of sailing mates.

We proceed to gather the paperwork once again to make our visit official. Going ashore to the port captain's office, we're never sure of the official response to our presence. The authorized office is located. We enter and sit in front of the large desk. Behind it sits a dour faced official, filling the room with his privilege of power displayed by a haughty demeanor. He continues to look at the pile of papers spread across the desk - ignoring us. This continues for seemingly endless moments. Don finally speaks; "we've come to this office to present our customs and immigration papers for clearance." The official looks up with disdain. Interrupting his busy schedule is clearly an affront to his position and office. He continues to shuffle papers. We continue to sit. This is the only office we can accomplish the customs procedure. Finally with exasperation and a sigh he grabs our passports and documentation papers. Now with exaggerated precision he spends endless moments leafing through our passports examining each stamp. Finally, without looking at us, gives his approval with a forceful thump of each official stamp. In addition, as we prepare to leave his uncomfortable presence, still staring at his desk, he warns us. "All the outlying islands are off limits to all visiting yachts. Stay in the lagoon." Period - No discussion.

As we make our way back to the anchorage, we stop by the other boats and discover each one has been restricted to this spot as well. Evidently there's an ongoing power struggle among the government workers. In this way they've made their statement loud and clear. The local tourist businesses are furious with the shenanigans of these few men who dominate the local politics. As a result, they call a meeting of interested tourists as well as local businesses affected by these new rules. After the meeting a telegram is sent to the King in Tongatapu. His immediate order to these officials demands they cease their political maneuvering. For years these islands have been christened 'the friendly islands' - inspired, no doubt, by the treatment Captain Cook and his crew received on one of the many stops they made here. We all are granted, within a week's time, the required cruising permits that allow us to visit the outlying islands of Vava'u.

As we cruise among the thirty islands that comprise this group, one impressive scenic view after another occasions us to stop and explore. Sparrow Cave outlines '*Horizon*' anchored outside it's entrance. We've taken the dinghy inside its dusky, cathedral-like interior to capture a unique frame around our photo of *Horizon*. Throughout the lagoon the exquisite coral formations reflect their beauty through the clear water. We snorkel through beds of sea fans, brain and stag horn coral alive with blossoms of sea worms waving their brilliantly colored petals. When we touch these small flowerlike creatures they immediately disappear into the tiny holes dotting the surface of the coral head. On the sandy stretches between the coral are star fish and brittle stars spidering a slow crawl as they forage for food. Looking under ledges and lifting stones we find shells attached with their mantels or siphons extended to find food. Many varieties of cowrie shells can be found here, as well as the spider conch in shapes I've not seen before.

The fish, however, are not that plentiful. Throughout the world this is becoming a problem that no country wants to address, including the industrial nations. Programs are being introduced to educate native populations with the relationship of fishing conservation to their livelihood as fishermen - a relationship that needs to balance nature's ability to replenish itself in order to sustain both sides of the problem. Lets hope it's not too little too late.

Of course there are beach parties. Perhaps one of the more memorable ones is the party we attend with about ten boats to celebrate Halloween, a festival unknown to the local folks. To not offend local customs, we find a remote beach where we come ashore in the most outlandish costumes we can piece together from our limited resources. The results are hilarious, there is the Sheik of Araby with a belly dancer close behind. Here is Wes, a solo sailor dressed as a rather attractive female with accusations hurled round him that he's been sailing alone too long. The children in the group, really quite a few, are scampering about as pirates and princesses. Don and I work hard on our costumes. We get out those cool duds we wore when we left Annapolis. With a long tail pinned appropriately on my blue, long underwear, I crawl into their warm confines as I try to ignore equatorial temperatures. Over my head I pull a pillowcase on which I've drawn a rat face, complete with whiskers and small ears. Don is garbed in a brown plastic garbage bag with a wide band of aluminum foil around his waist. On his head he wears the palm hat made by Hiti's family in the Tuomotos with more palm fronds decorating the brim. Together we are the rat that tried to climb the tin-girthed coconut tree. We are voted the most unique.

As we continue searching for enchanting little anchorages, we stumble into a hidden little lake with access through a cut in the rocky shoreline. After making ourselves secure in the small anchorage where a few houses are visible on shore, we learn of the invitation presented to all the yachts arriving here in Hunga. Saturday afternoon we dinghy towards shore in the wake of other dinks making way to a small dock. Instead of a carry in meal, we are asked to make a financial contribution to a fund the village is promoting. They plan to build a small shed that will house the many tools another yacht has donated, tools to help in the repair of their motorboats. Included in this tool chest is equipment for welding. It really is a sizable gift from this California yacht. Later, we heard that the bad tempered officials we dealt with on arrival were causing problems for the village of Hunga as well. They paid no duty on all this equipment. We never learned the outcome of the problem. But today everyone is in a happy mood as the hot coals are slowly roasting four small pigs in the pit called an omu. Vickie, one of the crewmembers on *Isis,* is leading songs that delight the folks with her inventive renditions on the accordion she is squeezing.

The little pigs look so scrawny; I can't believe how fatty they are when we are served the slivers of meat. Accompanying this are tasty fishcakes, roasted sweet potatoes and fried breadfruit with fresh fruit for dessert. It really is a large buffet of tantalizing dishes spread across corrugated tin sheets laid on sawhorses. Once again, the guests are served first while the villagers retreat several feet. By now most of the yachting community has become aware of this traditional expression of hospitality. We take small portions to make sure there is enough food for everyone. As we leisurely sit under the large breadfruit tree we enjoy visiting with the villagers. They invite us to join them for walks through their village.

We are surprised what a large village stretches along grassy paths on top of the plateau. The homes are built of wood, some include modern jalousie windows. Many are surrounded with fragrant frangipani and bougainvillea blooming in colorful profusion. Our guide, Vaha, invites us to attend church with his family tomorrow then join them for dinner after the service. We gladly accept his invitation. Tonga remains a very staunch religious kingdom. The missionaries, mostly English Methodists, established in the 1830's a strong presence in the life of the King and his subjects. Today the Sabbath is strictly observed as a day of rest. The only activity permitted beside worship is visiting friends.

Next morning wearing our best Sunday clothes, we arrive outside the small wooden building to wait for Vaha and his wife Mafi. They show us to the only seat in the church, a bench along the back wall. In front of us the floor is covered with mats of woven palm fronds, a table with a large open Bible stands at the front. Our hosts excuse themselves and we quietly sit on the bench. Two grandmothers come in with six children to sit comfortably on the matted floor. These women are wearing the distinctive traditional skirt, the ta'ovala, that we had noticed women wearing in Neiafu. It is a woven mat, much like the floor mats here in the church. This rather rigid mat is worn as a skirt that is secured with a decorative woven waistband. Occasionally we see men wearing them. Theirs are secured with a string of twisted coconut fibers called sennet. Some of these prized possessions look well worn and are barely holding together. They have been handed down through the generations, gaining value with each passing generation.

We hear the clanging of the church bell. As we look through the window, Vaha is banging on a discarded water tank hanging from the small tree outside the church. Almost immediately the little church floor is filled with families from the neighborhood. I notice a father wearing one of these mat skirts. He sits with two children beside him, while in his lap another child is sleeping. In front of us sits an elder of the church. His presence bears this out. In a few minutes, he leads with his strong voice as the congregation joins him in a glorious hymn. Glorious hardly describes what we are hearing. These hymns are sung without any written music. The harmonies are sometimes so intricate and complex that my college major in music is confounded by the glorious sound lifting these rafters. They sing with the support of a strong diaphragm that loudly proclaims the promise held in the verse. Nothing is sung in the quiet register. Everyone is singing except the small children. Unknown to them they are absorbing all of this glorious sound so that one day, they too will spontaneously burst forth with this same joyful noise they learned from their fathers and mothers. I am so fascinated with this magnificent choir I ask Vaha if anyone would object if I brought the video camera next Sunday to record the singing. I want to share this experience with our family back home. He seems to think there would be no objection.

After church we walk a short distance along flower lined paths to join Vaha and Mafi at their newly built home. The house, with its two large rooms, is supported above ground on cement block pillars. One of the rooms is their sleeping room with the grass mats, their beds, rolled out on the floor. The other is a sunny room with large windows reflecting sunshine across the shiny new linoleum covered floor. The only furniture is a long picnic table covered with a cloth where plates and silverware are laid. After grace is given Mafi serves roast pork, sweet potatoes, taro leaves with coconut cream and a new dish that I served many times after this visit. Mafi has taken papaya before it is fully ripe, cut it into cubes and just slightly sautéing it with onions turns out a wonderful, flavorful vegetable dish. The chocolate chip cookies I baked are served for dessert. All this cooking and roasting Mafi does outdoors in a small open sided cookhouse with an omu and a fireplace affair for top of the stove cooking.

We give them T-shirts, fishing line and a bright potholder for Mafi. Don suggests salt-water gargles for their son suffering a sore throat. Now as they proudly stand in front of their new home, we take their picture with our Polaroid camera. While they watch these photos slowly revealing their faces, it brings a smile to Mafi who has remained very quiet during our visit. After walking the paths through the small village and past two more churches, we say our adieus then return to *Horizon*.

Time to move on. Here it is the beginning of November with miles to go before New Zealand by Christmas! Joining us on this next leg will be another new yacht we met here in Vava'u, Bev and Mark aboard *Saturna* hailing from Vancouver, Canada. We make our way south through the low-lying atolls of the Ha'apai group. With more coral heads presenting wavering outlines through the water, it's important to keep a sharp lookout as we move through these atolls

In this Ha'apai group of islands, there is a mysterious island that rises above the water only to suddenly disappear below the surface. Tonga lies along one of the deepest valleys on the ocean floor. The Tonga Trench pushes against the Indo-Australian Plate making it one of the more volcanic prone areas in the Pacific region. It is thought this disappearing island is the birthing of a new volcano. We talked to other boat-crews claiming they saw the phenomenon of underwater radiance as they sailed through this central group of islands. The only extraordinary sight our two boats experience during this leg is the sounding of a humpback whale as it passes between us. Our yachts are only a hundred yards apart making the close proximity of this enormous leviathan steering a path between us, awe-inspiring. Its enormous length reducing the size of our two boats to bobbing corks along its sides.

The second day out of Vava'u we come upon a sparkling white beach stretching for miles along our path. The lay of the island offers enough protection that we decide to drop the hook and explore a bit. There don't seem to be any villages here. However, we do see a blue tent snuggled in under the bushes along the beach. As we approach in the dinghy, we see two kayaks pulled in beside the tent on shore. No sooner have we pulled the dinghy high on the beach than Susan and Jeff Sloss greet us. They are owners of a kayaking business and are now exploring possibilities for this paddle adventure beyond the Alaskan shores where they are based. The six of us spend fun filled days together walking this exquisite beach, snorkeling around the coral heads and sharing meals together. Several evenings we engage in scrappy contests of memory as we challenge each other to find answers to Trivial Pursuits.

'Alaska Discovery' has been a dream come true for Susan and Jeff after a lot of hard work. Now as they are expanding their knowledge of distant destinations for their clients, the challenge has become how to make these remote areas available. Susan tells us she is a descendent of Fletcher Christian of *Mutiny on the Bounty* fame. They had hoped to attend a family reunion on Pitcairn Island, however a strike by French airline employees erased any hope of getting to that remote island. The two of them are staying another week here on this island so we say good-by. *Saturna* and *Horizon* continue the last leg to Tongatapu, the capitol of Tonga.

Tongatapu is a large bit of land. Its outline is shaped much like a pork chop. If you curl the tip of the chop a bit, a large lagoon appears offering some protection. Following the well-marked channel to the quayside at the town of Nuku'lofa, we decide to anchor outside the breakwater protected harbor. The harbor looks full. The nice breeze we are enjoying just outside its outline suggests there could be sweltering days inside its boundary. Several other boats join us - *Solmar, Cool Change* and a few new boats we have yet to meet. There is only a short process to provide the necessary information to the well-behaved customs officials here. We inform them we have arrived from the Northern Groups and give them our proposed length of stay here in Tongatapu.

Visiting the marketplace we first see and enjoy New Zealand apples and canned butter. The other vegetables are locally grown and healthy looking. This island has a very productive agriculture industry built on the rich volcanic soil left from ash deposited centuries ago.

The island's silhouette is a sloping plateau with the southern shore rising above a rocky, coral coastline that descends gradually to the shores of the lagoon along the north shore. We join Ligia and Joao from *Solmar* to rent a cab with the driver as our guide around the island. The first stop is under a large mango tree in the front yard of a small house. Here a woman is sitting on the dirt yard as she works on a large tapa cloth spread in front of her. This cloth is made from the bark of a mulberry tree. Many times as we walk through villages, we hear the distinctive hammering of a thick stick against a log over which is draped the bark of this tree. By continuous pounding as it is pulled over the log, the fibers of the bark will be softened and made pliable. These sheets are then pasted together to make a very large canvas, yards in width and length. The lady working on this piece has almost completed the design. She is painting with a stubby brush made of coconut fibers tied together. The two colors she uses are made from natural dyes, one black the other brown. The designs are traditional heirlooms arranged by the individual artist to depict life as she sees it. Most of these large tapestries tell a story or myth about the origins of man on these islands.

The talents of the many artists in Tonga are well known. The guidebooks describe their creative skills, as do the recommendations of yachties here before us. We waited until we arrived here to purchase native art. We bought large baskets in the northern town of Neiafu and filled them with carvings, dolls and other handsome crafts to be sent home to our families. It was there that a large boat from Hawaii purchased one of these very large tapa cloths measuring twenty feet long by ten feet wide that he proposed attaching to the ceiling of his house in Hawaii.

Continuing our tour around the island, we pass the large buildings and beautifully landscaped grounds of the Church of Latter-day Saints. Our driver has few favorable words to say about this ostentatious display rising beside the modest homes of the natives scattered nearby. Further down the road we come by a cemetery surrounded by trees. The sandy mounds with outlines around the graves decorated with flags, shells, artificial flowers and most visible, the inverted beer bottles glistening in the sun. The frangipani trees around the perimeter of the cemetery are leafless now, but hanging from the branches are hundreds of fruit bats. Because this is the only country in the Pacific where this bat is tapu, sacred, it is the one place they are easily seen. The royal family possesses the only right to hunt the bat here in Tonga, while other countries kill the bats for food on a regular basis.

We stop for lunch at a little restaurant with only American hamburgers featured on its menu. The afternoon drive takes us along the higher south coast. This spectacular coast displays hundreds of blowholes where the ocean surges into the rocky coast forcing water through the many holes and fissures that comb the coral formations. It is windy today. Fountains of water dance along the rocky coast displaying curtains of translucent cascades. The spout of water shooting 50 feet into the air just ahead of us suddenly showers us with a spray of salt water that sparkles with a rainbow of colors. Dancing along the coast, these fountains display in endless repetition. Really outstanding! Our last stop for the day is beside the King's palace. This wooden Victorian style, large house faces the sea with the front lawn, now a bit shaggy, embracing two tall Norwegian pines.

We return to the harbor with a driver that is unhappy with us. He was sure all tourists gave generous tips. We explain the price agreed upon before we stepped into his cab was the fee we had agreed to pay. Plus, we added, the meal we bought him was beyond the agreed price. With a shrug of his shoulders he is gone.

The November temperatures are rising each day as we near the summer months here on the south side of the equator. Next day sitting in the cockpit with the sun shining on a calm sea, we are totally unprepared for one of our more harrowing experiences while anchored. With no warning, the wind suddenly goes from a calm five knots to a screaming fifty knots in the blink of an eye. The wind from the north is rolling into this lagoon with huge waves building and breaking on the coral shore behind us. Where our stern had lain away from the coral for a week, it is now dangerously close to the jagged heads exposed as the huge waves wash across their ominous surface. We have only one anchor out. The boat is beginning to hobbyhorse. First the bow soars high in the air, then the stern, in exaggerated motion, tilts skyward. I start the engine. Standing at the helm, I motor forward to relieve the pressure on the anchor and steer to keep the bow heading into the wind. Even this is difficult as the wind blows the bow to one side. Don, meanwhile is getting in the dinghy to drop the other anchor forward. I am alarmed as I see him struggling to release the anchor at the bow to unload it into the dink. The bow is making scissors movements against the dinghy. It looks very dangerous. I'm afraid he'll be badly injured. We can see our friends standing on the breakwater yelling advice, but there is no way they can come to our aid. The seas are awesome. Just as I decide to leave the wheel and go forward to help Don, I see two men swim by the hull and climb into the dinghy. With their help the other anchor is dropped ahead of *Horizon*. The boat seems stable now as distance from the reef is maintained. For two hours we monitor our position as the gale continues to howl around us.

These kind natives, when they saw our predicament, swam across that sharp jagged coral to offer their help. Now joining us in the cockpit to rest while the winds continue bashing, we learn they are father and son. They had been walking along the waterfront when, they too, were surprised at the sudden blast of wind. With no hesitation they crossed that dangerous reef and came to our rescue. We can't repay them; they refuse our offer of money or clothes and just quietly smile as we share drinks of cocoa and cookies. They leave as suddenly as they came. The next day we write an article describing the storm and its effect on us. Expressing the gratitude we feel for these two brave souls who came to our aid, we stop at the newspaper office to request they print our article entitled 'These *Are* the Friendly Islands'.

Cool Change had left earlier that day on their way to little Atata Island at the tip of the pork chop. They, too, were beaten by these same winds. Since they hadn't anchored yet, they continued to motor around the lagoon till it passed. But it was a tense time for them as well.

We join about a half dozen boats at the tiny anchorage beside the island of Atata. The dances that are performed at the hotel have drawn us to this place. These dances present the cultural story of Tonga. With much shouting and stomping, the dances by the men are again bold, suggesting warriors. Their oiled torsos glowing in the torchlight make a virile display of their strength. In contrast, the girls are modestly attired. They move only their hands and legs with none of the hip movements we have been seeing in previous countries.

We enjoy walking through the small village on this island. There is more beating of the tapa cloth heard in the distance. We walk through fields of vanilla plants; the long, purple beans not yet ready to harvest. Young boys are climbing the tall trunks of the palm trees with only their bare hands and feet to propel them to the cluster of coconuts at the top. Twisting them free with their toes, the coconut plops to the ground where an older brother takes a swipe with his machete and cuts a wedge from the green coconut. They pass them around the group, inviting us to drink the clear coconut water inside. On a hot day it's a very refreshing drink with only a light coconut flavor, rich in electrolytes.

As we sit at anchor this Thanksgiving morning, a magnificent sight rises through the morning mists. A tall three-mast bark ghosts its way along the lagoon. Passing us, it makes way toward the main anchorage we had left three days ago. Over the radio we can hear the captain of the '*Eagle*' being granted permission to enter the harbor. All its sails hoisted - here is a splendid sailing vessel from home, the sailing training vessel for the U.S. Coast Guard. With the Stars and Stripes flying, it sails by us on this day uniquely ours. It is a day not being celebrated by our British, Canadian, South African or Tongan friends. If we even remotely thought we who share the holiday with this great ship might be invited to share in a turkey dinner, we found the sun to set with nary an invitation. But these same friends from all corners of the world anchored around us, rallied together. Our six smaller ships, nevertheless, enjoy our own thanksgiving, celebrating friends well found.

Plans are now being made for the longer sail south into the higher latitudes, beyond the trade wind sailing we have been enjoying. Our captains are discussing routes, currents and the prevailing wind patterns for early December. All these factors influence the best time to make the passage to New Zealand. It is the last day of November '87 as we make our way out the pass for the second time. We hope the indefinable problem we are having with the engine overheating that has plagued us since leaving the States is now solved with our further tinkering. We pray the passage South will be uneventful.

Leaping a gale in Tonga, *Horizon* hobby-horses at anchor.

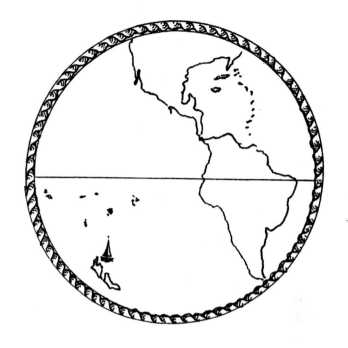

New Zealand

CHAPTER 8
A SUMMERTIME CHRISTMAS

After thirteen days at sea with no whistles or lights indicating an overheating engine, we sail into the Bay of Islands at the northern tip of New Zealand. We actually had quite good weather most of the way with sunny skies and moonlit nights. The winds were moderate but blowing us in the face. This forced us to sail about five hundred added miles east and west as we tacked back and forth to make some headway south. To tack, we bring the bow of the boat through the eye of the wind a hundred degrees on the compass to fill the sails with some speed toward a new direction, outlining a zigzag course on our chart. Some of these legs strongly suggested we were heading for Australia and demanded that we claw our way back to a more southerly heading.

A startling phenomenon held me spellbound on one of these tacks West. Scanning the darkness ahead, there seemed to be a boat showing its bright white navigation light directly ahead. I continued to monitor its passage - the light remaining fixed to our position. With just the white light visible, I knew I was looking at the stern of a boat. I continued to be bothered that it stayed at a fixed position ahead for such a long time. Finally, I realized Venus, the goddess of love and beauty had mesmerized my night vision to her magic once again. There was no boat, just the outstanding bright star's image holding me in her spell until the light of this glowing planet sank below the horizon. It has happened before and, no doubt, will taunt me again.

Finally on the 13th of December, close to midnight, range markers that lead us into the protected waters of the bay become visible off the coast of New Zealand. Seeing these working, modern navigational aids, we become aware that we can relax and enjoy a society organized much like the one that taught us navigational competence. These aids have three portions red, white and green that immediately give us visual direction. As long as the white light is visible, the course into the bay is being laid. If the red or green portion is displayed, a revision needs to be made to maintain the correct heading. When seeing a red light we are to the left of course or to the port side, the green indicates we are too far right, the starboard side. This is easy and straightforward enough to read even at midnight, when we are tired after the long passage. Making our way far enough into the protected waters, we move out of the channel to anchor free of traffic. Now we have time to look about us. The hillsides are dotted with Christmas lights twinkling about trees and doorways. What a sight . . . now for the first time I have pangs of homesickness. It is Christmas, a time for family gathering. Our family seems so far away tonight.

Next morning we continue the short distance into the customs dock at the village of Opua. The word had been spread back in Tonga that the New Zealand customs officials, upon our arrival, would confiscate fresh food, canned meats and living matter like plants. We made sure we ate all the eggs and canned chicken plus the few fresh veggies remaining before tying up to this dock. The officials come aboard, looking sharp in their uniforms complete with the shorts that are the signature of any New Zealand male, no matter how cold the day. It isn't long until they are joking with an easy manner that makes us feel welcome. However, the Christmas cactus I had been tenderly nurturing for the past year with pink buds offering promise of cascading brilliance, now is unceremoniously dumped into a plastic garbage bag with a nod of regret from the officials. And the one remaining can of bacon we had purchased in Tonga sits on the table for them to bury at a garbage dump. We are having such friendly banter that the bacon was forgotten. With no sense of guilt we enjoy it with our next breakfast of New Zealand eggs. The reasoning for all of their concern about the introduction of any product that might contaminate the isolated island agriculture makes sense. We remember quarantines in the States when a crop is threatened.

After the paper work has been completed, we move *Horizon* around the dock to the large anchorage now swinging with boats familiar and those unknown that we find an exhilarating part of a new harbor. On *Annette* we meet Gayle and Jerry Smith. He was pianist for Elvis Presley before taking leave of that job inducing stress, to one that invites the songs of the *Sirens*. We feel privileged to welcome Susan Hiscock aboard *Horizon*. Circumnavigating several times with her husband, Eric, they wrote the guidebooks many of us have studied. With their descriptions of a life at sea, they opened windows of possibilities for the rest of us. Widowed now, she continues to live aboard *Wanderer V* here in New Zealand - such a gracious lady. The sailboat *Crazy Lady* had shared anchorages with us before, but it is only now that we meet Betty Pierce, her captain. She is a savvy lady sixty years of age. To circumnavigate as a solo sailor takes some courage. She demonstrates this with no hint of 'crazy' evident to the rest of us sharing her waypoints.

The small village of Opua nestles amid gentle hills. This harbor seems to embody all the qualities that the term 'harbor' has always brought to mind. Its protection cradles the fleet in a large basin surrounded by these lush hillsides. We are anxious to walk and stretch our legs a bit. We walk by small homes reposing behind well tended front yards that feature new and outstanding landscape plants we've not seen before. In many of the yards we see the large, dramatic blooms of the protea bush. The streets are lined with jacaranda trees with its luminous lavender blossoms cascading through the green leaves. We are happy to see a dinghy dock provided that rises and falls with the wide ranging tides - when stepping off we are at the post office right next door to a small but well stocked grocery store. On the back-porch of the store are several washers and dryers that stay in constant use by this band of seafarers tired of hand washing.

There are buses available to the nearby towns of Pahia, Russell and Kerikeri but we decide it might be a smart decision to purchase a used car. We've heard of a dealer in Kerikeri who has promoted a business of selling then buying back these cars that are so much in demand. Most of us plan to stay in these latitudes for six months that will allow ample time to see the entire country. We find a little blue Morris that looks like it still has a bit of life left in its tires and an assurance from the salesman that its engine will get us to Fiordland in the mountains of the South Island and back.

There are so many of these cars now in the parking lot provided by the town that a new problem arises. Some enterprising local man realized the possibilities this new concentration of cars posed. Here is a source of available car parts that could be his for the taking. He hired gangs of unemployed boys to come at night and remove batteries, seats, whatever, to resell. Since the police are overwhelmed with this new bit of mischief the anchorage rallies. Watches being standard for seafarers, it's agreed we stand watch over our parking lot at night to notify the officers of any suspicious activity. This schedule continues for several weeks when the whole enterprising scheme is uncovered, arrests are made and the trouble is no longer with us.

It is here in the north of the North Island that the historical backdrop for the birth of the nation, New Zealand is cherished and restored along the quiet streets of Russell and Kerikeri. We enjoy walks through the villages. They have restored the oldest church in the country in the village of Russell. For a short while this little village was the capitol of the country with a history of violence and debauchery as the whaling ships seemed to compete with the crews of the trading ships to reach a level of lawlessness that shore leave often symbolized. In nearby Waitangi, a site is preserved marking the signing of a treaty with the native Maori chieftain that offered the protection of England and gave to the British Empire a new jewel in her crown.

On the way to Kerikeri we drive through kiwi groves. With their vines groomed on trellises they look much like grapevines until you see the brown, fuzzy fruit hanging from the vines overhead. Down by the water we enjoy lunch on the verandah of one of the restored homes of this earlier period. Standing nearby is the Old Stone Store where the early goods that were the staples of the British colonists in 1830 are displayed. Beyond the store is a restored Maori village with Maori guides giving interesting descriptions of native plants growing here and their use for medicines and food. Continuing over the hillsides at every curve in the road, we can see large flocks of grazing sheep. There are more sheep in New Zealand than the two-footed New Zealander, offering an extensive choice of mutton and lamb at the butcher shop. And later on when visiting the stores in Auckland the finest wool sweaters, shawls and scarves in lovely shades and patterns could be purchased. We survey the towns and trails that compose this picture book setting of a pastoral and quaint countryside. We plan to share this newly gained knowledge with family and friends planning to visit us here.

It isn't long until we have a chance to drive our 'new' car to the airport at Auckland, about a three-hour drive south. There we'll meet son Tom for his ten-day Christmas vacation with us. Since we haven't done much 'gunk holing' around the bays and coves here in the Bay of Islands we take this opportunity with Tom, to anchor in different little bays to explore and hike the hillsides. These offer us nice trails, some through woods and across pastures. We can't help but notice the local sailors, out now in large numbers for their Christmas holidays, with a passion to anchor close by our boat. Always very friendly but just a mite closer than we are used to in an anchorage.

Hidden along the back roads, we discover a place of unusual beauty. We repeatedly bring our friends to share its quiet majesty. An almost missed dot on the map indicated a nature walk. As one of the guidebooks to this country has expressed, "It's places in New Zealand that nudge your sense of wonder, that make you take a quick breath with a sense that 'Here and only here can I experience this'." As Don and I drive along the dusty back roads, around curves and over small hills dotted with sheep, we see small farms nestled along the way. The flocks of sheep embroider a woolen skein as they delicately weave together the farms across the hills of New Zealand's North Island. Trying to locate this small dot on the map keeps us back-tracking our way along the dirt roads. Ahead we see a trail-marker with a small parking space just barely scratched beside the road. Is this the dot we are looking for? Pulling backpacks over our shoulders, we chatter about the similarity of today's drive to the Bucks County hills of my childhood in Pennsylvania.

There is no name to the trail as we move from the sunshine of the road into the shade of an ordinary path through oak trees with some scrub at their base. Gradually as the path loses the undergrowth by its side, we become aware of a magnified dimension stretching ahead of us. The sun sends shafts of filtered light through the canopy expanding above us. Our chatter hesitates. We begin to whisper. With each step there is a spacious reach encompassing every step. Stopping, we listen. There is barely a sound - no bird song. With breath suspended, there's just a rustle of foliage restless overhead. The easy path curling around hills becomes a boardwalk as the ground underfoot becomes soft and spongy. The trees are changing from the ordinary to tall straight trunks that thrust overhead. It is a cathedral setting. These tall trees with their trunks stretching as columns support the green spattered vaulted dome overhead. There is no rose window. Instead a circumference of a diffused light lends spatial radiance. The colors take on a dimension of muted autumnal shades of moss green, ochre and russet outlined with deep chestnut browns. We have stumbled into this Kauri forest. Surely this is one of these places of wonder the guidebook suggests. The Kauri tree with the beautiful earth tones of its smooth bark, like rich tapestry tautly stretched over the straight trunk, grandly reaches to a very tall and majestic splendor. With no lower branches to interrupt its climb to the sky there unfolds an umbrella of foliage. We crane our neck to see a hundred or more feet high, the fractured sunbeams scatter through the patterned green leaves. It is a tree unique to New Zealand that was sought by early ship builders. Its strength and the lack of knots provided strong and smooth boards needed in the construction of seaworthy ships. Beneath their tall majesty, we see for the first time - giant tree ferns providing a delicate balance. The green fronds at the top of a sturdy trunk, six to ten feet tall, look like ferns we knew from the floor of the Michigan woods. These, however, are an exaggerated version. The large umbrella of lacy fronds with its diameter stretch of six feet or more could offer an elegant shelter from sunshine or showers. Where there are paths to be made, this little country constructs, with simple beauty, quiet trails that become part of the landscape. The trail stops. Now we step along a boardwalk that winds across a bog to an expanding deck surrounded with seats defining its outline. Stepping softly across the deck we settle amidst this splendor to eat our lunch. There is no echo of the surf here. Here the resonance of the land sends its own harmonies - the thrum of a breeze among the trunks is heard as the distant rustle of leaves lends a staccato duet overhead. The sea and the land compose, each one, their own unique compositions. We decide it is this gem of a place we will share as a favorite spot. For the host of friends and family coming to visit us over the next few months, can there be a lovelier place to enjoy lunch together - a place embracing such unrivaled ambience?

At this place we share quiet conversation with Tom. He describes his new job at Boeing as part of the large designing group for the new 777 airplane. Continuing our exploration of these hills near our anchorage, we climb a promontory that overlooks the Bay of Islands. A photo of the two of us overlooking the bay becomes our Christmas card for the year 1987. Succeeding years I design our cards to reflect our place on the globe. Another task I enjoy is painting a copy of the flag of each country we visit. This cotton flag is flown from our starboard shroud as an indication of our granted status as a guest.

Tom's ten days go too fast. Whether it was our absence behind a steering wheel for years or our negligence in car maintenance, we suffer a cracked engine block. We return to the dealer. After explaining that we need to make the trip to Auckland in time for Tom's flight with a subsequently planned three-week trip with our daughter - it presents no problem to him. He gives us a different car as a 'loner' for these trips. We are on the road again to Auckland knowing that in a week we will be back to welcome Linda for her three-week stay. When we returned a month later, our Morris was ready to go once more, its innards repaired.

With our suitcases in the trunk, we meet Linda at the airport - ready to travel. We spend the first day exploring the cosmopolitan city of Auckland and some of its shops. Most interesting is a Greek temple of a building high on a hill overlooking the harbor, the War Memorial Museum. Here are housed outstanding displays of Maori and Polynesian culture dating back a century. There are also fine displays of greenstone jewelry, the New Zealand variety of jade. A trip to the rose garden on the bluffs overlooking the city reveals a lovely dining room with views of the extensive garden of roses now in full bloom. We remember it's January, not a time for roses back home. The calendar seems topsy-turvy here south of the equator.

The next morning we continue to Rotarua, now a mecca for tourism. It's a barren wasteland of stunted vegetation that stands starkly by the bubbling cauldrons of mud spewing sulfurous fumes in plumes of clouds above the roaring geysers. It is one of those places that authors declare a resemblance to Hades, Dante's Inferno or fire and brimstone. This entire area is covered with thermal pools and springs. Many have been capped and channeled to provide heat for the hotels. Therapeutic pools and hot tubs are a widely advertised attraction for the tourist.

The history of the area dates back to about 1350 A.D. when the legendary voyagers of the Maori forefathers arrived in their enormous Te Arawa canoe from those far away islands of Polynesia now thought to be a part of the Hawaii group. Today the city has the largest concentration of Maori residents in the country. They provide informative displays of their traditions and culture. A beautifully carved war canoe under its protective pavilion sits amidst pools beside landscaped gardens, a backdrop of a gentler dimension than its documented history. We enjoy an evening performance of the dances still enjoyed by the Maoris. As a part of the dance, the men, their arms and legs and even faces covered with tattoos, stick out their tongues to accompany the most ferocious grimace the warrior can muster as feet stomp to the frenetic beat of drums.

Not far from the city we enjoy one of the many sheep shows that are the hallmark of a prosperous ranch. This one, however, is an Agradome with more of a research quality to its performances. We learn of the many varieties of rams. We watch an awesome contest of sheep shearing. The pelt is stripped in one complete fleece almost in the blink of an eye. But it is the uncanny working of the sheepdog that captures our attention. We are fascinated at the ability of these dogs. With the whistle command of his shepherd, an alert canine will work to corral a large flock. With deft moves it chases or leads the sheep to another pasture or herds them back to the yard with intelligent decisions. This may mean sometimes, the dog will run across the backs of the sheep to lead the flock in a new direction.

We notice the car's radiator has started leaking. Before we can continue, we start adding a product advertised to seal leaks. The problem persists until we return the car six weeks later. By then we are sure the resultant percentage of sealing liquid is much higher than the water content. These used cars we all thought to be a bonus, seem to harbor hidden shortcomings.

We continue south to Lake Taupo and the National Park at its southern head where three active volcanoes rise above the scrubby land. One has wisps of smoke curling from its summit. We take some hikes through the barren, brush covered slopes and discover how hot January can be here south of the equator. Linda is a hiker and puts Mom and Dad through their paces as we try to show her our 60 years can keep up to her 33 energetic years.

We stop at the little motels that provide a kitchenette and sitting room in addition to the bedroom. The eating area is complete with stove and a fridge that always holds a quart of milk when we arrive. We buy groceries in the evening. After cooking our evening meal at the motel room we pack a lunch for the next day's picnic. With this strategy we find traveling here can be quite inexpensive. For forty dollars a night three of us can relax in a comfortable motel. The few times we have eaten in the small restaurants, the culinary talents didn't persuade us of a natural talent. With all the great vegetables and dairy products available, the ability to create tasty dishes seems to have baffled the Kiwi cooks - except for their delicate, meringue-y dessert known as Pavlova. This becomes a delicious finale to an otherwise dull meal.

We continue south to Wellington where we'll cross to the South Island on the three-hour ferry. It beats its way across the windy and choppy Cook Strait to the small town of Picton. However, when we arrive without a reservation for the ferry crossing, we find we have three days to visit this 'San Francisco South of the Equator' before we can make the passage.

With cable cars crawling the steep streets of Wellington and old Victorian wooden houses painted in shades that remind us of that U.S. city at the foot of the Golden Gate bridge, we could be climbing the hills back there in '56, the year of Don's internship in San Francisco. It is a fascinating city that promotes the Arts. We are delighted to visit yachting friends, Mike and Sylvia Burch aboard their docked *Ngaio* in one of the marinas here. We first met them in Panama. They have returned to New Zealand after a long stay in London where Mike performed operatic roles with his outstanding tenor voice.

With still a few days left we drive around the hills surrounding Wellington. Several times we find our way blocked along the road as those smart sheepdogs are guiding large flocks of sheep to new pastures. With the windows open, the breeze is fragrant with the scent of fresh mown hay and pastureland. Nestled on the hillsides are beehives with cattle grazing nearby. Truly this is a land of milk and honey.

After crossing the boisterous Cook Strait to the South Island, we leave the ferry to find traffic less congested than on North Island. It is easier to sightsee as we drive along the magnificent mountain ranges that shelter sparkling blue lakes. Following the curved road, suddenly the deep cleft of a fjord or the broad stretch of a sound will spread before us. These outline the irregular coastline that Captain Cook so accurately charted on his second voyage in 1774. We marvel today as we view this challenging landscape that confronted those master sailors. As we drive along the Milford road to the famous Sound that shares its name we are denied the long views because of drizzle and clouds. After inquiries with the Park Ranger about the next available date for the four-day hiking trek into Milford Sound, we find the first open date will be after Linda's departure. She is disappointed. Nevertheless, Don and I make reservations to return in a week to hike the thirty-five miles over mountains and through forests to Milford Sound.

Linda leaves for her journey to Java, Bangkok and India before she returns to her medical residency in Minneapolis. We send her on her way from the airport at Dunedin.

Don and I decide to spend several more days in this Scottish town on the East Coast. Climbing a hill, we move quietly to sit hidden in tall grasses where we watch the giant albatross. Here on the high cliffs overlooking the craggy shore we had hoped to see this magnificent bird described in sea legends, take flight with the stretch of its eleven-foot wingspan. However, this is the time of year they protect their eggs. We can see their splendor even as they hunker down on nests in the tall grasses. With some disappointment, we leave. But there's another interesting bird along these shores bidding us to continue our search. Again our luck remains illusive. We hide in the beach grass above the sandy shore. Now we are hoping to see the small blue penguins that make this stretch of seashore their landing area. After several hours rubbing cramps from our legs, we are rewarded by a quick glimpse of one small little penguin. With erect posture, he waddles across the beach and immediately disappears into the pounding surf.

By evening our luck has changed. Our lodging tonight will be at the only castle in New Zealand, Larnach Castle. Although modest in size as castles go, we are delighted with the accommodations. The brick stables have been attractively remodeled into sleeping rooms. These overlook lovely gardens where peacocks display, with shimmering iridescence, the broad fan of their elegant tails. Beyond, we see the castle with its crenellated outline, a silhouette on the hill above. We spend two days here enjoying a tour of the interior rooms. The beautiful wood inlaid floors and walls that gleam with the warm luster of some this country's finest woodworking, have found the perfect setting. Ceilings and cornices of ornate plasterwork all present a small gem of architecture. The family now owning and restoring this mid-1800's castle are finding furniture of that period to refurnish its one time elegance. Here we enjoy the finest dinner we will find our entire stay in this tiny country. It is presented with all the accouterments one would expect at a castle. The waiters, a white napkin draped across the sleeves of their black suits, graciously serve dinner with fine china on starched linen; the silver and crystal sparkling in the candlelight. The menu features roast lamb prepared with awareness to seasoning that pleases our palate. We feel pampered after several years with dinners of beans and rice served in small quarters.

This area at one time rivaled our country's gold rush with the discovery of gold in the hinterlands. The rush of immigrants to reap the harvest of wealth made this one of the most populous areas of the entire country. As a result, the country's first university, first medical school and finest educational institutions were founded here beside the flourishing businesses and civic centers. For a quarter of a century it was a bursting, booming town - then the gold was gone. Slowly the centers of commerce moved north to the island across Cook Strait where weather and ports were more favorable. Now the reminders of that once prosperous time are hinted at with graceful architecture and tree lined streets that shelter universities and churches of the early Scottish influence. There is a statue of the poet, Robert Burns, his back turned to the churches, as he stands on a tall hill amidst trees to gaze with a serendipitous glance towards the nearby pubs. It is today a graceful city.

It's time to retrace our drive across the Island to get ready for the Milford Trek. We rent backpacks and buy inexpensive sleeping bags at the village of Te Anau. The local stores carry interesting dried foods that we add to our backpacks. With instructions to carry out everything we carried in, we decide against backpacking canned food. Instead we pack the dehydrated meals in foil packets and add apples for munching. We start out with our sturdy hiking boots laced. Wearing shorts and a light jacket this cool morning we join the other thirty-eight hikers that will be our companions these four days. Since there are an allotted number of sleeping spots available in each hut at the day's end, this is the number used to set up the total daily reservations.

The hike starts out with gentle inclines through woods along the outstanding trails carved into the terrain by the New Zealand Park Service. The hut at the end of the day's ten-mile hike is a welcome sight. Provided are burners to heat our dinner and facilities for washing up dinner service and bathing - all with cold water - an automatic regulator of lengthy bathing. It is our responsibility to make and maintain the wood fire that is the only heat for the hut. We spread our sleeping bags against each other on the floor of the loft. Everyone is tired. There are only short conversations before we snuggle down into our sleeping bags to get rested for the hike tomorrow. This first night, as I start to doze, I am alarmed to hear Don snoring beside me. Soon there are quiet complaints and rumblings from around the room to 'stop the noise'. With nudges and pokes to Don's ribs, I can only make small differences to the sonority of his noisy background. I don't remember if I was at all successful at stopping the rush of snores. Having been familiar with this accompaniment to my sleep for many years, I fall asleep. Next morning there's much talk about someone disturbing the peace. We eat our meal in silence.

At each hut there is an explanation of the terrain we will be covering the next day. The percentage to the incline you are about to climb is noted along the trail. This information I could very well do without on those steeper climbs. The third day of hiking becomes the hardest. Amidst a dusting of snow these last two hours, the trail leads straight up to the hut on the windy top of the mountain. By day four we are rewarded with the slopes stretching below to some of the more spectacular long vistas we have seen as we scramble around large boulders on snow covered craggy peaks. Reaching sea level again we stop at wonderful waterfalls then hike through lush rainforests. Passing along the last little stretch we lose no time as we hurry through swarms of biting 'no-seeums' that attack our exposed legs and arms. Our calves are aching and Don's heels are really sore. The sight of a waiting boat for the trip across Milford Sound is a welcome sight. Finding a seat, we take off our shoes and relax to enjoy the grand and majestic views of this fjord-like Sound. From here we are bussed back to Te Anau. Hot showers and a soft bed at our motel restore our enthusiasm. We are ready once more for the drive along the mountainous western coast of this spectacular island so near the South Pole.

We return to the North Island and to our anchorage on its northern tip at Opua. After returning our loaner car, we are once again bouncing around the back roads in the little blue Morris with its repaired head.

More guests are expected and our date to haul the boat out of the water is approaching. There is a flurry of busy days to get the boat pulled up the railway tracks centered on the narrow beach.

Dick McIlvryde, with his heavy-duty motor, hauls *Horizon* out of the water. The whole bulk of her sits exposed on shore with braces holding her upright. The mast is nestled in among the branches of the large tree rising from the steep bank just ahead of the bow. We are an unlikely sight as we sit perched here together with the birds, viewing the grand oversight of the small bay. In a few days we will have the hull draped in a long skirt. Such humiliation for our grand barque. The discouraging diagnosis is that the hull is covered with a pox of blisters. These blisters contain water that has seeped by osmosis through the skin of the fiberglass. Each one will be ground open to allow it to dry out. With the skirt in place, heat can be added to hasten the drying process. Before the skirt is in place there is a week of grinding with the accompanying cloud of fiberglass dust that is layering everything aboard. It is not an environment where we care to hangout. We spend most days seeing more of the countryside and catching up with some medical and dental problems. By evening the dust has settled aboard *Horizon*. We sweep up the day's dust to sleep in our messy nest.

A dentist from Sweden addresses our dental needs. With his dentist chair fixed in a cabin aboard his sailboat docked in an Auckland marina, he is supplementing his income with fine examinations to the dental needs of the yachting community. We comprise quite a large number. There are other yachties who also find employment here in New Zealand to boost the sailing 'kitty'. The crew aboard *Oniva*, Claude and Margot, whom we met years ago in Venezuela, have found work here. Margot, a young physician whose home is Germany and Claude, a multi-talented man from France, continue to work in this tiny country as they still write us nine years later. There are a large number of young people that have chosen to interrupt their careers and take this voyage of a lifetime. They realize their incomes will be reduced and take such opportunities as these to work their way around the globe in order to make the dream come true. We are using savings and retirement funds to carry out our dream, but I think a majority of our mates in the anchorages we share, are living on shoestrings and feeling satisfied that they can create the finances that make it all work for them.

Here in the anchorage at Opua is a tiny sailboat twenty feet long with a small cabin only high enough to sit in. Its freeboard is only inches above the water, but '*The Boat*' has sailed here from the U.S. with its crew that appears to live on air. None of us are sure how they survive at sea or on land. The majority of boats we have seen are 37 to 45 feet in length with crews ranging in age from 30's to 50. We seem to be in the group over 55 that number the fewest of sailors, which surprises us. These folks are not waiting for retirement to step away from the security a job may offer. They are doing very well as far as we can determine. I must say, finances are rarely a part of the discussions that take place when we get together. In fact, for much of the group, the previous occupation is unknown, as is an awareness of last names or marriage status. We seem to be a group of individuals who share a common interest in the world and possess the competence to discover our planet with our skill as sailors. It's a community that respects the individual and the choices each might make but will come to another's aid if such help is requested. This family of new friends is a comfortable bunch.

Back to our dusty boat still 'on the hard', Don is replacing the chain plates to make them as water tight as possible. These plates secure to the hull, the shrouds that support the mast. The water tank lying under the sole (the floor) of the cabin has developed leaks. It will be removed to be welded before it is replaced on spacers to keep it off the interior hull. Here it is mid-March and we are still drying out those blister holes. During a hurricane that goes through the area, we watch from our shore perch, relatively secure, as boats in the anchorage tear loose from their moorings. Dick McIlvryde is out in a runabout working to corral careening boats as he tries to make some order in all the chaos.

It's been a rainy season that adds to the delay in the drying process we had hoped for. But there are more friends coming. Our days are occupied with fun times showing Pete and Hulda Classen all the favorite spots we've discovered. Pete is a physician and Goshen College grad like Don. Both set up their medical practices in the Elkhart area and both of us have children the same ages. We shared a lot of years together. When Don told the medical staff of his proposed retirement, we later learned they gave us six months before he would be back in their midst once again, stethoscope in hand and prescribing pills. It was no surprise when Pete told Don that a place on the staff was still available if he wanted to give up this lifestyle. Don's response was a hearty chuckle and declaration there was no way he'd give this up for that! We celebrate Don's 61st birthday while they are with us. Don proposes a toast to Pete in celebration of Pete's work ethic. These worker-bees contribute to the retirement fund known as Social Security that Don hopes to begin drawing next year.

The spunky Morris makes the trip to Auckland to get them to their flight home. In four days we make the same trip back to the airport to pick up Don's sister Thelma, and her husband, Weyburn. The boat not being a hospitable place for any human being, we have scouted the area nearby and found a lovely bed and breakfast for their lodging. The host, an artist and boat builder with his Hungarian wife offers a delicious goulash dinner for the four of us one evening. The same sights and walks that we have been sharing with the family over the past weeks are also a part of this visit. It is while they are with us that we make a call to my sister. When Lynn answers the phone, he tells us that Anne's cancer is spreading. He suggests I might seriously consider making a trip home. We immediately make plane reservations for my flight to Denver. Weyburn and Thelma are with us a few more days before we drive again to Auckland, pleased with the performance Morris is giving.

I choose to take the bus to Auckland just two days later, since the four previous weekends have been traveled by car. The trip to Seattle is a twelve-hour flight with a three-hour layover in Hawaii. Spending four days in Seattle with Dale, Linda, Amanda, now two and a half years old, and Lindsey, just celebrating her first birthday, gives the trip a happy beginning. Tom entertains us in his apartment overlooking Puget Sound with some of his delicious home-baked apple pie.

Then it's on to Denver where Lynn and my brother, Richard, meet me at the airport. They bring me up to date on the unsuccessful surgeries that have been performed to halt the spread of Anne's cancer. She meets me at the door. Her cheeks are pink. She looks healthy. And yet when I draw her close for a hug, the pain she is suffering is apparent. It has been years since this circle of family surrounding her have been together. It's hard to watch Mother's concern for her youngest child. Anne continued her teaching until last week. She is still involved instructing the substitute teacher with her plans for an upcoming music performance. More surgery had been proposed - then canceled. X-rays have revealed the cancer has spread to her brain. She maintains a resolve to get better. I promise her I'll stop back after visiting with son Steve and his family in Indiana. My heart is heavy as I leave, but with a cheery note she waves goodbye.

Embracing small, healthy granddaughters restores a balance to life. Natasha, four years old, is bouncing around her younger sister, Michelle, with sounds of laughter - full of energy. Three days surrounded with such liveliness reaches a somber note when I receive a phone call that Anne died this morning.

This return trip by her family is not as we had promised Anne. It's now a journey of sadness. Our youngest sister and daughter will no longer share her exuberance for life we had all come to cherish. This *joie de vivre* was still radiant when she returned to me the well marked travel guide to Fiji she had outlined, saying, 'We probably won't make this trip this year.' After her funeral I sadly retrace my way back to New Zealand. These long hours give me time to remember a beautiful sister. It is hard giving up plans we had talked about sharing in our retiring years. We enjoyed each other so much.

In my luggage I have a new toy for the boat, a weather fax machine. By plugging it into the ham radio, it will produce visual graphs of weather patterns that make it easier to decide on passage making. The printed pages extend the knowledge accessible for making wise decisions. Paying attention to weather has become our primary focus. With this information offering us intelligent choices, we insure a safer passage.

When again I see *Horizon,* now rocking gently in her more familiar surrounding, the water laps the new cafe au lait colored hull. I am not at all sure my choice of color for the new paint job is very attractive. But so be it, it's done. Paint now covers layers of resin and fiberglass smoothly faired over the blister- repaired hull.

The weather is turning more favorable. The time is approaching to move on. We get busy stocking the boat once again for a long passage. Don takes Morris for its last ride to sell it to the dealer who took advantage of an eager market. We sell it for $600, a bit less than the $900 purchase price of Morris. But we agree it's a pretty reasonable price to pay. To travel about a beautiful country at our own leisure for six months makes this a worthwhile expenditure.

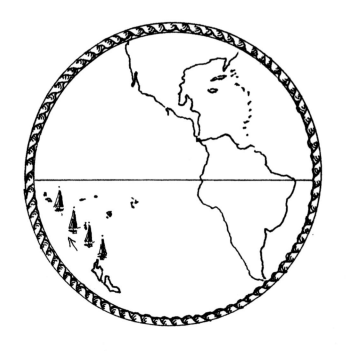

Minerva Reef to Fiji

CHAPTER 9
A HAZARD TO NAVIGATION

W e are embraced with fog this Friday morning, May 27 as we search for channel markers leading out of the Bay of Islands. Free of land we once again feel the force of wind and waves on the boat. This feel embodies the joy of hearing a favorite sonata one more time, a rhythm deep within the ocean's soul reviving again a special cadence in our daily composition. As we return to the South Pacific Ocean after keeping our feet dry for six months, we find hopping into our sail-pants takes some adjustments. Don and I have been fortunate that seasickness has never been a problem, however, on that first day back at sea, we do spend most of the time in the cockpit. To regain the balance the horizon offers, we continue to watch that distant rim while the boat heaves and rolls through the waves.

With the full moon casting its silvery glow across three-foot swells and sails straining to pull us through the water during the balmy days and nights, we experience one of the most exhilarating passages to date. The knot meter is displaying speeds up to eight knots, the first time since leaving Panama this instrument has provided such exciting information. We are making twice the speed we made on the sail south to New Zealand. After nine days the wind becomes even stronger with a steady thirty to thirty-five knots. We reduce the amount of sail and continue to move not only as fast but recognize this improves the heel of the boat. With less sail flying the boat regains a move towards a more perpendicular posture and assumes a heel of ten to fifteen degrees. I can tolerate this skewered dimension to life aboard. Sailing on the side of a hull where every move on the boat means hanging on for dear life along the deck or around the cabin, has never been my favorite point of sail. Down in the galley the stove maintains a balance as it rests on gimbals, allowing the top to be level at any angle the boat acquires. This insures the soup stays in the pot and not on the floor or, even worse, across the ceiling.

Minerva Reef is an unusual place in the ocean. Along the undersea trench known as the Tonga Trench, there is a seamount that thrusts from the ocean floor to just scratch the ocean's surface. With a low tide, perimeters of coral formations are visible as the sea breaks against the coral walls but when high tide arrives the ocean rolls across these obstacles unhindered. They disappear and give no clue to their dangerous presence as the waves sweep across this perilous place, a formula that has caused untold numbers of shipwrecks. Here at Minerva there are two coral reefs about twelve miles apart. Each of these has a break in the coral so access to the inside lagoon is possible. This is our destination.

Since we are making such good time, we heave-to fifty miles from the southern reef for a safe margin of distance that will allow a good arrival in daylight. About three a.m. we check the sat-nav, hoist the sails and set our course for 23.56.45 degrees S. and 179.07.45 degrees E., putting us on a bearing for this mysterious rendezvous in the middle of the ocean. At noon we see the breaking waves in the middle of this vast oceanscape. We drop the sails and motor towards this '**hazard to navigation**', as it's noted on our chart. We look for the flat water between the breaking surf. Our search is made much easier when we see the mast of another sailboat resting in the moderately placid lagoon, sheltered inside the reef. *Niatross,* from British Columbia, welcomes us. In the months ahead we'll enjoy the generous hospitality of Frank and Lis and their two children, George and Julie.

The anchorage on this southern reef doesn't offer much protection as winds of thirty-five knots continue to strain the anchors. Next morning we both decide to move northeast to North Minerva. The current between these two reefs is so strong that we find it difficult to keep our heading and not be pushed too far west. In order to make the pass through the northern reef, we start the engine to assist the sails in hopes of getting a more easterly set. I feel sure we're going to miss it completely but with some short tacking into the wind, we finally screw our way through the pass and into this large lagoon. This northern reef is circular in shape, while the southern one is shaped like the figure eight with only one of the circles accessible for anchoring.

Where the deep cobalt blue of the ocean has been our canvas these last days, now the sandy bottom, just twelve feet deep, has changed the seascape to turquoise. Indeed, we experience a most unreal, almost surreal feeling of being transported to another world. We sit in the center of this turquoise carpet with a rim of coral outlining protection from the cobalt depths dashing against its perimeter. This watery expanse at high tide stretches for three hundred and sixty degrees from the lapping water at our hull to that distant horizon of sea and sky, etching a distant, undisturbed line in one circumscribed circle. There is no smudge, no hint of land as I scan that encircling horizon. With a sense of wonder I gaze at that unwavering line that surrounds my point on the compass. At high tide there is rocking and heaving of the boat as the swells wash across the reef and over the shallow water. But at low tide with the reef exposed, acting as a breakwater, the quietness here inside the reef is a special gift. We welcome this with amazement and gratitude.

There is a crowd here now. To find what secrets might be discovered here, six sailboats have made this successful journey from paths between Tonga and New Zealand. *Canowie* has arrived - we are assured of parties once again. Beach parties, however, seem out of the question. Even at low tide all that is available to walk and explore is this sharp and jagged exposed reef only fifteen to thirty feet across at its widest point. A planned picnic on a rather flat bed of coral is canceled when the wind continues to roar across the area. Since casseroles and desserts are ready to be eaten, we decide to enjoy the picnic aboard *Canowie's* welcoming deck.

After four days with strong winds, the gale subsides and a soothed lagoon becomes calm. Six dinghies now scoot around this new playground. Don is having success spear fishing and adds to his reputation as an accurate marksman with remarkable breath capacity. . . a real bag of wind! One night with our lanterns spattering light across the exposed reef at low tide we wear sneakers to search for lobster. With gloved hands we catch fourteen lobster as these tasty guys walk across the reef. This means we will enjoy a New England lobster feast tomorrow. We're surprised at the amount of meat in the legs, all the legs together providing as much meat as the large tail. The warm waters in these latitudes around the world harbor the spiny lobsters. Any New Englander would immediately see our delicacy lacks the large fore-claw they are used to harvesting.

On one of his diving forays, Don finds a beautiful and rare black tun shell as big as a grapefruit. On calm days during low tide, most of the gals walk the reef searching the coral to add new gems to our shell collections. Thinking this remote spot will offer an abundance of shells we are disappointed in their absence. Bjorn, captain of the Swedish sailboat *Orkestern,* has found a large whale tooth wedged in the coral walls. He later commissioned a Fijian artist to scrimshaw his ship's profile in a beautiful design along its long ivory length. Because the unique dimensions of this place fascinate us, we stay three weeks with the winds gentle some days or screaming at us with forty knots on others.

By June 23 with east-south-east winds a comfortable ten knots we depart this special place with *Elron* and her Seattle crew, to carve a path toward Fiji. The swells remaining from a month of strong winds are so huge that our two boats lose sight of each other even though we are only a hundred yards apart. The top of their mast vanishes behind the wall of water climbing between our two boats. At other sightings *Elron* perches like a bird ready for flight as it mounts the summit of an expanding reach to disappear again into a deep trough of the sea's wrinkled face. After three days of good sailing on a broad reach, we are searching again, this time through showers, for the reef with its marked entrance into the large harbor at Suva, the capitol of Fiji.

A year ago there was a military coup on these islands. When the British, all those years ago, added Fiji to its crown, they brought a great number of indentured Indians from India to work here in the fledgling sugar plantations. Many stayed on after this policy ended. Now, with the population of Fijians of Indian descent overtaking that of the native Fijians, conflict has arisen. The Fijian Indians were gaining power not only in Parliament but holding positions of power in the market place as well. The 44% native-born Fijians felt they were losing their native born rights although they owned 80% of the land. The ownership of land is very complex. We understand there is no public land. It has been divided among the native Fijians.

The only vestige of last year's disturbance for us is the boarding by the Navy to see if we are carrying any firearms. We have none. We chose never to have any aboard. A sense of anxiety still exists among the population because the military can search without a warrant and arrest without much cause. However, as we walk the streets of this bustling cosmopolitan city, life seems quite normal with few signs of a military presence.

We, as the yachting community, are here to enjoy the sights, not to spend our days involved in any politics. The Suva businesses are geared to help this unique group of tourists. A directory has been distributed among the fleet listing all the services available in Suva. We take advantage of the expertise available to have the leaking refrigerating system repaired. We also have the life raft undergo the required inspection as we continue polishing, painting, greasing and spending the many rainy days improving our good ship. You might say, 'but you just did a complete overhaul in New Zealand.' 'Tis true, but 'tis also true, there is no let up in this damp environment that keeps us constantly spending money on this 'hole in the water'.

This large island of Viti Levu, lush and green with its mountainous peaks in the center, has showered us with rain a majority of the days. We understand when we sail around the south coast to enter the large lagoon on its western side, we will face a drier climate.

Before we make that trip, however, we have gotten the required permission from the Prime Minister to visit some of the outlying islands. We are interested in the Lau Group of islands that stretch north and south along the eastern boundaries of Fiji. While in New Zealand we met Ron, a solo sailor, who told us of the warm welcome he had received at the island of Kandavu. He gave us photos to take back to the village of Mauni as a reminder of his visit. Through the narrow pass in the reef then following a well-marked channel, we slowly make our way just off this village and drop the anchor.

It is just at sunset on Sunday. We decide to wait until morning to present our gift of kava, a prerequisite to visit any village. Decisions change, within minutes of dropping the anchor, a canoe paddled by three men has come alongside. By the time we get topsides, they are all aboard. Had not Ron assured us of the friendliness of this village, we'd have had great concern at their boldness. We invite them to come below. Koresi, their spokesman, asks for our landing permit. With the formalities completed to their satisfaction, we give them Ron's photos of the villagers. Immediately the atmosphere becomes relaxed with a great deal of chattering and laughing. One of the men, Daniella, son of the chief, tells us a bit about the village, Mauni. He explains that Monday evenings the chief and male members of the village meet to plan work projects for the following days. The first week of the month is spent solely on community needs like mowing the grass or roof repairs and so forth. The rest of the month is spent working on their farms. Native Fijians have been granted a parcel of land to develop. Here the majority of the families have chosen to farm their lands. We later note the absence of any Fijians of Indian descent living on this island. The often repeated phrase, 'this is the Fijian way', is spoken in a way that implies the superiority of THE native way.

Our first order of business next morning is to present our gift of kava. In order to enjoy any part of their land or water, we need to take part in the 'sevu sevu' ceremony performed in the presence of the chiefs and his elders. We've brought with us bundles of dried roots from the kava bush that we purchased at the market in Suva. This is a member of the pepper plant, the spice pepper. As we walk into the village properly dressed, which means I wear a skirt with a modest blouse while Don wears shorts and shirt, we are met on shore by a young male who will take us to the chief's mbure or meeting place. Tevita introduces us to the chief, a tall man with Polynesian characteristics who displays the bearing and presence of a leader.

We stand in a large room with few windows that gives it a dusky feel. Sitting on grass mats arranged in a large circle on the floor, twelve men are sitting cross-legged. In the center of this austere circle of elders is the kava bowl, a large wooden bowl a yard in diameter, resting on its stout carved legs. Attached to the bowl and stretching across the floor is a long strand of sennet made of twisted coconut fibers with a large, white cowrie shell attached that rests at the feet of the chief. We are motioned to sit to the left of the chief, being very careful to sit with our feet tucked under our body. The pointing of toes to any Fijian is taboo. I sit kind of sidesaddle while Don crosses his legs as all the others are doing. Before sitting down, Don has laid our bundle of kava at the feet of the chief, who then chooses to receive or reject it. We are hoping for the former or we'd have to leave the village immediately. One of the elders speaking Fijian, is evidently introducing us to the chief as we recognize the word 'American' frequently being used. It is a long speech. When it's concluded all the men around the circle clap hands with accompanying grunts. Another elder speaks to us in English explaining the ceremony and councils us on our behavior as we participate in the proceedings. The chief rises, nods and indicates he is pleased with our offering. Speaking Fijian he proceeds to welcome us to his village where his protection and care of us is assured. In return we are asked to respect the customs and traditions of this village.

Now the time has come to share in the drinking ceremony. Our woody kava roots are mashed into tiny pieces and squeezed as water is added to them in this large kava bowl, called a tanoa. This ancient ritual involved young virgins who gathered to chew the kava root then spit the concoction into the tanoa, ready for the drinking ceremony. We appreciate the changing patterns of customs and traditions. A lengthy process of hand squeezing these roots in the water continues until a muddy looking liquid fills the bowl. Using half a coconut shell as a cup, the chief is served first, followed by several of the elders. We notice, as we had been instructed, the entire content of the cup is swallowed in one draft. I never thought much of the capacity of half a coconut shell, but as I watch Don take the cup offered, filled with that muddy looking water, I marvel at his ability to quaff that amount with such poise. Next it's my turn. Guided by Don's performance, I clap my hands once before accepting the cup. Then, taking this shell, I notice my portion is less than Don's had been, I proceed to swallow the potion in one gulp. I hand back the cup and clap three times. The taste is much like I suppose muddy chalky water would taste. There is a definite tingling to my lips. The cup is passed around three more times. Our participation is approved - we are greeted with smiles and handshakes. One of the elders, in fact, with a twinkle in his eye, teases me when he asks if I think kava is as good as Coca-Cola. I reply I didn't think Coke had anything to worry about. This brings chuckles from the group.

We give a bag of medicines and bandages to the chief. Much discussion takes place as Don discusses the use of the medicines with the elders, each being satisfied he understands the directions. Finally the long morning is over. Tevita has waited for us outside the mbure the entire morning to escort us back to the beach. We sense it is important to the village that we enjoy this companion, not so much to check on us, but as an expression of their hospitality. They couldn't have chosen better, Tevita is a most gracious host and guide.

Tevita takes us under his wing and proudly shows us his village neatly tended. He points out a cave carved into a hillside by the beach some distance beyond the village. Here, he explains, when cannibalism was still a part of Fijian life years ago, this cave was used to lodge an elderly member of the village who could no longer contribute to the welfare of the community. A procession would bring this senior villager here to the cave without food, his or her legs would be broken and the villager would be left to die. Some of the oldest members still living in the village have memories of cannibalism and practices like these. No longer is this kind of thinking a part of the modern customs of the villagers. But it does remain a part of the history. It was cause for legends like that of Capt. Bligh of the Bounty, whose epic voyage took him through these waters. With skillful tactics he eluded capture by these Fijian warriors in their swift canoes to escape a fate worse than hunger.

Tevita shows us the five acres allotted him that crawl up steep slopes. This in no way discourages him from tilling the entire acreage with only the long, narrow blade of a hoe and his sharp machete. As we walk over the hills in our bare feet we can feel the loose, loamy soil producing these healthy looking vegetables, taro, cassava, onions, sweet potatoes, pineapples and kava. He shows us how he transplants much of his crops from the existing plants. Since it's a sweltering day he climbs one of his coconut trees to supply us with the refreshing juice of the nut.

Further down the dusty road away from the village, Tevita brings us to his home where he introduces his wife, Vani. Here they reside adjacent to her parent's home. He shows us through his tidy home constructed of cement block. In the bedroom, as he pulls the mosquito netting aside from the large bed, he proudly shows us his two-year-old daughter, Atalaite. When asked, Don's diagnosis is a bad case of scabies now visible over much of her body. Although we are unable to offer the needed medicine for Atalaite now, Don promises to send some when we return to Suva. Before leaving this 22 year-old father, we meet their parents, Vani's and his, to enjoy afternoon tea together. It's obvious this is a family that enjoys each other as they joke and tell of their plans for the day. Tevita's father had been employed in Suva for twenty years in government work but decided to return to his village here to insure that his children would retain respect for their roots. His wife was not too keen about the move. It meant giving up electric, refrigeration and inside plumbing, but she was willing to try. They now seem content and adjusted to a much simpler life here on this island apart from the bustle of Suva.

On our final day at Mauni, we watch their rugby team with Koresi as captain, compete with the village from across the lagoon. It is interesting to watch the elders as they sit protected from the hot sun on the porch of the school, drinking their kava and trying to stay interested in the game. This drink is heavily consumed by the older members of the village and, as a group, the effects from years of imbibing kava is seen in the dazed and confused condition of their movements. The whites of their eyes have taken on the muddy hue of the drink as they lazily blink with thickened eyelids. The younger generation is making an effort to stop this tradition. They are aware of its effects on their fathers.

We say our farewells to the villagers. Tevita has remained absent these last days. We miss him. We'll not be able to thank him for his generous care and quiet hospitality during our visit here. No doubt Koresi has been taunting him about the days he has spent with us. Koresi has a dominant personality with a manner that can be abrasive. For shy Tevita to evade such a presence posing possible conflict is appropriate to his quiet ways.

We leave Kandavu to sail north along the Lau Group. This will be an overnight sail. As yet we don't have radar and must depend on the sat-nav to guide us through these islands. Although the charts of Fiji are well done and accurate, the currents and tides affecting a passage demand we maintain a sharp watch as we continue the trip. We look through the darkness of night for any darker shapes that might indicate land nearby or the hazy white spume that might warn of a reef in our path.

By morning light, we are relieved to see the buoys that mark the entrance into the lagoon surrounding Vanuabalavu. What a great tasting language we are hearing around us. Just say this island's name. It's pronounced the way it is spelled - Vanuabalavu - just feels so good as you roll it off your tongue!

After our presentation of kava the half dozen boats in the area will be free to explore this large island. There is a corner of the lagoon called the Bay of Islands (another country that bestows this familiar label to such a group of islands) where we can anchor behind our own mushroom shaped islet. Each one has been carved by tidal changes over the centuries.

The days are spent looking for shells, snorkeling and spear fishing or walking the lovely beaches. We make visits to tiny villages where we're treated to our first taste of jackfruit, a large elongated fruit with a white pulpy texture. It has a hint of banana and citrus flavors. In the evening, we could set our watches with the whooshing passage of hundreds of fruit bats as this churning dark cloud leaves the surrounding caves in search of their night meal.

Aboard *Maxine*, we enjoy the new taste of a shark dinner. Jill soaked the steaks in milk to get rid of the uric acid that's present in some shark flesh. They join us on the overnight ninety-mile sail back to Suva. Careless preparation on our part finds us wallowing in the swells while we fill the fuel tank with diesel from the jerry jugs tied to the lifelines. We have run the fuel tank dry. This means the fuel line has an airlock. The long time it takes Don to bleed the system becomes an exercise in frustration as we toss and heave with the swells. We are to learn, miles and miles ahead, a more efficient and speedier process to rid the fuel line of air. Not only do we run out of fuel on this overnight sail, we also drink the last glass of water that drains the water tank dry as well. Son Steve told us years ago, anyone worth his salt needs to have learning experiences - but so many?

Needless to say, the familiar markers showing us the way to the harbor at Suva are a welcome sight. It's September and we are anxious to move around to the drier part of this island. Before we leave, we join Frank from *Niatross* who is alone since his family has returned to Canada where the kids will attend high school. He has been invited to visit the homes of two Indian Fijians. We spend the early part of the evening at the lovely home of Dr. Rabat where we enjoy an Indian meal with their friends Yitsuf and his wife. Dr.

Rabat, an optometrist, explains some of the political problems and the effects they're having on the Fijian Indians. Many have been devastated by the demands placed on them as a result of the coup. He estimates 28,000 Fijian Indians have fled to Australia, leaving the business community at a loss. Together with the native Fijians, just a few years ago, they had built a vibrant, emerging new economy with a bright future for this small country. Now uncertainty prevails.

As I replenish the food stuffs aboard and can more chicken, Don is spending this last day at Suva in the various offices getting permission to move to the other side of the same island and new ports. We are boarded once again, this time by the army for what reason, we are never told; guns, drugs, a stow away, we don't know and never catch a clue. It does make leaving this attractive place a lot easier. We've met nice folks and visited lovely places but this atmosphere isn't comfortable.

We leave Suva and sail along the southern coast of Viti Levu to a small bay. Here is the hotel we had planned to spend time with Anne and Lynn - the Fijian Hotel. I wear a shroud of sadness remembering Anne. We take part in a short sevu-sevu ceremony then are free to make use of the hotel facilities.

One of the attractions nearby is a fire-walking ceremony presented by the natives of Mbengga, a small offshore island. This ceremony contrasts from the one we attended in Tahiti. This one is not a part of worship rites. There is a festive and jubilant celebration to the occasion. The Fijian warriors in splendid garb, with much ceremony, fan the coals to a fiery glow. They are laughing and almost dancing as they stride across the glowing coals. When we look at the soles of their feet after the ceremony, we are amazed to see smooth skin with no blisters or calluses evident as they proudly hold their feet up for our inspection.

It's only thirty miles to Musket Cove, the popular anchorage inside the reef on the western side of Viti Levu. Musket Cove caters to yachties. Dick, the operator of Musket Cove Resort, a sailor himself, offers among all the other amenities at his spot the hassle free service of sending and receiving boat parts that need to go through the red tape of customs. He keeps the atmosphere of this small resort low key with a Wednesday night barbecue he offers for $2. He spreads a bountiful buffet excluding meat. This you provide for broiling over the hot coals he provides. Since the anchorage offers protection from every quarter it is usually full of yachts. Since we're not real fond of full we move on after taking advantage of the buffet, laundry, showers and fellowship.

We sail on to discover a very special little island, Vomo, with an even smaller Iti islet to its west that's connected by a narrow isthmus. Some of the most beautiful coral we've found is off its beach. In fact there is so much coral that we spend considerable time looking for a sandy spot to drop the anchor. We meet Matia as we come ashore. He lives on this island with his wife, Bali. They are the only residents of Vomo. He and Don spend time snorkeling and before long they bring to our boat a good sized octopus all nicely tenderized with the rock beating process we'd seen those months ago. We invite Matia to eat with us. Bali has gone to the mainland, where they own another home, to visit their eight-year-old son attending school there. Following his instructions, I steam the octopus, tentacles up, until all is bright red, then turn it over for another ten minutes. After it cools enough to cut it into small pieces, coconut cream is added and all is simmered for a few minutes. This recipe differs from Michelle's, who, back in Mopelia, added onion and ginger to his sauce. Both ways are delicious. We compare the flavor with that of lobster. We thank Matia for his hospitality and suggest we might bring our daughter back to meet him on this bit of paradise. This seems to please him. He hopes Bali will have returned by then to welcome us as well.

Since we are expecting Linda's arrival with her friend Paul, we head back to the Regent Hotel anchorage. It's a sheltered bay along the western coast of Viti Levu. On the way we stop at Navandra, a small u-shaped island with no villages; thus no kava presentation. It looks like it should offer good protection for an anchorage, but after hours of hobby-horsing in the large swells rolling onto the beach, we decide to move on to the large island of Viti Levu and the Regent Hotel. Here we can do our laundry, pick up mail and get ready for our guests. Nadi, the town just a short bus ride away, offers good markets and butcher shops. Fiji Meats sells good local grown beef. They cut the roasts into steaks and label them whatever you are asking for- not real tender but good flavor.

We get up early. It's 5:30. The taxi is waiting for the ride to the airport to meet Paul and Linda. With only a ten-minute wait, we see them walk through the custom doors looking slim and relaxed, with no signs they've traveled half way around the world. They are carrying, besides their luggage, all the boat parts we had asked them to bring. It's all a part of the price you must pay to spend a South Seas holiday aboard *Horizon*.

We soon are enjoying breakfast in the cockpit. Conversation and pictures are savored with the pancakes and fruit. Family aboard is one of those exceptional moments that add a special ingredient Don and I have been fortunate to enjoy. There are crewmembers on boats in anchorages we've shared that tell of their families rejecting them for embarking on this journey. As we made plans to take this voyage, our children, my mother and our siblings all cheered us on. They bestowed their blessings to go and discover with no regrets. It is a gift Don and I treasure. We took it for granted until we started hearing the grief some other boats were experiencing.

Thinking the kids would want to rest, at least until lunchtime, we hadn't taken into consideration the resiliency of youth. The two of them are on the foredeck ready to haul the anchor. We are off once again to Vomo. It's just a nice day's sail. We drop the anchor at sunset, again finding that only sandy patch.

The next morning, with a lot of splashing and laughter, we are diving off the boat to snorkel through the exquisite coral formations. Through the crystal clear water huge heads of brain coral surrounded with a forest of jumbled branches of stag horn coral display underwater grandeur. A contrasting background of waving large and lacy fronds of purple sea fans against flashes of brilliant colors of damselfish, angelfish and the iridescence of parrotfish all bombard our senses. While we rest on the beach, Matia strolls towards us. With introductions made, we spend a jovial visit as he shares some of the local legends with us - he's a happy fellow. He invites us to join him and Bali for the evening meal at their mbure, just a short walk as he points through the trees. We gladly accept.

This is Oct. 28, a calendar day for me. It's the whole number year that heralds my 60th birthday. To satisfy my sweet tooth, I bake a cake. Searching in those deep corners of the boat, I find six candles to decorate the frosting. I'm ready to celebrate. Linda and I chop some cabbage for coleslaw to take to the evening feast as well.

As we make our way through the trees, we see ahead, almost hidden in the tall grasses, the small square mbure, their home. The walls are made with mats woven of palm fronds. The roof is made of the same palm branches tied to spacers. An opening on each side provides doorways. Inside, the room is divided in two by a curtain. The room we have entered is their living space. On the other side of the curtain, a bedstead indicates their sleeping room. A window flap is thrown open over the bed

We are invited to sit on grass mats on the floor as Matia begins to mash kava roots in his kava bowl. During this ceremony a young goat kid ambles across the room, relieving itself next to Linda. Bali jumps up and shoos the lovable animal outdoors as she cleans the mat, apologizing to us. Meanwhile, as the water in the kava bowl begins taking on the muddy color, I notice Linda staring at this whole process. We had forgotten to clue them to this part of any visit. We weren't sure it would be a part of an informal visit. Matia explains that the kava ceremony is a gesture of the Fijian hospitality. We each take our one big draft as the coconut cup is passed - except Linda. She takes a sip as though it was teatime.

She is even having difficulty with that amount and as graciously as she can, declines the succeeding offers. We linger over the kava as the evening dusk settles over our shoulders. While we talk and learn more of Matia's life here on this tiny island, I begin to worry that we misunderstood the invitation for dinner. Bali is lighting the kerosene lamp in the darkness. I did notice when we arrived there was a large steaming kettle resting over the coals of the low fireplace beside the house. But perhaps that was not preparation for this meal, so I ask Matia and Bali to join in the celebration of my birthday as I take the cake out of our backpack and light the candles. With a flurry, Bali jumps up and goes to the bedroom, pulling from under the bed a large mat like the one we were sitting on. She presents it as a birthday gift to me. I am touched by her thoughtfulness and thank them for the gift. Chuckling, Matia says, "Bali, you better give Linda one or she might take her mother's with her". So Linda is given one as well. We then enjoy bowls of broth as a first course. The fish that had simmered in this rich bouillon follows. Along with rice and the coleslaw, I can't imagine anyone enjoying a birthday dinner more than I did at this special place with such good friends. Truly a memorable sixtieth.

The Yasawa Group of islands beyond beckons so we leave Vomo the next morning and work our way north. Naviti Island contains a lot of villages. We are realizing these islands here along the Northwest outline of Fiji have been exposed to large cruise ships in ever increasing numbers. This has taken away the spontaneous friendliness we have been enjoying up to now. No doubt the villages are overwhelmed with sightseers who peer into their daily life at every turn. When we bring our kava to the chief, his response is one of boredom. He seems truly relieved when we don't linger. We make a few other stops to visit a church known for the outstanding hand carved decorations. Another village is distinguished for the beautiful flowering trees and bushes along its paths. The winds remain strong as we sail between islands each day. This gives Paul, who has been at the wheel, the feel of a weather helm that commands a display of some muscle.

Finally, we sail into an outstanding anchorage with the turquoise water and the glistening beaches of a rich man's paradise. An American millionaire bought Turtle Cay by the Blue Lagoon. With its advertised luxury and pampering, the only way one gets ashore is by invitation or reservation. The waters, however, are free so we drop the anchor. Very shortly a motorboat approaches us with its smartly uniformed crew inquiring about our planned stay here in paradise. When they are satisfied we intend them no harm or intrusion, we are left to our own pampering for the next several days.

In this beautiful setting, with the evening sky awash in pastel aureoles, Paul and Linda give a performance on the deck one evening. As Paul places a bouquet of beach blossoms in Linda's arms, they burst forth singing to the tune of 'She's Getting Married in the Morning'. The new and appropriate verse they composed announces their engagement. An April wedding is planned. We are instructed to learn how to wear shoes in the meantime.

With strong vocalizations we roundly harmonize 'Merrily, merrily down the stream' as we make our way back to the Regent Hotel for their approaching departure. With a nice dinner at the hotel, compliments of the youngsters, we all remark what fun we had together.

Now we make plans to move on to Micronesia. Most of the boats that have been sharing our anchorages are also moving on. This multitude, however, is making paths toward Australia with stops in New Hebrides and New Caledonia en route. We choose to go North to the less visited islands of Micronesia. The traditions and customs of these islands are uniquely different from those of Australia that share a similarity in culture to our own. It is apparent as we make our way across the islands of Micronesia stretching over two thousand miles on a northern parallel to the equator that we will be alone most of the way.

To add to the safety factor for sailing through atolls and reefs, we become convinced that radar would offer an added quotient of protection. We have John Potter send us one. Whenever a newly purchased part from overseas is installed on the boat it can be excluded from duty fees. With the good assistance of Musket Cove's Dick, this process was simplified. We spend the next week learning how to use and adjust the radar. With it we can see not only the outline of the coastline ahead of us, but the hidden bays and coves not easily picked up visually. These are clearly displayed on the monitor. Behind us we are also able to pick up the breaking waves over the outside reef. This really 'makes our day' and adds to our sense of security. And the few showers that come through are easily read on the radar where it shows the outline of the storm and the density in its center. We are really feeling this new addition to our arsenal of tools is going to reduce the stress we faced when approaching the coast or a storm.

With the last minute details of buying stores for the boat and checking out of customs carried out, we leave Lautoka Dec.3. This is my sister Emily's birthday. Our efforts to wish her a happy birthday with a phone patch using the Seattle ham contact are unsuccessful. There is no answer to our phone call to her.

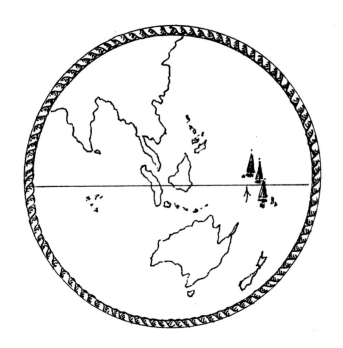

Marshall Islands

CHAPTER 10
NORTH ACROSS THE EQUATOR

We estimate it will be a two-week sail to cover the thousand miles north to Majuro in the Marshall Islands. It takes us two days to sail beyond the Yasawa Group and out of Fiji. Free of land and sailing towards the North Pacific, the first two days favor us with an east wind of ten knots giving us good speeds of five to six knots. But, alas, the wind dies and we motor for a day. When the wind picks up the following day, we are faced with a northeast wind. This is almost on our nose so we pull the sails as tight as we can to make headway. Even then we are sacrificing the preferred heading in order to get some speed. To add to the problem there seems to be a current pushing us east. It's slow going and at times I feel like we are clawing our way through a tunnel. The winds aren't high, about ten knots, and the seas are not rough but our progress sure is slow. A week later off the islands of Funafuti and Tuvalo, we discuss stopping to wait for the better winds that had been predicted, but decide to keep going and not make the trip any longer. We crab by these islands as we watch them vanish on the radar. Now we are beginning to have squalls pass through more frequently. When we see that threatening line of clouds ahead, we reduce the amount of canvas our sails are carrying - not to be overpowered when that band of thirty to forty knot winds tear by us.

The radar is really turning out to be a comforting companion. We can pick up atolls twelve to fifteen miles away and have been able to recognize the pattern of squalls. This makes it possible to avoid some and make preparations for those that are going to be a direct hit. We are glad we have it because the sat-nav seems to be having difficulty picking up good fixes here near the equator. Depending on dead reckoning, that traditional way of making a rough estimate of our heading, once more becomes our navigational tool.

Without ceremony, we sail across the equator to the northern hemisphere once again. We will continue to curve a serpentine path ten degrees either side of this noble marker for the next several years. With the radar as backup we find we are closing on Kiribati (pronounced Kiribas) and decide to stop here a few days. The outline of the island has been on radar for quite awhile. At sunrise we can see Tarawa, with an island in its lagoon ahead of us. Tarawa is one of the atolls of the country Kiribati. We make our way through the well-marked entrance of the reef. Looking straight into the morning sun, we blindly pick our way to the anchorage. Looking across the surrounding reef, the rusted remains of World War II guns, boats and planes are still scattered about. The winds are roaring across the lagoon with waves piling up on the wharf. Don, in the dinghy, does manage to find a protected spot behind a wall and get ashore to the customs officer. The dock master, very laid back, says not to worry about customs, we can take care of that when we leave. The varied customs practices and attitudes of immigration officials at each country we enter continue to amaze us. We spend a restless night here at anchor and decide, after a quick walk through the village next day, we'd rather be sailing than bouncing around in this harbor. The delayed customs is completed and we are off.

As the days pass, we start seeing birds ahead, a good sign. Surely the Majuro atoll is near. The clouds are changing color with a definite yellow-green cast along the underside of the towering cumulus, reflecting a shallow lagoon lying below. We are learning to recognize such markers to the presence of land approaching. These last days have been glorious sailing. The wind moved back to the east and we are on a broad reach making seven knots most of the way. This was the kind of wind that had been forecast when we left Fiji. Don claims the weather fax is only as good as the weatherman feeding it the information.

By early dawn we can see the lights of Majuro. It takes us the entire day to sail west fifteen miles to find and enter the pass into the lagoon - then motor that same fifteen miles into that same contrary wind to drop the anchor off the town of Majuro, the capitol of the Marshall Islands. There are two more boats beside us. Jim and Barb from Chicago aboard *Serenity* are now working here. The other sailboat, *Mr. John*, rocks at anchor with John the solo sailor aboard. At one time, John was the first mate on that luxurious 350-foot yacht, *Sea Cloud*, a birthday gift to heiress, Merriwether Post. We all meet at a very nice small restaurant called The Tide Tables that serve some of the best food we've enjoyed since the States.

It is Christmas 1988. Two years have sailed by since leaving home shores with our charts revealing almost ten thousand miles penciled across the pages. Still tired from the nineteen-day sail, we relax in a calm cockpit to enjoy a quiet morning on the boat. Handle's Messiah is playing on our tape deck while we enjoy funnel cakes with our coffee and cranberry juice. Don scrambled around town yesterday looking for my gift of a very attractive T-shirt with a Majuro design and a tape of the Mills Brothers, the closest sound to classical he could find on this remote island. Having thought it might be a problem, I looked for his gift in Fiji - a Sony Walkman, that I knew we would both enjoy. Listening to tapes when we are on watch helps to pass the time. It's especially on a day when the boat is stretching in long strides across a glistening sea, that we thrill to the combination of a Mozart symphony or Brahms concerto and the effort of the sails. We celebrate the sum of mankind's creative spirit soaring with nature's creation surrounding us.

Our new friends describe the rousing experience that captures the hearts of the entire community - Boxing Day - to be held tomorrow. There is no doubt when we awake next morning - celebration is in the air. We join the stream of folks shuffling along the dusty street to a large shed of a building. Inside bleachers rise on three sides with seating in the center that faces a stage. Noise and bedlam erupts as we enter, bombarding the senses as teen-agers shout greetings to their friends across the large room. In fact the entire audience is in a greeting frenzy. Adding to the confusion, the space above our heads is raining candy. It's being tossed back and forth from the large bags everyone is carrying. Choirs and dancing groups from the churches gain some semblance of order while performers and schools provide their presentations. Each group dressed in a distinctive costume, swings down the now narrow aisle. With arms in the air, they sway this way - then that, as they sing and dance their way to the platform. Here with a final flourish their performance of Christmas songs accompanied with graceful movements is acknowledged with applause. While the candy is still soaring the noise climbs even higher, its echoes float across the entire lagoon. We sit squeezed between active teenagers for three hours then decide it's time to head for the peace and quiet on *Horizon*. The sounds of celebration continue drifting across the water all day. We understand it hung in the air through the night while we slept.

Walking around town a few days later, we are approached by a young man, his blonde hair and Caucasian features prominent among the many strollers. When he stops and asks about the boat from Indiana, we lay claim and introduce ourselves. Because his face seems familiar, we ask where in Indiana was his home. A shrug of the shoulder, 'Oh, just a small town you've probably never heard of - Goshen. My name is Joe Lehman'. As we shake hands, I have to chuckle as I chide him; his memory isn't any better than mine. He sang in the church choir I directed before we left the States. Joe is married to Anna, the daughter of the Speaker of the House here in the Marshall Islands. They met when Anna attended Goshen College. Married, they returned to her home. Joe is a lawyer, one of the public defenders for the country. His job, he says, is mostly taking care of traffic violations; the Marshallese are gentlefolk with little inclination for violence.

As we sit under the Poinciana tree now blooming with brilliant red blossoms, Joe talks of the role the U.S. government has played in the development of Micronesia. As a part of the settlements that took place after World War II, this group of islands that stretches for a 2400 miles just north of the equator was assigned to the U.S. as a Trust Territory. This Trust bound our country to promote economic well-being and self-sufficiency to the inhabitants. The unstated strategy of the navy and military establishment, however, was to build military bases and conduct nuclear tests while the welfare of the villages was only considered in relationship to this primary purpose. As a result we poured a lot of money across this large American Lake, as it has sometimes been called. We essentially made a welfare state out of these tribes who had fed and managed their survival on these remote islands for centuries. Now they depend on canned tuna and corned beef and rice for their sustenance. There is a surfeit of civil service employees as more and more government jobs are offered. We now have instilled political dependency as well as economic lassitude. You can see it in the town here. The streets are littered with flying paper, rusty cans and old vehicles with their rusty shells pushed to the side of the roads to deteriorate in the salty air The pride of noble tribes can no longer be seen.

In 1969 the Micronesian legislators surprised the U.S. with their resolve and political astuteness by rejecting the American offer of commonwealth status. This would have allowed 'big brother' eminent domain over areas it needed for military use. In 1978, after years of maneuvering and trying to break apart the cohesion of purpose these islands were displaying, a statement of Free Association was signed and the Trust Territory was dissolved. This Association could be compared to the two pieces of bread in a sandwich with a tasty filling between. Choosing to form political entities of their own, this new compact now established three entities, The Republic of the Marshall Islands to the east and the Republic of Belau on the western edge, while sandwiched between lies the Federated States of Micronesia consisting of Kosrae, Pohnpei, Truk and Yap. While we move through this part of the world, the future is still uncertain as we hear of legislative moves by all sides to consolidate power.

We spend time with Joe and Anna and their four-year-old daughter, Fern, inviting them to visit us on the boat. Their nine-year-old son, Chris, is living with Joe's mother while he attends school in Goshen. I believe Joe could have spent all his evenings in the cockpit with the quiet stillness a real contrast to the bustle along the streets. We had invited them aboard for supper. The next day they encourage us to see the rest of the 15-mile stretch around the lagoon with a drive along shaded roads. We pass tiny hamlets neatly tended where life seems more tranquil. We promise to get together again after we make visits to some of the out-lying atolls.

At the end of the first week of this New Year as we make arrangements to sail to Aur, an island about ninety miles north of Majuro, Don begins to show flu symptoms. We delay our departure for four days until he feels strong enough to leave. In the meantime an official from the Out Island Affairs Office contacts us asking if we would take 40 twenty-five pound bags of rice to the island. We agree to do so. But when it comes time to leave there is a great deal of confusion. He tells us the bags will not be going. There is no explanation or discussion. So we leave around three in the afternoon for an overnight sail to Aur. With the wind from the southeast we are on a 'peachy' sail once more. As we approach Aur the wind picks up. Our noses become another tool recognizing land nearby, wood smoke invariably touches this sense before vision. With only sketchy charts to navigate by, we drop the sails and motor along the outside of the reef for five miles until we find the pass through the reef. There are no markers at these out-island passes. It's a rather long pass through the coral reef. With no tide-tables available here it's obvious that we've missed slack tide as water rushes through the pass. Since we will be heading almost into the wind we hoist the sail as insurance in case the engine should falter. We're only making two knots with the engine and sail both trying to pull us through the pass. All the while we keep watch not to be swept to either side onto the coral easily seen through the clear water. Finally we're through the pass then head towards the south of the lagoon. We drop the anchor off the village.

Before the anchor is set a motor boat is beside us and the mayor, Rissen Hansen, is asking for our landing permits. When we hand them over he relaxes and invites us to come ashore. We explain the need to set the anchor first before we pay him a visit on shore. The slope from the shore to deep water is steep. We have to reset the anchor several times before we feel it has made a good purchase. Even then we stay aboard another hour to make sure it will hold. As we pull the dinghy on the beach, Mr. Hansen meets us. We both try very hard to converse. He speaks very little English and the few Marshallese words we know make understanding each other difficult. We have learned the greeting, 'Yokwe', and use it, probably excessively, as we meet villagers along the neat paths. The homes are made of wood or tin. Mr. Hansen points out the school and churches along the way. It's a clean place with paths between the houses that shelter about two hundred kinfolk. We stop at his home for a cool coconut drink and delicate portions of deep-fried bread, not sweet but very nice. When I pass out candy to the children I'm overwhelmed with small hands reaching and grabbing. Some children get only a few pieces while others push to get more than their share. A poor decision on my part, not well thought through. An idea I discarded, never to use again.

We move along the lagoon hoping to find better anchoring conditions. Every little motu has a very narrow sandy beach steeply plunging to deep water. This doesn't allow much of a margin for safe anchoring. At one sandy spot where we drop the anchor, we notice, after several hours, the boat is adrift. Hauling in the anchor we swear it has a truck attached. The anchor is wearing a mass of old twisted line around its flukes as we hoist it aboard. We keep moving along the islets looking for a better spot until we are at the far end of the lagoon. Here is the only other island cradling a village. There does seem to be a broader area here that looks promising for the anchor.

Once more we dinghy ashore and are greeted by a large group of children. As a chorus they are saying, 'Hello my name is—, what is your name?' We answer, of course, and continue asking questions until everything becomes confused. There are giggles and shoving as shy faces study the circles they're drawing in the sand with their toes. A tall, blonde, young lady is running to meet us. Nancy, here on her two year Peace Corp assignment, welcomes us to Tabal. With her instruction the children are learning some English, we became part of their eagerness to try this new knowledge. The village is looking forward to welcoming visitors that might find their tiny island.

She speaks the dialect here and interprets as we stroll through this village. Again we walk along shaded paths. With cool breezes sweeping across the yards and the fronds of palm trees swaying, we drink in this South Seas atmosphere. Their small houses are simply made of wood with quite a few thatch homes scattered between them. Nancy explains she has been working with the women to teach them how to grow vegetables. By composting the debris that is swept each morning from the pathways and yards she is hoping to get soil for the gardens. If the supply ship is late arriving, she says the natives will go hungry instead of fishing as they used to do. We tell her of the request asking us to bring rice here. She nods and explains this island has been very unhappy with the management skills Mayor Hansen provides in affairs affecting the villagers on both islands in this lagoon. He, no doubt, again failed to get the money to Majuro in time for our delivery of rice.

She walks beside us interpreting as we visit with the friendly folks. We meet Etami, the cultural teacher, who keeps alive the traditional lore. He is passing on folktales to the children at school. Under the very large breadfruit tree, sit a half dozen elders of the village. Several are carving with their large cumbersome looking machetes small canoes they will send to Majuro to sell. Butto, the police chief is leaning against his bike. He tells us his staff of four policemen is not very busy here. The biggest problem they have is the drunkenness that comes from drinking the fermented coconut tree sap called tuba. We have seen bottles tied to the palm trees at a slash cut in the trunk. The sap, funneled into the bottle, will ferment in the sun. Nancy tells us the men are discussing plans that will keep the young men interested enough to remain on the island. So many of them are bored. As a result, alcoholism is an emerging problem here. As we are leaving, Etami, with a smile says, "If you will come to live with us, I offer you an island that's mine west of Tabal". We are touched with his generosity but assure him we choose to live near our family. He understands this. Family is treasured here as well. When we invite him to visit us on the boat later, he said he would share more of the folklore of the islands with us then.

Along the way we meet a teenager with a stack of palm hats on her head. The women of the village weave these. Several have an intricate blue design woven around the crown. We ask how she gets the blue color. Smiling, she says they noticed the pretty color of the carbon paper the school was throwing out, then discovered by boiling this paper in water they had a new source of dye to use.

Investigating still more, they found rusty cans could be another source of color to add to their palette of dyes. Here they use the pandanus plant for the beautiful weaving of placemats, hats, baskets and mats for sleeping or wall hangings. This is a source of income for the villages. Many of the homes here are made of this woven frond.

As we walk by a very attractive and tidy one, we meet Medrik the wife of Butto. She is the midwife for the village and also a very fine basket weaver. On her lap is an attractive tray basket on which she is weaving the finishing touches. The rim is decorated with the small white money-cowrie shells found on the beach. When I ask if she would sell it to me she agrees. Nancy says the six dollars I paid is twice what she would get from the wholesaler who buys the island crafts sold in the States.

Nancy tells of the island custom called night crawling. After dark, a young man crawls quietly to the home of his favored lady friend. With a long carved bamboo stick, he pokes through the grass walls to lightly touch his love in hopes she will join him outside on the beach. There is a certain amount of strategy involved. He needs to be familiar enough with the sleeping arrangements so not to lightly touch her brother or worse still, her father, at which point the crawl becomes a mad scramble. Nancy reveals she was the object, several times, of such endeavors by the young men of the village. She doesn't share with us her response to these touches. I purchase one of these delicately carved sticks when we later return to Majuro.

We enjoy a last visit with Nancy and three villagers who pay us a visit aboard *Horizon*. Etami misses the visit because, we are told, he has left the island on a visit elsewhere. Nancy suggests he may have been forbidden to join us. The stories he tells of their ancestral heritage are guarded treasures not to be casually shared with the world. Assuring Nancy we will phone her parents in Michigan when we return to the States in April, we bid this most pleasant place farewell.

Beyond Aur just north, is the atoll Malolelap, our next stop. Here is another great 'tasting' name! We anchor in the quiet lagoon at the southern village of Airik and meet Anne, the Peace Corp worker here. We walk again through a tropical setting with shaded paths and a light breeze teasing the palm fronds overhead. We pass the grass houses with the dirt yards all brushed with palm branches to be litter free. We are invited inside a house to see the single room with its swept dirt floor is absolutely bare. Only the rolled up grass sleeping mats lie in a corner. Outside, beside the house is an open sided cook shed. The stove is a hole in the ground where they cook with coconut hulls as fuel. There may be a shelf stretched between the corner posts where cooking pots and eating utensils, bags of rice and cans of tuna and corned beef are stored. We are surprised how little English is understood beyond Majuro. In fact one very gracious lady we visit, never off her island, is surprised that we don't speak Marshallese. She thought it was the language of the whole world, much as we assume everyone should speak English.

As we continue walking along the path, a lady motions us to come inside her cookhouse. Her daughter is squatting by the fire rolling little balls of dough and dropping them into a kettle of boiling coconut milk. They invite us to share breakfast with them. We sit on mats on the ground. She kneels before us to place banana leaves on our laps. These little boiled dumplings are spooned on this attractive plate. The flavor is much like you'd expect dough of flour and water to taste, not very interesting, but their genuine desire to share is delicious. They also share with us boiled fruit of the same pandanus tree that is used for all their weaving. The flavor is much like a sweet potato. However, it is so fibrous that we are pulling strings from between our teeth the rest of the day.

We had planned to visit one more island before returning to Majuro but Don has become very sick, stretching my limited nursing skills to care for him. After breakfast this morning, still at Airik, he's suddenly overcome with chills. His temperature has spiked to 105 degrees with bouts of nausea and weakness. His diagnosis is a kidney infection, probably associated with his spell of sickness a month ago in Majuro. He outlines for me the regimen for his treatment and contingency plans if this doesn't work. I go ashore and check with Anne about any flights back to the hospital in Majuro. She says there is supposed to be a flight every two weeks that makes a landing on a narrow strip of beach but even this could not be counted on. I then ask her to find several fellows who can help me get the dink aboard in case we decide to sail back. In three days his temperature recedes and he starts eating better. In this pleasant place we just stay put for another week before returning to Majuro. Most of these days Don sleeps while I spend time ashore with the video camera. With Anne as guide, I take videos of life on the island. I am trying to get on film as many of the villagers as possible while they work, play and attend Sunday morning church. While I sit on a grass floor mat in an open sided pavilion during the church service, the camera captures the restless children squirming beside their mammas. The singing strains my ability to concentrate. The decibels climb close to shouting level. This shouting is the testimony of the women and children alone; very few men are in the congregation. Knowing the mayor owns a VCR, I make a copy on tape to leave with him. They will be able to watch themselves working and playing around their village.

Back in Majuro, Don goes to the hospital to have tests taken at the modest lab there. When we return to the States he will get a thorough series done at Elkhart Hospital. It's time we begin making plans to fly to Minneapolis for Linda and Paul's wedding. The local travel agent arranges the ticket home on Continental Air, the only airline flying this route. We also are fortunate to find Dan, a young Bostonian on a working vacation, who agrees to live aboard *Horizon* while we are gone. After dinner aboard, Don explains to him the various systems, electric, plumbing, fuel line and most important, the mechanics of the bilge pump! He would like to crew with us on our return when we will sail the next 350-mile leg to Kosrae, the neighboring island to the west.

We take the flight out of Majuro the last Thursday evening in March and arrive in Hawaii Thursday morning. How is the body clock supposed to adjust to all this fast shuffle crossing the dateline? We head for the Northwest Airline desk to purchase our reserved tickets and find nothing but grief. The desk clerk refuses to sell us the tickets we had reserved in Majuro. They are a reduced fare for nonresidents on a round trip ticket. The details at this late date elude me. I do remember, however, feeling discouraged. The possibility we would not be a part of our daughters' wedding seemed real. Don hung on tenaciously and finally persuaded the clerk's supervisor that we had been assured the legality of our status with a statement signed by an American lawyer in Majuro, our good friend Joe. Finally we are sold the tickets. However, this ticket restricts us to fewer legs than the cities we had planned to visit. After a two-day stop in Seattle to do some catching up with our new granddaughters, Amanda and Lindsey, we arrive in Minneapolis.

For two pretty salty sailors to suddenly be immersed in the flurry of formal wedding preparations causes us to take deep breaths. We are not at all sure we won't embarrass our family. Although parents of the bride traditionally carry the burden of organizing and paying the big bills, these two kids had arranged and planned every detail. All we need to do is get a haircut, see a hairdresser and put on our shoes. A wonderful reunion with our side of the equation before the wedding is a special gift. We take this opportunity to visit with Don's sister, Thelma, and her husband Weyburn. Our abbreviated ticket cancels the visit with them in Ohio. The time we had hoped to spend with Lynn and Dana in Denver has also been cut. Having all of us together at this happy time suggests the quality of a string quartet with each instrument blending rich harmonies. The wedding is lovely, as is the bride. With Paul by her side, they make certain this celebration is a joyous occasion for everyone. When the honeymooners leave for Florence, Italy, we all go our separate ways, with the two of us on our way to Elkhart.

Dr. Pete and Hulda have offered their guestroom for us the week we will be here. We catch up with the state of our finances - Don signs up for Social Security - he has his tests done at the hospital - we both have teeth and bodies checked, the whole works. The final analysis - the *Horizon* crew seems to be in good shape when all is completed.

The Classens have invited fifty of our friends for an open house that really reassures us that friends are forever. We enjoy a nice weekend with son Steve, our daughter-in-law Linda and our other two granddaughters, Natasha and Michelle, while we catch-up with their busy lives. Hugs are shared and pictures taken as we say goodbye. I might explain, at this point, Lindas abound in our family. Beside giving this name to our only daughter, we find we now have two more Lindas, daughters-in-law, to grace the Miller registry. Sons Steve and Dale, each brought to the Miller family tree these additions. Linda means beautiful, a fitting description adorning our tree.

Then it's off to Doylestown, Pa. to spend time with my family. This catch-up time with all these special ones never have us feeling that anyone thought it was time to come home and live a sensible life. There may have been doubts about our safety, perhaps, but nary a word to us of their doubts. Having some experience being a mother, I couldn't help but feel that my Mother must at times have lived with great anxiety about us, but she never expressed it in her many letters to us. It is the letters I wrote her that I now find a great source of information as I write this journal. While we journeyed I maintained a loose journal but I am finding our letters home provide concise descriptions of the highlights of our trip around the world.

Since Annapolis is close by, we stop to get John Potter's advice on a new anchor windlass. Because we are dealing with U.S. postage in Majuro, we decide it will be easier to mail it rather than carry the very heavy bulky apparatus with us. Using all the allowed legs on this ticket we head back to Seattle.

We have time for a sail aboard *Horizon* 1 now resting in Dales lapping bays. As we sail San Juan Straits with snow capped peaks on the distant horizon, memories return of those early learning days exploring the Great Lakes with our four children squeezed into its small quarters. We leave Seattle for Hawaii. A two-day layover gives us time to visit college friends, John and Lois Bender. John teaches at the Univ. of Hawaii. With his major in language, he spent several years in the Marshall Islands listening and writing the first lexicon of their language. The last leg back to Majuro gives us time to process mentally the emotions and feelings of this past month that have crowded into our subconscious. It allows nurturing to heal the separation from family and friends.

We fly over atolls with their oval reefs of coral and turquoise lagoons that we have sailed across. To look at them now from this perspective, this fairy tern's view, it looks so simple. Looking forward from the deck of a heaving sailboat towards waves washing over a reef ahead seems complex by comparison. As we circle one of these small spots in the vast ocean, we realize we are landing on Majuro as the sun is dipping close to the western horizon. By the time we get through customs and catch a taxi to arrive at the shore near *Horizon*, it's almost dark. We can't attract the attention of any of the three boats still in the harbor. The only means of getting out to *Horizon* seems to be a battered rowboat of questionable floating capabilities pulled here on the beach. With no owner visible we 'borrow' it to ferry all our luggage. Dan was not aboard but his note on the pile of freshly laundered linen said he had a job offer and decided to leave, assigning the care of *Horizon* to Barb and Jim on the boat beside us. Everything looked in good shape and spotlessly clean. When we checked with *Serenity* next morning they reported no problems while we were gone. We get settled in and make plans to leave as soon as the windlass arrives.

The heat continues to be oppressive. The showers we take are short lived. Our bodies glisten with perspiration. I take advantage of the offer Lehman's have made to use the air-conditioned coolness of their mobile home to can chicken before we leave. As soon as the windlass arrives, we'll be off. If it doesn't arrive this week we will have to get an extension to our visitors' permit. It doesn't and we do!

To relieve the 'treading water syndrome' while we wait - then wait some more, we plan to sail to Mili, an atoll about eighty miles south. Our lawyer friend, Joe, has asked to join us for the overnight sail. His enthusiasm for the boat has been keen every time we see him. Weighing anchor to sail moderate seas, we are surprised how seasick he remains the entire trip. He's at the rail continuously. His head comes up, and with a weak grin he says 'It's not too bad'.

We've been invited to this island by an American couple who started a business raising clams, the giant tradacna clam. They hope to get the local men interested and knowledgeable enough about the production of these enormous bi-valves so that this new industry would allow them self-sufficiency. It is a complex program requiring knowledge of the fertilizing process of this clam. In tanks of seawater on shore the tiny shells are constantly monitored and nurtured until they grow to be four to five inches across. When they are large enough to have a chance to survive they are moved to the protected lagoon just offshore this very small island. We are shown the tiny clamshells in the tanks on shore; then don snorkels and masks to swim over the long rows of the larger clams standing on the floor of the sandy lagoon. It is awesome to see these dramatic specimens of bi-valves as they siphon water through their open halves. We look into the beautifully colored thick frill of the exposed mantle that edges the wavy contour of the shell. The speckled mantles shimmer with hues that have been borrowed from the rainbow as the sunbeams send fractured prisms of light through the clear water across these open clams. It's truly a magnificent sight. What makes it so breathtaking is the size of this shell, many of them three to four feet across. There are stories of unwary swimmers stepping into one of these open clams to be locked in the grasp of these valves that close with a very quick reflex. There is a Japanese market for the food of the clam. The shells alone have a price tag around $50.

For three years Ron and Susie with their two sons Ocean, five years, and Forest, three years old, have made this tiny motu their home. Both of the boys live in naked splendor - brown as hickory nuts. With ease they scamper over coral in their bare feet, up palm trunks as swift as any monkey or crouch under birds nest ferns to watch for coconut crabs. Grabbing my hand, Ocean insists I take a tour of his small paradise. With a first stop at his tree house, he then beckons this sixty-year old grandmother to follow him over fallen trunks and under bushes to poke our long sticks into piles of fallen palm branches where surely we'll find the elusive crab. And sure enough, he teases a large one out of the burrow. His small hands grab the fearsome thing with its awful looking large claw waving in the air. With no hesitation we dash across the island to present to Mom his choice for supper. Meanwhile little Forest has collected a bucketful of hermit crabs hidden in their borrowed shells. He's been busy with a hammer, smashing them into small pieces. He'll feed this mess to his six chickens until their craws are full. I feel I have enjoyed a visit with Swiss Family Robinson.

Poor Don missed out, not only on most of the excitement of this island life but also seeing those extraordinary clams. He is now suffering with the pain and fever of dengue fever. He said the common term 'bone break fever' aptly describes the pain he is experiencing. Mosquitoes transmit it. We now become more religious in our use of spray when leaving the boat. We are able to keep the interior of the boat screened. He is beginning to feel the Marshall Islands have a real grudge against him. Having to wait around for a boat part that is lost in the mail somewhere between Annapolis and this Pacific country only increases his frustration with matters that seem to be beyond our control.

119

When we return to Majuro we're told that a dispute has arisen between Continental Airlines and the island government. Because the Marshallese have been exploring possibilities to operate their own air transport to Hawaii, Continental is holding all mail in Hawaii to force their contract.

More time on our hands - twiddling our thumbs. Don spends a lot of that time puttering around the boat and declares it beats mowing a yard. During these long days a special display captures our attention. As the day's brightness slowly transforms to the softer colors of twilight, the heavens burst with the sparkle of fluttering white wings. This signature of the tiny fairy tern fills the canopy overhead as flocks perform lissome acrobatics that hold us spellbound each evening. Especially enthralling is the *pas de deux* ballet as pairs of these small white 'fairies' soar in perfect synchronized turns and dives adding dimension to the heavens. This heavenly beauty rivals the splendor we are enjoying underwater.

It is six weeks before the part arrives. We are fortunate the windlass arrives complete. The box it traveled in is in tatters with small parts loosely banging around the interior. Installation of this heavy equipment challenges our muscles and 'know-how'. In order to secure the fittings and bolts to the deck, we lie on our back, feet in the air, to take turns holding the motor against the roof above the bunk at the boat's bow as nuts are tightened. Then, following Potter's diagrams, Don hooks up the electric power. This is energy that will supplant the back power Don has used to haul the anchor these many years.

It takes a week of hot sweaty hours before we press the button and hear a reassuring hum as the windlass slowly spins. We anticipate our journey will be even more comfortable with this new energy. We take on supplies, fill the water tanks and start the engine to motor across the lagoon to the fuel dock. Almost immediately there are ominous thumping sounds - a sputtering - then quiet. What is it about this place!

When we ask the locals and the 'rebellis' (white man) for a good diesel mechanic, there's always a long pause before we get an answer. We locate the man most recommended. He comes to the boat several afternoons and stands, hands on hips, giving instructions to Don. Don is the one getting greasy hands - he's doing all the work, replacing injectors and taking the head off that still looks good. Following the 'guru's many instructions, the engine still won't respond. Our mechanic shrugs and says, as he leaves the boat, 'You've got a sail boat, get on with it.' 'Tis true, but we have changed our environment. All of this electronic wizardry - a sat nav, radar and now a windlass - requires

120

electricity. A working engine has become essential to our path westward. Old Joshua Slocum would have said, 'Told you so!'

Meanwhile the ham radio is getting repairs. We discover the young man doing these repairs had worked as a diesel mechanic for ten years in California, and specifically on Yanmar, the trade name of our engine. We say a quiet prayer of thanks. As soon as possible we get him aboard. Don reviews all the steps that have just been tried to find the problem. Without a pause, he proceeds taking apart the juncture of the exhaust pipe at the engine. Here he finds a large buildup of gunk caused by exhaust. He cleans this and reseals the joint. With a turn of the key, the engine comes to life, able to breathe once again. We are off, finally.

Kosrae to Pohnpei to Truk

CHAPTER 11
SAILING THE AMERICAN LAKE

The weather isn't great - rainy and squally. But we are on our way, the 13th of July. After a day of clouds and a lot of sail changes to accommodate these squalls, the weather does become more favorable. The sun starts sneaking peeks at us and the wind has stayed a steady ten knots, pushing the boat on its stern quarter, my 'peach of a reach' once again. By late afternoon, the third day of sailing, we can see the faint touch of land making its presence felt along the horizon. The sat-nav tells us it is still thirty miles to Kosrae. Rather than make an arrival in the dark at the unknown harbor, we decide to 'heave to' for the night. The next morning we sail the remaining miles to this lovely island with the tall peaks of Mt. Finkol, over 2000 feet high making it possible to see the island those thirty miles back. We motor into the harbor at Leluh Harbor, the only sailboat to grace its quiet seclusion. Around the perimeter of this small bay is the village. As we squat under a tree beside the customs official we carry out the usual permission requirements for our visit. Kosrae is one of the most unspoiled and unpretentious countries in this necklace of jewels stretching across Micronesia. The pace is unhurried, the smiles are easily shared and a spirit of innocence blows gently across any encounter we are fortunate to share.

We decide to walk the three miles into Tofol, the town with a market place and we are told a very nice restaurant. It isn't long until a truck stops to give us a lift. The lady driver, who speaks English, tells us about the town, and 'be sure to try the good oranges that we grow here'. The small market has a nice selection of fruit and vegetables. The oranges, we discover, have green skins with the usual orange fruit as sweet as the more familiar ones we know. There are also pineapples, bananas and large yams - some shaped like a melon. Just as we are leaving, a farmer brings a basket full of smooth purple eggplant that completes our purchase today. We do stop at the small, very tidy eating-place and enjoy a simple but tasty lunch of hamburgers, coleslaw and fried slices of sweet potato. We have puzzled frequently over the table decorations used in the restaurants in the Pacific. With all the exotic flowers growing in wild abandon along the byways, plastic substitutes grace these tables. It's pleasant to have windows here to view the lush vegetation climbing the slopes. So different from Majuro where the eating places had few windows. As we start our walk back to the anchorage, it begins to rain. A family with two children stops to offer us a ride in their car. The father, Stan, is very well spoken, telling us he attended University in Hawaii for two years. We make an appointment with him to take a tour of the ruins at Leluh tomorrow morning.

It is rainy today but Stan is ready to show us the dramatic ruins of a civilization that was once the most stratified society in Micronesia. It was a feudal system with only a few chiefs owning most of the land, the lesser chiefs as managers and commoners doing the hard labor. The ruins that we are looking at date back to 1400A.D. They are quite remarkable. Filling in low coral areas, using essentially slave labor, a capitol center was constructed. The king's domain and various worship platforms are the prominent features. All of the structures were built on a remote corner of this forty-two square mile island with basalt stone hewn into log shapes. The partial walls are still standing. Outlines of the large platforms are visible through entwined vines hiding much of the scope of this once royal complex. During its period of regal majesty there was a vast network of canals, remnants of some still visible, that made access to the far reaches of the kingdom possible. These also made it expedient to leave the walled city by canoe to protect its ocean boundaries. Only recently is there enough interest to sift through these ruins in order to catalogue and display the artifacts that are just now being discovered. Stan feels the history of his people will be lost; prompting a sense of urgency to take the time to copy remembrances of their older citizens. A small museum has been opened. It struggles with the apathy of the native population that shows little interest in contributing to its wealth of artifacts. Stan invited us to attend, this weekend, a special performance of cultural dances and singing. To this day I regret that we didn't stay to attend. With our overlong stay in Majuro, our haste here was misguided. After just a week here, we use our nifty windlass and leave this special quiet domain.

With a three-day sail in light winds, we find we are using the motor to make the passage to Pohnpei in reasonable time. We arrive at the north pass of Pohnpei to see it is well marked with the distinctive volcanic plug, Sokehs Rock poking its head skyward - a landmark for sailors. We follow the buoys to the dock where we tie-up. Within a half-hour the cockpit has eight officials squeezed aboard ready to clear us into their country. Half of them are vague about their official status but all proceed to scribble 'pertinent information' on the backs of envelopes or scraps of paper. They all insist on seeing the interior of the boat and do so with courtesy and politeness. Swiftly and with efficiency they stamp the necessary papers. They remind us to notify them a day before we leave to receive our important clearance papers. Still at the dock, a grand rain shower proceeds to sweep across the decks washing away the salt and dust of the recent voyage. With our makeshift dams of rubber foam blocking the drains in the gunwale, the rain rushes into the open access to our water tanks.

We leave the dock with only vague directions to the anchorage that, we are told, lies ahead after several turns around obstructions. We hug the coast, thinking we are in good shape, when we feel that ominous thump and hear the crunch of coral. We are sailing these last weeks without a depth sounder. We sent it to the States for repairs. The water in this harbor is so muddy that there is no hope of reading the water. We are now sitting on top of a large coral mass. Trying to back off does no good - going forward will just shove us further onto the reef. With a sigh, we start the long process of inflating the dinghy. We'll row a distance to drop an anchor, to kedge off. During this process, we notice some movement of the boat. Dashing back to the helm we put the engine in reverse. The tide has risen enough to lift us sufficiently to steer away from the danger. Now gun-shy, we slowly ease our way towards the few boats we see anchored just around the next bend and drop the anchor in the muddy waters. Surrounding the little bay are steep hillsides spilling their lush tropical foliage to the waters' murky edge. This second largest island of the

Micronesia chain boasts a rugged, rain forested, mountain terrain, 2500 feet tall. Torrential streams are fed by endless precipitation dashing over rocks to form spectacular waterfalls.

No one seems to be aboard the other three boats anchored here, so we begin preparing supper. About seven o'clock there is a knock on the hull. Poking our heads through the companionway, we see a large dinghy with a smiling Canadian, Del, welcoming us to Kolonia. With him is his wife, Urene, a young native gal who looks to be about sixteen years old. He dropped his anchor here and hasn't been able to get it up after finding the joys of Urene and a job as administrator of civil aviation for the Federated States of Micronesia. As his wife sits on his lap stroking and kissing his cheeks, he gives us directions for walking to town, telling us the locations of the market, laundry and post office. He continues to stop by each evening. We enjoy chatting about sailing and the lifestyle we both have chosen. On a sunny Sunday they pick us up in their truck and escort us to a thatchy, lovely restaurant owned by two Americans. We enjoy a gourmet brunch of eggs benedict and blueberry pancakes. Then we tour the island, past unique volcanic plugs looking like phallic symbols scattered over the landscape. We stop to hop across the streams on slippery rocks to the thundering waterfalls spilling between thick foliage. We finish the day of sightseeing with a visit to the newly constructed government buildings. Pohnpei is the capitol for the Federated States of Micronesia, consisting of Kosrae, Pohnpei, Truk and Yap. These attractive buildings are constructed of basalt logs with architecture resembling traditional native longhouses.

Walking along the streets of Kolonia, the largest town in Pohnpei, we find displays of carvings expressing a distinctive interpretation of culture on this island. With U.S. postage still available, we decide to send our family the carved mobiles we see. With fish, birds and animals carved in teak; they hang as floating ballast, swimming through air as gracefully as their water counterparts. The friendliness that surrounded us in Kosrae is absent here. We especially notice a more aggressive disposition of the men at the helm of their motor launches racing as close to the anchored sailboats as possible. There is endless circling of an anchored sailboat to see how much rocking can be achieved. This is the sport for an evening.

In order to recapture some of Don's snorkeling and spear diving skills, we leave the muddy lagoon for a small out island, Ant, just twenty miles southwest of the big island of Pohnpei. Del suggests the clear water in that lagoon might harbor some fish. We find the lagoon, indeed, to be crystal clear but depleted of fish. The small 'big-eyes' that Don was able to spear offered the good taste once again of fresh fish. Since all the surrounding land is private, we can't stretch our legs on a beach-walk. We decide it's time to make way for Truk. We return to Kolonia and contact the immigration official about our proposed departure. A young boy tells us to stay at the dock overnight; the official will clear us in the morning. With all the emphasis concerning the importance of clearance papers given when we entered, we are surprised when the official arrives late in the morning. Displaying a bothersome hangover, he just waves us away muttering, 'You don't need any more papers'. Since we have papers outlining our stay at this place, we hope these will be sufficient to clear us into Truk.

Here in late summer we are finding the prevailing winds to be light. Motor sailing becomes the *modus operandi*. It's been two days since we left Pohnpei. Checking the chart we note a small island that might make a nice stop. The surrounding reef with no sign of trees, is visible on the horizon. Since we don't have a detailed chart of this atoll, Oraluk, Don climbs the mast. He sits on the spreaders in order to see ahead and locate the entrance through the reef. Following his hand signals, I steer our course through the pass, motor inside and round a low sandy spit that stretches inside the lagoon. Our newly repaired depth sounder displays the depths as we look for a sandy patch to drop the anchor. We circle several times looking for any sand. There isn't any - the anchor will drop amidst coral heads. We hope it won't be too challenging when it's time to haul the anchor. There is no wind to be concerned about so Don dives over the side with his spear gun to look for fresh fish for supper. I swim to the sand spit to look for shells. I'm greeted by a host of screaming terns diving at me for trespassing. The same dainty fair terns we watched turning exquisite pirouettes in the sky are now squawking in dissonance as they protect their territory. Their beauty has not found expression in their voices. Not long after searching unsuccessfully for that special shell, I notice a dark squall line forming a threatening line just to the south. The waves start growing. I am not sure I can swim back to the boat, since I had dislocated my shoulder for the fourth time while in Majuro. My shouts to Don go unheard. His head is under water most of the time. We have the wind generator running on *Horizon*. Very soon it is spinning at a furious pace. Within moments the vane that holds the propeller into the wind, blows away. Finally, Don becomes aware of the turbulence around him. He dashes back to the boat, stops the generator, and gets the dinghy off the deck to pick me up. We decide to put a second anchor down. Now we feel more secure in the thirty-knot winds that blow all night.

After a night of pitching seas, we try the new windlass in the morning. The speed and ease with which it brings the anchors up are quite remarkable. To get away so easily from the tight boundaries which we find ourselves is a new experience. The wind is still kicking up its heels. As we take a last look while motoring through the pass, the engine suddenly stops. Immediately, Don hauls the sails aloft. He scrambles below to see what the problem is and discovers the fuel tank is empty. We seem to be slow learners. There is no gauge to check the amount of fuel in the tank, but with each fill of the tank we do keep a written record of the hours logged on the motor. And sure enough, the fuel log confirms our predicament. With all this motoring, we just hadn't made a recent check. As the sea tosses us, we fill the tank from the ever-present jerry jugs tied to the lifelines.

As it turns out, we don't need to run the engine for the remaining forty-eight hours of our passage. The first thirty hours are squally with winds to thirty-five knots, just off our nose. I fret that it's going to take us a million years to get there. We are making only two knots - with two hundred miles to go. I hate every wave. I wish the wind would shift or quiet down. After thirty hours the wind does back and becomes a more friendly fifteen knots that allows a better point of sail. Sometimes we are scooting along at seven knots, with clear skies and stars sparkling overhead at night. About noon August 7 we can see the white pyramid shaped markers ahead that mark the entrance to the large lagoon of Truk

We move across this large lagoon along the well-marked channel to the commercial dock, planning to complete the customs process there. Drawing close to the wharf, we see a tangle of swinging, loose boards from rusty iron projections reaching out to attack our hull. With several fast motor launches creating waves and turbulence, we quickly steer one hundred-eighty degrees - this is no place for dockage. We'll take the advice a sailor had given us back in Majuro and continue to the anchorage off the lovely Continental Hotel. Don goes ashore here, phones our arrival to the customs and immigration offices then, following their directions, makes a trip to their offices. He receives all the necessary papers without any official even caring to see *Horizon*.

This large lagoon, forty miles across, was at one time a large volcanic island that sank below sea level. The remaining fifteen islets within the lagoon defined by the outer reef, are the tallest peaks of that long ago island. Moen, the island where we have dropped anchor is the capitol of Truk and its commercial center. We are at the southern tip of the island and away from the town, so we take advantage of the pickup trucks that ply the roads. These provide taxi service for the outlying villagers. The other passengers sitting in the back all neatly dressed and well groomed, welcome us to their country with smiles and good-hearted conversation. So we are surprised when we arrive in town at the dirty streets and debris filling every corner. We thought Majuro was dirty but these folks seem even less inclined to come to grips with the garbage they care to live with.

We enjoy sharing experiences with the small group of sailors anchored here. Kelly on *'Far Side'* is employed here, working with the legislative body using her skills as a lawyer. She is frustrated as the body of representatives struggle with the disposition of the money the country is receiving from the U.S. There seems to be a lack of understanding for the need to spend this money on their infrastructure. A lack of a good water supply and poor roads to the outer villages are a common complaint of the people. These men prefer, instead, more ostentatious projects that would be hard to support or maintain.

For years this lagoon has attracted divers from around the world. In the depths of these waters are sheltered the remains of over sixty Japanese ships sunk by a US Navy air attack February 1944. Because this large lagoon with few entrances offered protection, it had become the Japanese Imperial Fleet's safe haven for many years. These boundaries finally became their trap. So today, some fifty years later, these hulks are camouflaged with mounds of coral that make spectacular diving sites. Don joined some of the fellows on several dives to these eerie sights, resting from thirty-five to one hundred feet below the surface. The guns now outlined in soft corals.

We find the craft shop located in a back corner of town. Here the proprietor, David, displays the many crafts and local shells that are for sale. He has been responsible for searching out the crafts created in the surrounding villages to offer them for sale. We purchase a storyboard. We have been hearing about these carved pictures of legends and myths, beautifully designed on large slabs of the breadfruit tree trunk. We choose the legend of the magic breadfruit tree originating from Babeldaop in Palau. *This legend speaks of Milad, a young woman who possessed a magic breadfruit tree with a hollow trunk that reached down to the lagoon of the islet. Occasionally a huge wave would wash a large fish through this hollow, providing food for the entire village. In time the nasty head of jealousy raged through the village. The jealous hands with clamshell axes, cut down Milad's magic tree. The ocean poured in, drowning the village. Slowly sinking into the sea, the islet, Ngibtal was never seen again.* This storyboard, with its beautiful design carved in fine detail, catches our attention. We decide to purchase this one, rather than wait until Palau also known for it's fine carvers. In the past, waiting to purchase unique art, has left us empty-handed when only meager choices are later available. David invites us to his village, Udot.

After exploring Moen for five days, we sail ten miles to the island of Udot, and his village Penia. Children swarm around us as we bring the dinghy ashore. Young Roxanne takes us to David's carving workshop where he arrives shortly. David is a native of Tonga. He came to Truk as a Bahai missionary, then stayed here after marrying a local girl. Finding there was no local economy, he took on the task of teaching carving to his neighbors. As a result, they now support themselves with this talent. Although the local chief is given monies by the legislature to provide water catchments and sewer facilities for the village, they still have to haul water long distances, wash clothes in muddy streams and use privies. The chief's home, meanwhile, gets larger with added modern facilities. The village is angry, yet their traditional manner has them conditioned to accept circumstances imposed on them. The village has a sorry appearance.

David's generosity, however, spills over with his commands shouted to the many youngsters crowding around us. They scamper off to round up gifts of food to send us on the next leg of our journey. Boys climb to the tops of the palms, screwing the green drinking coconuts off with their toes. Two small boys struggle to bring a full bunch of bananas. Still others bring a large watermelon and papayas for us. We comprise a happy, noisy parade as we all march down the dusty road to our dinghy, giggles and singing filling the air.

As we wave farewells, Don climbs the mast to sit on the spreaders once again. He keeps a lookout for coral heads and shallow spots as we leave this joyous crowd. We make our way through the reef and on to the ocean passage towards Yap.

In two days we arrive one hundred-fifty miles west at the tiny atoll of Pulawat. We have been reading about this distinguished island and the magnificent skills of the ocean navigators living here. David Lewis in his book, 'The Voyaging Stars' , vividly describes the accuracy of these voyages. Using their knowledge of wave patterns, the stars, clouds and birds, these men, for centuries, traveled great distances in their canoes to commerce among the islands of the Pacific.

We arrive in the protected lagoon and drop the anchor. There is no other boat sharing this paradise, we are alone. It's not long until a small out-rigger canoe with two men paddling comes to the stern. One of them is shouting greetings in excellent English. 'Bingo' is his name. With a broad grin he proudly shares the fact that he had spent three years in Walla Walla, Washington, attending college. After an exposure to the pace of life in a foreign environment, he decided Pulawat and fishing was really where his heart yearned to be. While we are enjoying their stories and sipping lemonade, a 'boom-boom', an apt description for their fishing boats, roars alongside with a very large man at the helm. He introduces himself, Uromo. With our invitation he climbs aboard. This is something to behold. I am guessing the three hundred plus pounds that heaves over the lifelines with only a tiny loincloth covering a narrow strip of flesh, exposes more buttock than I have ever seen. While we visit, we become aware of his great intelligence. A quiet courtesy conceals his curiosity about the world beyond Pulawat. He is the teacher of Junior High students. We enjoy the stories he shares about the cultural richness of his small island and the history of their people. They were one of the most feared tribes in this part of the Carolina chain of islands. Now he is a model of the gentle giants these islanders have become since the missionaries arrived in the late 1800s. This small island has seven hundred inhabitants that are divided into twenty tribes.

Next morning we go ashore to give gifts to the two chiefs. Beside the traditional chief, Manipi, there is the elected chief, Erlan who we find to be the friendliest with a keen sense of humor. In contrast, our visit to the large canoe house of the traditional chief, Manipe, is a formal, serious affair. There are no smiles as we sit before his stern presence to present our gifts of coffee and fishing lures. David Lewis, in his book, describes Manipi as a chief who uses manipulative skills as his source of power.

The loincloth is the standard male attire. The women wear only grass skirts or sarongs, some pulling scarves across their breasts when we pass them on the paths. Bingo guides us to Uromo's large canoe house. We are invited to share with his family as they dine on fish, taro and breadfruit. This is served on a large leaf placed on our lap as we sit on the ground. Children giggle and stand shyly around as Uromo explains the making of the large canoes and the voyages they undertook. Tomorrow, the men will assemble to repair one of the canoes. He invites us to watch. It's ok, he says to film the process with our video.

He becomes a frequent visitor to our boat in the evenings. Many times he brings tasty breadfruit boiled in coconut milk - much like a fritter - for us to enjoy. It's delicious with its accompanying smoky taste. All the cooking takes place in a pit in the ground using coconut husks as fuel. Smoke, that navigational tool, is also integral to the food we're eating. Most of the thatch, plywood or corrugated tin houses have a pig tied near the door and chickens roaming freely. As a result, clouds of flies move with us as we make our way through the tall grasses.

We feel privileged to watch the men, each with his special skill, gather next morning to repair the large canoe. We suspect Uromo has made our intrusion into a rather sacred tradition, possible. In front of us sits an elder taking fibers he has picked from coconut husks to twist into long strands called sennet. These will be used instead of nails to tie together elements of the canoe. Another group of exceptionally handsome young men is fashioning a new outrigger. Their tools are handmade awls, hammers and knives. With expert skills the joints are completed with precision and a tight fit. It's hard to believe that as late as 1965 many of these men had a reputation of piracy in these waters. We show them pictures in the Lewis book. This brings smiles and teasing as they recognize members of their village shown on the pages. We give them the book to enjoy and share with the rest of the village.

As a last gesture of Uromo's hospitality, he invites Don to join him in the boom-boom for a fishing foray outside the lagoon. Don seems pleased to go. So I'm surprised when they return and he says he wasn't at all sure it was a good idea to go. Uromo has been such a generous host and to turn down his invitation seemed insensitive. It's not uncommon that their motors stop working. They seem to have limited knowledge about getting them started again. Usually the natives don't take oars as a back up or even some kind of sail to limp back to port. We have towed native fishing boats back to their villages from their stranded positions several times. This time all went well. Even the chicken feather lures Uromo uses have caught some nice fish for supper.

With Don's hand signals we are through the pass.

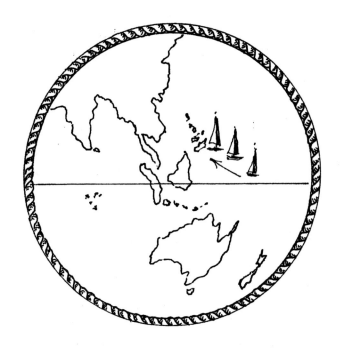

Pulawat to West Fayu to Palau

CHAPTER 12
TO BE or NOT TO BE ... STRANDED

We leave Pulawat about noon Aug 25 and continue west for one hundred fifty miles, arriving at West Fayu the following evening. Between squalls we manage to slide through the pass and drop the anchor in thirty feet of water with a sandy bottom promising good holding. This is a small circular lagoon with a tiny island on its northeast corner. No one lives here. Only an occasional fishing boat stops to rest during their ocean forays. We are alone. The wind has started picking up. Don is letting out more scope on the anchor lines. Both anchors are now beyond chain, riding on line only. Secure, we go below, have supper and watch a movie on the VCR. There is a bit of a chop and the wind has shifted to the south. Now our stern has swung towards a lee shore. But with still enough distance between *Horizon* and shore, we feel we are secure for the night. It is a bumpy night. Don gets up several times to check the anchors in the dark.

What a surprise when at 7:30 next morning we feel that dreaded thump, gentle but definitely there. Dashing topsides we discover we are adrift, bumping across the sandy bottom and moving towards the reef that stretches from the island. Both of the anchor lines have chaffed through. Just frayed stubs of line stare at us at the bow. They evidently bounced off the rubber anchor rollers that provide chaffing protection for the anchor line. My immediate thoughts struggle with the image that we are going to be stranded at this isolated spot in the ocean, for heaven knows how long. . . with a damaged boat . . . to be spindrift or flotsam on the beach.

As we scramble to the stern to get the third anchor with its three hundred feet of line ready for use, we seem to be all thumbs. The boat continues bumping towards the reef. *Horizon* is beginning to heel over as she plows along the rough bottom with less and less water to support her upright. Feeling we might still have time to get some help from the engine, we turn the key. The engine roars alive and immediately chokes to an ear splitting quiet as the prop seizes with the dinghy painter (line) wrapped around the blades. We didn't notice the dinghy, tied to the boat, had drifted across the stern dragging its line across the propeller. With the adrenaline now really pumping, Don gets into the dink, cuts it loose from the painter and pulls it beside the boat. I lower the large fisherman's anchor into the dinghy, then he proceeds to row as far into deeper water as line will allow, in order to kedge off. Meanwhile, I lead the bitter end of the rode (anchor line) over the bow and around the windlass. The tide is going out making matters worse. The boat is beginning to list still more to one side. As each wave passes underneath, the boat bangs against the hard bottom with reverberating thumps resounding along its ribs. High tide seems so far away as each thud shudders through our bodies. We feel we can't wait for a high tide lift. In fact, we're not sure when high tide is and where in the tide cycle we are. As the boat heaves a bit with a wave passing underneath, we wind in more anchor line using the new windlass. Very slowly but deliberately the bow strains forward, creeping by inches toward the anchor. The boat starts regaining its upright position. With accompanying crunching sounds, we claw our way across the bottom. The mast is almost vertical once more. Finally, with *Horizon* afloat in deeper water, close to the anchor, Don dives on the propeller to remove the entangled line. Free at last after four hours of hard work, we can use the motor, take up the anchor and move into forty feet of water where we re-anchor.

Completely exhausted, we take time to eat cheese omelets and savor hot coffee before we begin the search for those two lost anchors. We think about the fragility of this fiberglass bottle that we ask to protect us as we bound across the oceans. Without floating capabilities, it is useless. Demands this lifestyle dictate, keeps us alert to solutions.

Our problem solving continues - Don is in the water, holding on to the back of the 'dink', to peer through his facemask at the sandy bottom. I motor in a grid pattern across the wide area where we thought we had originally anchored. It's four hours of this frustrating process before he finally finds both anchors nicely dug in as if holding *Horizon* safely in their flukes! They are dug in so well it strains the little dinghy and its small motor to pull them loose. The winds die. We relax for two days before starting the sail to Yap five hundred miles away. Not to be stranded here . . . this day . . .

This passage offers occasions to appreciate the radar. Not since leaving Florida have we seen so many freighters and fishing boats. One night on my watch, the lights of a fishing boat gradually move closer. We have been seeing them quite often with Japanese names on the transoms. Their erratic paths, as they search for fish, usually don't bother us. They seem to have us in their sights and stay clear, but this one continues closing on us. As I watch on the radar screen, it's obvious we are on a collision course. I change our heading and watch him continue on his course as he quietly glides by us. I assume their autopilot is on while the crew is sleeping, all the while unaware of the danger they pose. I pat the radar for its eyes that have not only steered us around squalls, ships and islands at night, but also delivered peace of mind tonight. This leg from Truk to Yap has thrown challenges across our path that we've managed to solve without succumbing to panic or fear.

We arrive off the surrounding reef of Yap September 4. It's late in the afternoon with a monster thunderstorm swirling around us. Visibility has diminished to zero with curtains of sheeting rain streaking across the bow, making it hard to find the pass through the reef into Yap harbor. The clutter on the radar monitor is frustrating, offering no more information than our vision across the bow. The storm is monster in size, not in violence, but visibility has gone to nil. We heave-to for an hour while still eight miles from the entrance. Slowly visibility improves. Now, with the help of radar, we proceed until we can make out the reef line to follow it towards the pass. We can see fishing boats ahead and follow them through the pass. They point the way to the anchorage to our left. Since it's late, almost dark, we will do the paper work in the morning.

Once again, we are amazed at the number of people that come aboard for this process. Without exception here across Micronesia they have been courteous. When the immigration officer arrives, it is with great difficulty that we all work to get him aboard. He is a very large man and with great difficulty makes his way into the cockpit. He then insists on going down the companionway to the cabin. He continues to chew his betel nut while puffing on a cigarette at the same time. When finally seated he stares ahead vacantly, not moving a muscle. Don really is afraid the man will have a heart attack here on the boat. After long quiet moments, he looks in his lap and says, "Oh, I brought the wrong papers". Still quietness . . . then pushing himself up, he looks about, dazed. Eventually, ready to leave, he says we can pick up our papers tomorrow at his office. He heaves himself off the boat.

This voyage across Micronesia has launched us into discoveries of cultures and ideas that we had never before even been aware. Such provinciality on our part. To not be curious about the splendid variety brought to the family of mankind here on this tiny blue globe brings a humble spirit to our journey of discovery.

Yap offers a singular thread to this tapestry. As we step gently along these centuries-old paths, we become aware that here is a jewel set apart by its particular desire to keep faith with these same century honed patterns for living. The tradition of stone money has survived here. These huge donut shaped stones standing upright in the yards along these old paths are reminders of the strength of tradition. A strict caste system is adhered to. The traditional chiefs wield as much power as the elected ones. A visitor is welcomed, yet is reminded that wandering around their island requires their permission. So with patience and respect, we gain permission to visit some of the remote villages to talk with the shy, courteous and proud folks.

There is a lot of organization to this society, with a definite caste system in place. There are seven or nine castes prevailing. The lower ones serve those of higher rank. An entire village is most likely to be one caste. Another manifestation of this order in societal matters is evidenced when we see the woman always walking behind the man who, indeed, may be her son. A sister cannot step over her brother if she needs to move across the room. She waits till he moves. The women do not fish. In some villages the men and women eat and even cook separately. The males dress in loincloths, although not as brief as Pulawat and always in one of the three colors - blue, red or white - that signifies their caste. Leaving their breasts bare, the women are garbed only in the lava lava wrap around skirt that is beautifully hand-woven on body looms. Photo taking is not easily done. It may be forbidden in some villages.

We are able to photograph a plaza-like area with the stone money standing in rows, each varying in size and design. This sacred spot is called a money bank. These huge stones, as tall as a man, have been brought by canoe from either Palau or Kosrae across hundreds of miles of ocean. With these stones on a precarious balance across the canoes, they surely threatened a safe passage. It is no wonder these donut shaped stones are highly valued and represent the riches of the family that has arranged such a voyage. There are times these stones settle a dispute between families when they are offered as payment for an offence. They are considered the crown jewels of this society.

Exploring the small town and capitol, Colonia, we meet the new batch of Peace Corp workers just arrived. They are now waiting for the island freighter to transport them to their assigned islands. We've enjoyed their visits to our boat while they share more about this most unique culture of Yap.

The betel nut we've been hearing about is prominently displayed on the streets of Colonia. At first, the crimson blotches splattered along the street make us think a bloody accident has occurred. It is everywhere we look. As we stand in the shade of the porch at the small market, perhaps we see a clue to the mystery. We watch as men and women, with cheeks bulging, are spitting great gobs on the street. This is a result of the abundant, brilliant red saliva that results from chewing this betel nut concoction. The nut grows on a palm-like tree. The nuts are green, the shape and size of a pecan, and hang on fronds much like a date palm. Using their teeth, these folks from Yap bite off the end of the nut to crack it open. It's sprinkled with lime made from finely ground coral then wrapped in a green betel-leaf. With relish, it's popped into the mouth to be chewed or lodged in the cheek, much like a wad of chewing tobacco. The men and women talk to you with this wad in place giving a hollow sound to their voices. A period of chewing produces an abundance of brilliant saliva that stains the gums, teeth and mouth with an attention-getting crimson. It has a narcotic effect that can be habit forming. We notice some of the Peace Corp volunteers are already trying the stuff.

With more thought and care than we have seen in the other countries of Micronesia, the ruling party of Yap has moved cautiously, introducing VCR's and autos with care as easy money comes from the States. With an eye on their tradition and wisely noting the energy of their youth, they have built a covered basketball court that always seems to be echoing with the squeal of basketball shoes racing for that perfect shot. In the evening it becomes the local theatre where movies are shown for the enjoyment of the villagers. Nearby is the new facility donated and built by the Japanese. Here they process and freeze the tuna they catch using the training provided by the Japanese. Japan buys the tuna - both countries benefit from this cooperation.

It's been some time now since we've hauled the boat out of the water to repaint the bottom. We have had our eye on Yap as the best, maybe the only, spot that offers a railway to do the job. So we make the arrangements with Mario and his crew. Their railway is new and they are anxious to show us how well they can handle *Horizon*. With their facemasks on, they dive underwater and guide us as we center the hull onto the rail bed. Pulled high and dry with the braces in place, Don teases Mario. Throughout this entire process, the crews have all been chewing their betel nut while they continued to breathe through their snorkels.

Wow, I had forgotten what a red bottom *Horizon* has enjoyed since it was painted in New Zealand. I suspect *Horizon* has been secretly chewing betel nut as we crossed the sea waiting to expose its crimson bottom to folks who appreciate such colorful taste. I'll be glad to cover it with the nice modest brown bottom paint we were able to get in Majuro. Don and I work hard scraping and sanding the bottom before slapping on three coats of the new paint. All the while we have a gallery of onlookers that joke and cheer us on. It's not often they see a women doing this kind of work. Finally, after 4 days out of the water we slide down the railway until we are afloat once again to anchor for one last night. We take this opportunity to enjoy our last meal ashore at the new yacht club. With care to detail, they do a great job of spreading before us a delicious dinner in the soft glow of candlelight.

Three days later we are making our way along the intricate yet well marked entrance to Koror, the capitol of Palau. We have reached the most western fringes of land that outline this American Lake, Micronesia, stretching all these 2400 miles since Christmas. Arriving here in October we will be treated to some of the richest flora and fauna of Micronesia. The one hundred fifty mile-long reef cradles some of the most unique rock formations that we have ever seen. There are mushroom shaped islets of coral that have been undercut by tide changes over the centuries. These 'Rock Islands' are scattered across the large lagoon south of the large island of Babeldoab. They are made up of two hundred islands that wear caps of lush jungle vegetation shrouding overhanging arches and caves while hiding inland lakes. Meanwhile the larger islands shelter crocodiles in the marshy swamps that comb their coast. In the trees, flocks of cockatoos and other exotic birds perch among orchids dangling from branches. Underwater, we see exquisite gardens of coral. Especially enchanting is the magnificent mass of soft corals in their gentle shades of peach, green, purple and yellow. They always seem to be punctuated with the darting brilliance of tiny wrasse and angelfish and a delicate ballet of cuttlefish. This sapphire lagoon holds in its wavering depths many varieties of underwater elegance.

Here we have another gem of a spot that has teased the wandering dreams of our family to join us. When Linda and Paul find a medical seminar on water emergencies and treatments being offered here, they take advantage of the opportunity to add a visit with us. I had marked the date of their arrival on our calendar. Since they plan to stay at the hotel here, it simplifies preparations for their visit. As we sail off the beach of their hotel looking for a spot to anchor, imagine our surprise to see a launch whiz by with surprised guests wildly waving at us. Looking closer, we see it is our two kids in their diving gear ready to take their first dive of the session. Dateline dementia must have fogged my senses to mark their arrival a day late. We make up for the delay that evening and join in many of the lectures during the week. Dr. Don joins them in most of the dives sponsored by the group.

Diving the "Blue Corners" is especially challenging. A sheer, vertical drop-off of a coral wall offers some of the most spectacular diving in the world. These waters are the meeting place of three ocean currents and can pose serious threats to divers. Linda is caught suddenly in one of these current downdrafts. She plunges 80 feet in a moment. Able to think clearly enough she is able to swim up to a shallower depth to regain her equilibrium and stabilize her ears. Another diver was not as fortunate. She was rescued and taken, unconscious, to the pressure chamber, where blood gases are stabilized.

Palau boasts four times the number of coral species as the Caribbean. We see the immense tabletop corals, huge manta rays and sea turtles while sharks cruise around the dusky fringes. Shots of sunlight plunge through this emerald world to spotlight the radiance of moving colors through the coral and highlight the abundant sea life darting through its shadows.

Another magical world we share with son, Tom, when he arrives several weeks later, is Jellyfish Lake. Here, in the middle of one of these Rock Islands, is a mangrove- edged lake that shelters a unique jellyfish. We don our snorkels and fins and push off from the mangrove roots tangled along the cloudy shoreline to swim into the sunny part of the lake. As the water clears we suddenly are surrounded by peach colored jellyfish with bodies the size of a dinner plate, their tentacles pulsating as they glide about us - hundreds and hundreds of them. I am wary knowing the small ones in Chesapeake Bay and the Bahamas always sting when touched. These, we were assured, do not sting. Trusting this information, we look at each other through our masks and shake our heads with amazement and relief as we realize it is true. We reach out to touch them as they glide away with a scarf dancer's grace. They move across the lake to stay in the warmth of the sun. As we float among this pulsating mass, it is truly an eerie experience.

The next day Tom and Don decide to do more snorkeling among shallow coral beds. Since Don has a head cold, he's decided to float at the surface to peer through his mask at the coral. All of a sudden he feels something rub between his thighs. In an instant it is gone. When he looks up he is stunned to see a shark gliding away in front of him. He realizes this is the source of that sandpaper feel on his inner thighs. By this time Tom had already seen the shark's path. He leaped into the dinghy, ready to call it a day. Don assumes it was an expedition of curiosity on the part of the shark and, thank goodness, not a need for food. Paul, in his next letter, suggests his father-in-law start wearing swimming trunks of mail during future diving forays.

It is Thanksgiving once again. We are invited to share this feast with ex-pats living and working here in Palau. The District Attorney and his wife have opened their home to this group of seafarers found on their shores. We supplement the roast turkey with our carry-in dishes. Tom is fortunate to not only share this feast but also joins another celebration at Abby's Place, also known as the Palau Yacht Club. Abby, a Palauan, is serving the American traditional turkey dinner. He encourages us to try their island delicacy, roasted pigeon, which shares the menu. The most prized portion of this bird is the intestine. It is full of tart red berries that the pigeons were force-fed before their ultimate end in the roasting pan. We find the meat delicious and do some fudging on the berries.

After a Christmas spent with other yachts in the Rock Islands, we limp back to Koror leaving a trail of black smoke from our exhaust. This prompts us to inquire about the availability and the quality of engine repairs here. We are directed to Mr. Takesi. He is a small Japanese man with only two or three English words in his vocabulary, yes - no - and stop. He squats in front of this hunk of metal on our boat as he lovingly strokes its parts with knowing hands, listening to the groans it's making. He sighs. With his Palauan wife translating, he tells us that two of the valves are burnt and need replacing. Fortunately, he has a new engine like ours that he used for parts on another job; he still has new pistons to replace ours. He proceeds stripping the engine, carrying it back to his shed in an array of tuna cans. In the past our luck with repairs by local mechanics has been a sorry history of grief. Now, as we watch our large engine leaving *Horizon* in these small cans, it arouses a certain amount of dismay and anxiety about our engine returning with parts missing. Three days later he is back on board. With his quiet determined manner he proceeds to put this iron horse together. This includes dropping it back on the motor mounts and aligning the prop shaft. We sit back and marvel at this small man while he casually maneuvers this heavy animal and aligns it to the proper parameters. At one point he uses a screwdriver to make delicate adjustments to the injectors. Later, when Don asks him if he wants to use our torque wrench to tighten the head, he shakes his head indicating his arm muscle will recognize the torsion needed. He is truly a craftsman who delights in his ability to solve problems. A few test runs and *Horizon* is ready once again to slip free of land to steer towards its distant namesake. This American Lake with all its variety and beauty will now drift to the East leaving ripples of images that will forever stream across our consciousness as we sail West to dip into still more cultural reflections of our global family.

Philippines to Hong Kong

CHAPTER 13
THE CENTURY'S LAST DECADE

A new decade has arrived. January the 9th, 1990 finds us making our way out of the northwest pass through the reef of Palau. With lovely 15-knot winds from the NE pushing us on a broad reach for four days, we arrive at the pass just north of Mindanao in the Philippines. From here we day-sail for a week as we make our way towards Cebu, one of the larger islands in the middle of the more than 7000 island that make up this country. With protected little bays to anchor at night, we day sail among these islands. Spending the day with binoculars handy, we view the lush islands as they pass. There is evidence that the old slash and burn farming and the logging methods are causing erosion along some of the coasts, leaving the water stained with silt. This causes damage to fish and coral.

We pass a mirage. At least it seems so. A giant insect is stepping across the sun- shot waves. A closer view outlines a long island gliding by - just one long narrow strip of sand. This is the foundation for several hundred shacks built on stilts. Squeezed so close to each other they appear to be built one upon the other. This stilt-supported stretch of wooden huts takes on the appearance of a giant centipede, its many legs stepping along the dazzling sandy stretch. There are no trees and no spare land - only this beach offering an open margin around the village. We wonder what dynamics must be at work in a community with societal pressures such as these.

As we continue sailing through these fascinating islands, outrigger canoes of every size and description stream by us. Some of the smaller ones are stacked with fish traps so high it's difficult to see the man standing to paddle a course. There are others with a plastic sheet or a quilt of discarded clothes hoisted as a sail. And the noisy ones, the 'longtails', sporting a lawnmower motor with a long prop shaft stretching behind the canoe are spitting forward with attention-getting speed.

By the 19th of January we drop the anchor close by the ferry landing that services the large city of Cebu. Anchoring in a channel where swift tides rush between islands, it becomes a boisterous patch of water when the passage of large ships adds to the confusion. Taking the dinghy ashore, we meet friends Dr. Don and Bev Rock. They have been living here since his retirement from the Navy. Years ago in Tarpon Springs, Florida they had come aboard *Horizon* while they were researching their purchase of a new boat. Now anchored close by is their Tayana due, in part, to that visit. With their good advice we are able to find our way around the city. Transportation here is provided by the colorful 'jeepneys', a truck with two rows of seats along the sides in back, sporting psychedelic roofs overhead. Seating is crowded back here, hip to hip, sometimes even hip over hip. As we drive along the dusty, littered streets and see the miserable homes along the way, I marvel at the personal cleanliness of my fellow travelers. We're sitting almost on top of each other yet everyone smells fresh, their black hair shines and the white shirts and blouses they are wearing are spotless and clean.

We are impressed by their ability to fabricate and make almost anything. While in Palau last month, we noticed small freighters from the Philippines collecting the discarded junk lying in vacant fields - scavenging all of this to bring here and recycle into new parts and machinery. Now, taking advantage of their talent, we have several stainless steel parts on the boat repaired or replaced, as well as new canvas for covers and cushions restored. We are happy with their work and their reasonable prices. They are industrious and eager to please us. I am surprised, though, dealing with the sail maker we have engaged to replace the cockpit cushion covers. He seems so quiet and shy - I can't understand why he seems to be flirting with me. Whenever I ask a question his eyebrows become an exercise in up and down movement while his glowing eyes make contact with my own . . he's making eyes at me. Bev informs me this facial exercise is merely a sign of affirmation. Without words, he is answering yes to my questions - it's not a response to my beauty - Ah well . . .

It is a country of contrasts. One of the indicators of wealth here seems to be the girth of a few of its citizens. The majority of the folks we see along the streets are thin. We pass stalls lining the streets with the small braziers glowing. Here a woman is roasting on skewers chicken feet or pigskin to sell. Another delicacy we see for sale in many stalls along the way are fertilized eggs with the un-hatched chick ready to be eaten right from the shell. We look and shake our heads as the tiny head with its beak just breaking the shell is offered to us. The laundry stretches on lines across the dirt yards displaying bright and clean clothes tossing in the dusty sunlight.

Although our stay here has only been three weeks, I hesitate to write my impressions. The more we travel, the more I realize we Westerners are quick to judge the conditions we happen to see during our limited stay. There are so many factors contributing to the composition of a community. The society we view as visitors passing by cannot reveal its true character to our fleeting glance. The disparity between rich and poor, however, is much in evidence here.

And now the country has to adjust to the recent election. Mrs. Aquino has been elected to lead the country to a more democratic solution. There are demonstrations by the college students against the U.S. and our country's influence with the ousted Marcos regime. The armed forces are in rebellion. Many doubt the ability of Mrs. Aquino to stave off violence. Still, those we meet treat us with friendly smiles and helpful advice. We are fascinated that the question everyone asks us is, 'How old are you?' We haven't discovered the significance of this question but it does seem important to these friends.

By the middle of February we are anchored in a pleasant and protected little bay at Cuyo Island. It has taken us four days to get here after leaving Cebu. This path took us around the southern tip of the large island of Negros and into the Sulu Sea. Roving throughout the more southerly areas of this Sea are the pirates and sea gypsies that for centuries have been able to lure an unwary boat into their lairs to fall prey to the danger of their murderous ways. But our track takes us north as soon as we clear Negros to make our way towards Cuyo. Here we find an unspoiled island away from the tourist trail. We walk along clean streets lined with attractive homes either painted in vibrant colors or made with bamboo walls woven in fascinating designs. A small, clean market offers fresh vegetables and baskets of fresh shrimp.

Walking further down a shady street we stop for hamburgers where we meet Juanito Jutare. Mr.Jutare engages us in conversation with his precise English and carefully constructed sentences. He expresses concern for his country, hoping his countrymen will be patient and allow stability to once more return. He realizes economic growth won't happen before the streets are calm and safe. As we talk, he shares a bowl of warm, freshly roasted cashew nuts with us. We were hooked. This is one of the main crops here on Cuyo. We find it hard not to over indulge.

A tall and fair complexioned young man warmly greets us on an early stroll. 'P.I.' a young Norwegian who, after much research, found Cuyo to be one of the areas in the world that harbors steady, prevailing winds most of the year. Reason enough for his family to spend six months here to pursue his hobby of windsurfing. The other six months he and his beautiful blonde wife, Lizabeth, spend in Norway, where he earns enough money as a carpenter to fulfill his surfing dream. "Call me PI," he chuckles, " your American tongue is unable to pronounce my Norwegian name." There are many pleasant evenings spent at their thatched beach-side home. Relaxing together peeling and eating pink shrimp, we enjoy good conversation, as baby son Noah rocks in his hammock. This is also a good area for great diving and spear fishing, which always has Don ready to jump overboard.

We leave this tranquil and beautiful spot with strong winds pushing us further into the sunset. The sunset becomes a hallmark to this voyage of ours. I know if we keep to its direction, we are bound to complete the circle where gems of memories are collected - a necklace forever mine to wear.

Sailing on, we are anchored off the village of Coror. The harbor is filled with brilliant and skillfully painted longboats. These boats are the most highly decorated we've ever seen with their intricate designs beautifully detailed. This hillside village is part of the long chain of the Palawan group of islands that define the western boundary of the Philippines. Much like Cuyo, these outlying villages are neat and clean in contrast to the cities. We spend another four days finding neat little anchorages and visiting mostly with the fishermen that stop by our boat to chat and sell or barter their catch. By the last day of February the weather fax is reporting favorable winds for a heading northwest towards Hong Kong.

This sail towards Hong Kong has been one of the more pleasant ones even though we are sailing just off the wind most of the way. With a strong West current trying to push us east towards the Philippine shore once more, we constantly monitor the compass so that a North heading is maintained. Even so, we are able to make six to seven knots for a good part of the voyage. The six hundred-mile trip is completed in less than five days.

The night before arriving, we are faced with a daunting challenge. Ahead of us is a sea of lights bobbing and moving in every direction. We have sailed into the midst of a huge fishing fleet, hundreds of boats harvesting the sea. To get through this maze of lights, we decide to just hold our course. We will assume these boats that spend their nights dodging each other as a routine matter, will see our navigation lights as just one more hazard they need to avoid.

The next morning, with the chart of Victoria Harbor Channel at our fingertips, we sail between the rocky islands at the entrance and around sweeping curves to suddenly see a panorama of skyscrapers stretching across the horizon. They form a backdrop to the broad and bustling harbor. Large container ships overshadow the small sampans sculling a path between majestic junks - it's a throbbing, teeming traffic jam. While overhead large jets are making noisy landings at this unique airport stretching along the harbor, adding another ingredient to the commotion. Cautiously, we make our way into this confusing mass. It has been years since we've been part of such Pandemonium. We anxiously keep watch on every quarter to avoid collisions. Dodging the traffic, we continue to look for a large YAKULT sign painted on the wall of one of these tall buildings. The guidebook suggests it will provide us with a clue to the location of the Royal Hong Kong Yacht Club that's hidden along this swarming waterfront. We see the buoys marking the entrance and motor around the breakwater to tie at the dock. The dock master points the way to customs and Don is off. When the formalities are resolved we move to a mooring. Now whenever we call, the means of conveyance to the dock becomes a small sampan.

We have fallen in love with this city. It's so alive and vibrant. We get busy with the guidebook. A couple from New England who have spent ten years sailing these waters also share good information with us. After the remote cultures of Micronesia we will now survey this ancient one with its art and music flourishing around us. We take advantage of as much as we can. There are tours of the Art Complex and Symphony Hall. We enjoy concerts, Chinese dance and music that fill our days and nights. We visit a village depicting dynasties from 1200 B.C. to 1937 A.D. And, of course, a new suit for Don made by the enterprising tailors advertising on every street corner. We stroll the noisy, lively streets where the open stalls and bazaars display their wares, exotic and mundane. Reading the menus in the windows of restaurants offering tastes of varied nationalities, we savor new flavors. Every sense - hearing, seeing, smelling, and even touching, with our strokes to the burnished lion statues that protect large buildings - is stimulated with the colorful environment surrounding us.

The highlight of our stay, however, is a three-day trip into China. We cross the Zhu Bay aboard a fast moving hydrofoil to Macao. There is only time for a very fast tour of this Portuguese City before we cross into China with a minimum of fuss. Along with two other couples we meet our guide, Mr. Fong. This province has been granted special status by the Communist government to experiment to some degree with capitalism; some private enterprise is encouraged.

Although the tools are basic, a hoe and shovel and a bullock pulling a plow thru the paddies, the blossoming countryside is lush and very tidy. The Pearl River bounds these small farms. As far as we can see the green rectangles surrounded by irrigation ditches form a spectacular quilt in varying shades of green and yellow. Many of the paddies are now being planted. Figures bent at the waist, their large cone shaped hats almost touching the water, bring to reality the many Chinese paintings we've been enjoying. We walk along narrow streets through small villages where homes of hand- made brick or whitewashed mud line the clean cobbled street. A gaggle of geese waddles by as a small lad guides them with his long stick, creating an enchanting picture. Mr. Fong points out the raised door threshold at the entrance of a home. It is placed here to hinder the entrance of an evil spirit. There's also a wall or screen just inside the door around which those spirits would again be foiled of easy entrance. Other signs of obeisance to the spirit world prevail as we travel through this ancient culture. There are bowls of oranges or flowers placed before a shrine in shopkeepers' windows or along roadways. Joss sticks waft their incense fragrance as we pass street corners. On the sampans passing along the waterfront, streamers of red ribbons are fluttering from the bow post as homage to spirits.

Bicyclers crowd the road as we continue through the countryside in our van. At the modest home of Sun-Yat-Sen, the humble beginnings of this bold leader who was instrumental in dynamic changes to society is detailed. He discouraged binding the feet of young girls and encouraged men to cut off their pigtails, a symbol of a man's submission to his Manchu rulers - both of these gripped in centuries-old traditions. His many ideas brought about the end of China's last imperial dynasty, the Manchu Dynasty and were the founding stones on which Chiang Kai Shek built his rebellion against the Communist regime. This resulted in Chiang's fleeing to Taiwan with many followers.

We visit temples, a silk weaving factory, jade carvers and fascinating, bustling marketplaces. Here fresh vegetables are on display beside 100-year-old eggs that have been stored in lye and straw. There are hard-boiled eggs soaked in tea; fresh fish swimming in tanks will be caught fresh for the evening meal. There are eels and frogs; dogs and snakes, ducks and chickens in all stages of preparation - fried, pressed or crackling fried duck skins. There's no refrigeration in the homes, so the housewife makes her way to the market twice a day, with a promise of fresh food on the table.

At night we stay in luxurious hotels. The 'White Swan' in Canton surrounds us in elegance. A central courtyard is complete with a waterfall cascading from a towering loggia to a pool three floors below. Surrounding the pool are elaborate large jade carvings six to eight feet tall that present a spectacular centerpiece as we gaze from the registration desk. We enjoy new flavors at dinner. One of these is Dim Sum, a meal consisting of a kind of Chinese hors d'oeuvres that offers a variety of tastes from sweet to sour.

Upon our return to *Horizon* in Hong Kong, we start making preparations for the next leg to Singapore. We move from the bustle of the Hong Kong harbor, sailing north around the peninsula to the protected anchorage of Hebe Haven - a quiet spot to wait for the four gel batteries we had ordered. Meanwhile Don gets busy making an entertainment center using the available teak lumber found here. Now secure on this new shelf above the couch our new TV set rests. We purchased it in Kowloon. It accommodates the 3 systems used around the world to access local TV. Finally all ordered parts are aboard and installed. With one final ham contact to Linda confirming her date of arrival in Singapore, we haul the anchor April 10. Six glorious weeks has immersed us in an ancient, rich history.

As the hazy hills of China recede we sail from the rugged coastline. The many Chinese paintings of dim mountains outlined through mist are revealed. Watching the land recede, I recognize the source of this beauty. The Chinese artists surrounded with this beauty take delicate brushstrokes to canvas and paper capturing its mystical, misty quality. Sailing through the hazy day, I feel a part of this ancient panorama.

The wind is light but we are on our way with a 'peach of a reach' for three days. Ever so slowly, though, the winds are off to other places. By the fifth day, we find we are windless and drifting on a flat sea. The noise of the motor begins its monotonous droning as the electric autopilot works to hold the course. Gradually the large container ships and tankers are also sharing our point on the compass with seeming little regard for our path. We have had to change course three times to avoid collisions.

At night, on my watch, I stay alert with sky watching and learn ten new constellations with their magnitude stars. The skies are clear and brilliant with that canopy of stars thrown over us begging to be identified. During the day we trail the fish line and catch a lovely mahi-mahi, a few barracuda and one tuna. So our dinner table is nicely supplied with the sea's bounty.

We move south along those Palawan Islands that we had visited weeks ago. There's no hint of a breeze. We continue motoring off of Kota Kinabalu at the north end of the Malaysian region of Borneo Island. Checking the fuel log, we are concerned about the fuel remaining after all these days of motoring. Sails just flap with this fluky wind but we decide to fly the spinnaker. It might possibly catch any feeble breeze out there. Momentarily this enormous sail will billow as it pulls us along. Then, breathless without wind, it collapses on itself as the seaweed swirls around us in the still water. With erratic behavior this gossamer balloon continues to fill and collapse as we haltingly make progress. By changing our heading we sail close to shore, perhaps we can find those illusive offshore breezes that might nudge us along. We want to save what little fuel is remaining in order to maneuver into the harbor at Brunei. This was not a planned stop but the choices seem few.

Brunei Bay offers the best possibility for an easy stop. We find we are able to sail deep into the broad bay and drop the anchor for the night just off the entrance to the channel. Next morning we motor up the channel to a large fuel barge just ahead. The fuel tanks and jerry jugs are filled as the rough water bangs us against the black tire bumpers on the barge.

A U.S. couple directs us to follow their boat to the small yacht club where we join them for dinner. The next day we take the bus into Bandar, the capitol of Brunei, to tour this Muslim country. It is the richest nation in the world; this wealth acquired from their huge offshore oil reserves. So the homes we pass are fine structures but littered with garbage on the lawns and street corners. Evidently no one wants to haul garbage as a profession.

We explore the possibility of sailing up the Igan Batang River in Sarawak south of Brunei. The agent outlining the trip discourages such a passage with the short time frame we have available before arriving at Singapore. Walking about town, we search for the office of the father of a young man with whom we shared an anchorage back there in Fatu Hiva. Dr. Peter Hart now 72 years old, had been the physician to the royal family for years until the queen mother died. Now he is in private practice here.

While looking for a cab, a lady stops her car inviting us to see the palace and the city as her guest. The palace is a very, very large low structure with a glowing, gold dome. The sprawling edifice is not architecturally as attractive as the many mosques we pass. Cynthia drives by a unique town in the middle of the large river. The wooden homes, all on stilts, are connected by walkways also on stilts - the streets becoming water corridors - a kind of Venice in the middle of the river.

With our grocery bins full once more, we hoist the sails to leave the coast of this Borneo Island country. Cautiously we make our way through a carpet of floating logs, looking carefully for the 'dead-heads' that float just below the surface We hope their hazardous shapes, as they lie in ambush, will thin ranks as we move away from shore. Finally with these obstacles behind us, a new challenge rises from the ocean's surface. As darkness falls lights are strewn across the sea-scape ahead. It's not long until we realize these are the source of Brunei wealth. Oil rigs are scattered towards the distant horizon. With these light winds, maneuvering through this maze is made easier while we motor-sail an erratic path along our course. The next six days remain near calm as variable winds continue to control our progress.

Each day we seem to be attracting freighters like bees to honey. The path to Singapore is truly one of the world's busiest crossroads. Large ships with their transoms hailing ports around the globe keep us company. We stay with these big brothers to anchor in their midst when we arrive off the Singapore coast as night-time descends. The lights ahead of Malaysia and Singapore fill the night sky.

Following the channel markers next morning, we make our way along the northern boundary of the island of Singapore to pick up a mooring at the Changi Yacht Club. This is temporary, however, for all the moorings are assigned. We move further down river around Fairy Point to the anchorage filling with transient boats. A warm welcome is extended by Bob on 'Kim'. He's an American sailor, who thirty-three years ago helped build roads through the jungles of Thailand and Viet Nam. His insights and vast knowledge of these countries, charming so many sailors to stay and enjoy, have been valuable to us.

The fast, efficient and clean transport system that takes you to every corner of this small country becomes our mode of travel. We can't help but compare the many aspects of this city, Singapore, to our recent stay in Hong Kong. Here everything works and works well. We see beautiful landscaping throughout the city, rubbish free streets and cars of recent vintage. All is quiet and controlled whether we ride the trams or walk along the streets. In contrast, Hong Kong lives among the noise and the bustle of people; a vitality that fairly shouts to the visitor. Here in Singapore, as part of their organization, we can be arrested for jaywalking or for failing to flush the toilet in public restrooms. There is a kind of sterile, restrained quality to life here.

One of the guidebooks suggests that Singapore might be compared to a fine piece of cloisonné. The many colors of its traditions are fused together but each remains well defined just as the brass threads outline designs on the elegant vase. Over 76% of the population are Chinese, with Malaysians about 15%, while Indians and other ethnic groups each contribute to the kaleidoscope of this society.

We pick up our one letter waiting for us in the luxurious post office, its plush carpet on the floor and chandeliers with prisms sparkling overhead. A stroll along the waterfront on the south shore brings us to the famous statue that symbolizes Singapore. Here by the Singapore River, poised and rising over twenty feet is the statue, Merlion. A mythical beast with a lion head carved in regal splendor balanced above its fish body, the tail curved to its shoulder. Cascading from its mouth to the sea beneath is a fountain of water. Another signature building representing past British influence is the magnificent Raffles Hotel displaying the elegance of English prestige even today.

As we get ready for a three-week visit to Indonesia with Linda and Paul joining us, we hurry once again to repair parts before they arrive. We need a new compressor for the fridge that broke a month ago, new brushes in the anchor windlass and replacement of the alternator on the engine. It seems we go from port to port to fix or replace parts. Our passports by this time have stamps on all the pages. We are pleased to learn pages can be added while we wait at the U.S. embassy here. The week passes quickly while we make arrangements with Customs that assures them the boatyard here will be responsible for *Horizon* at anchor while we fly to Indonesia.

The airport adds to our impressions of the beauty of this country. Cascading from the lampposts lining the entrance, baskets of flowers in rainbow hues flutter with the breeze. Even as we stroll indoors, flowers - many of them orchids - continue to beautify the many balconies throughout the terminal. Standing and staring about us at this arboretum display, we almost miss Linda when she comes down the ramp. Since she has arrived on her birthday, we celebrate with lunch at a quiet small Indian restaurant we discovered hidden down a tiny esplanade. We enjoy delicious curries and lassi, a delicious yogurt drink - great food presented with, alas, poor service. It's unbearably hot on the boat when we return, demanding we start the fans to get some sleep before the early rising for our flight to Sumatra tomorrow.

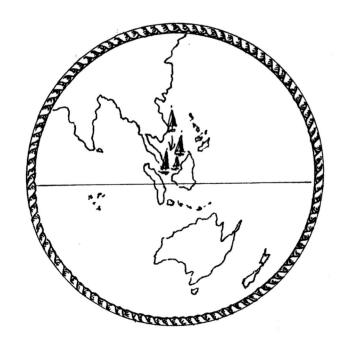

Brunei to Singapore to Indonesia

CHAPTER 14
WITHOUT SAILS

After a two-hour flight across the Straits of Malacca, we land at Medan, the capitol of Sumatra, one of the larger islands of Indonesia. After scrambling around the streets, lugging our luggage, we find a bank that will exchange money for us. With rupiahs in our pockets, we stop at the tourist office to gather information about Lake Toba and a bus to get us there. All three of us manage to squeeze into a small cab attached to the back of a bike, called a 'becak'. We now become part of the busy becak traffic pedaling along the highway to the bus depot. As we stand about waiting for departure, we are bombarded on every side with some locals willing to offer more advice. We shortly realize this advice is not free. With a shake of our heads, we decide Linda has all the knowledge we need to find our way. Scrambling to find seats aboard the old bus along with the crowd of passengers - enough, it seems, to fill two buses - we try to make ourselves

155

comfortable in the cramped space. The wildly painted Chevrolet bus is full as we depart for Prapat. It is a five-hour ride on treacherous roads through jungle and past lovely vistas of slopes and rivers. There are frequent stops along the way. We can only assume the process of osmosis is being used to absorb still more passengers.

It is late afternoon when we arrive on the shore of Lake Toba. With the help of a young girl we find places on the ferry to Samosir Island in the center of the lake. We arrive at Carolina's Lodge to find a nice clean room with three beds waiting for us. The lodge was built and designed by the native Batak Indian tribes that live here. It displays unique architecture with the eaves at each end of the roof rising to peaks, forming a deep saddle between. Outlining the peaks and the wall underneath are intricate carvings, many times painted in black, red and white to enhance the design. Our cabin has a lovely perch on the hillside giving us a clear view above the trees to the lake below. It is a large lake, almost an inland sea, claiming to be one of the deepest and highest in the world, lying some twenty-seven hundred feet above sea level. The depth has still to be determined. There are birds singing and fragrant blossoms surrounding our verandah.

On Sunday we take a boat trip to Simando, a village nestled along the banks of the lake. As we speed along the shoreline, the captain is singing with a loud cadence, his arrival to the villages along the way. Stepping ashore at Simando we are guided to a pavilion to enjoy the dances of the Batak Indians. These depict life from birth through courtship, their fighting customs and finally, death. The dancers form a long line. While tossing grain in the air they shuffle their feet through the dust as they dance with a bobbing of the torso. Behind the dirt stage, the orchestra of mostly woodwind sounding instruments, accompanies the dance. The long performance becomes almost hypnotic with the repetitious pulse of this music. The final dance includes a life-size human-like wooden puppet that is jerked about as it's pulled on a wagon. Its grotesque movements signify that the corpse has entered the realm of the dead, never to haunt the living any longer. Members of the audience are invited to join the dancers in their long line. Linda has the video camera ready. Throwing the traditional shawl over one shoulder, I then try to imitate the movements of the tribesman ahead of me as I add my step to this dance.

Back at our lodge we enjoy walks through groves of clove trees. The cloves are drying on sheets spread on the ground, giving the air a lovely, spicy fragrance. On a morning walk, we see in the distance, a long row of women swinging long hoes and moving in unison across a field. They are singing as they till the soil. It becomes a ballet as we watch the delicate sweep of their hoes in time with the graceful, balanced step of the women.

The small village of Tuk Tuk, with its many stalls, gives us a chance to try our bargaining skills. I bargain for a nicely carved ukulele that will be a nice addition to my collection of musical instruments. Linda purchases an antique carved horn used as an old medicine repository. Along the narrow paths on the hillsides small houses or stone statues that are the tombs of loved ones, stand in haunting isolation.

We leave this unique island and return to Prapet the next morning to board a bus for the six-hour drive along the lake to Brastagi. As we pass large rubber plantations, I am surprised to see such a small trunk - only ten to twelve inches in diameter - supports a tall rubber tree. Looking down the long rows of the plantation, we see tin buckets hanging at the slash made on the trunks. Beyond are sheds where lines with the white sheets of rubber hang to dry. The bus trip today is pleasant with more room to sit. Along the way we pass groves of palm nut trees that provide oils used in soaps and food. It is a major crop for this country. Arriving late in the afternoon, we decide to stay in the old Dutch hotel that advertised 'Old World charm'. This is lacking. However, we discover a new and delicious fruit drink served here, the margarita, tasting much like a nectarine - very refreshing these hot days.

By chance, during an evening walk, we find, tucked in a remote corner of town, long wooden houses built high on stilts with roofs of thick thatch. As we stand looking at this unusual sight, a man motions us to climb the ladder and join his family. There is a dusky feeling inside with only the open door giving light. As our eyes become accustomed to the dim light, we see mats for sleeping stretched on the floor. Midway to one side is a brazier resting on a bed of sand. In a far corner a man and child are playing music on an instrument of gongs called a gamelan and a bamboo flute, almost birdlike in quality. It seems very fitting to this nest-like dwelling floating here above ground. Their tiny grandmother clasps my arm and gives me hug as we leave. We are enjoying the hospitality of this culture.

Another bus ride has us rolling and swerving along mountain roads back to Medan. Boarding another bus, we rattle away from the bustling city to the jungle. Our destination is a National Preserve dedicated in rehabilitating orangutans to a forest habitat. Many of these animals have been in zoos or domesticated in some fashion. No longer wanted they are sent here to relearn lost skills of survival.

We settle into a lovely setting in the middle of the jungle. We sleep in a loseman, a kind of motel. Nearby, we enjoy dining on the verandah by a stream with fast rapids filling the air with mist and soothing sounds. The food being served at a leisurely pace, is excellent.

Our guide is instructing us to be quiet this morning while we hike a half-hour into the jungle. Suddenly overhead there is a crashing and rustling of leaves. Looking up we see two large orangutans swing through the trees with a destination definitely in mind. As we move silently ahead we see their mission is to swing to a platform built high in the trees. Sitting crouched in one corner of the platform is a ranger with several buckets beside him. As these gorilla shapes ease cautiously down beside him, they reach for a banana or a bowl of formula. Our guide whispers that gradually this food is restricted, encouraging the orangutan to forage on its own. The men handling them make no eye contact and gradually retreat to fewer and fewer contacts. This retraining takes a minimum of three months to wean them of domesticated habits. Before we leave, there are a dozen orangutans swinging above us. Several of these are mothers with babies clinging confidently to their tummies while they enjoy the swinging sweep from tree to tree. We quietly depart this sanctuary and enjoy one last evening in the jungle.

Next morning we climb aboard the bus. We are a part, once more, of the crowd that becomes the body of this conveyance. Lashed to the roof , cargo is stacked again as high as the bus. Stacks of lumber, bags of cement, a wheelbarrow, crates of live chickens are all tied down on the roof over our heads. What a swaying contraption we become as we cross rickety bridges and lean around mountainous curves. Setting foot in Medan after the seven-hour ride, we appreciate the stability of land. Even dear old *Horizon*'s slender keel offers more security and peace of mind than those four (or were there eight?) wheels afforded. A night's rest in the Garuda Hotel restores our holiday mood. This time, we board a plane and leave Sumatra for the island that has enticed authors and playwrights to reveal its charms - Bali. Paul should be waiting for us at the airport, having arrived in Bali a few hours before us.

We taxi to our lovely hotel and find beautiful bas relief carvings decorating the walls of the porch. Through an ornately carved door, our rooms are a welcome sight. Kuta Beach, where we are this first night, is geared to the tourist, with the usual glitz and glamour that attracts commerce. Whereas Sumatra is primarily a Christian professing island, we are now in a predominately Hindu country. With a guide Linda has arranged to drive us around this small island, we plan to enjoy an ancient culture. She had visited this country two years before and became a knowledgeable guide as we moved through this old and spiritual kingdom.

When the van meets us next morning, our driver, Cebra, has a lovely tribute of woven leaves, some cut into intricate designs, arranged with fragrant blossoms and rice kernels in a small basket on the dashboard. He tells us this is homage to a specific god to insure a safe and pleasant journey for his new friends. In our reading, we observe that the Balinese are haunted by the spiritual world in every aspect of their daily life. And it does seem so. We immediately leave for the city of Depansar to enjoy a performance of the Barong dance. The Barong, in an elaborate lion costume with two performers under the imaginative and descriptive drape, symbolizes good. It is in constant conflict with Rangda, the evil witch with her fearsome presence. The performance, with its elaborate costumed dancers moves across the outdoor stage in exaggerated posture and rhythms. From grotesque to elegant the dance is accompanied by a gamelan orchestra with its resonance of gongs and bells in overlapping sonorities.

For months to come, even to Thailand, we will see the story of Ramayana inspiring art, sculpture, architecture, theater and even naming buildings, trains and toys. This is an Indian epic of over 24,000 verses, written over 2000 years ago - as old as Homer's Iliad. It is a Hindu legend about the abduction of King Rama's wife and his complex battles against the evil King Rawana to restore her to his palace. The dances and elaborate costumes make this an astonishing performance that we continue to see in varied productions from puppet shows to ballet, to mosaic walls, to any aspect of life where these cultures have been influenced by Hindu thought. Especially extraordinary are the hand movements of the dancers as they portray with elegance and beauty, the delicacy of the story's emotions; almost hypnotizing in the slow grace of each movement. The Lalong dancers are girls aged five to nine years, specially trained to take this story and reveal with their very controlled and graceful dancing, a dedication to an old tradition of story telling. Here their exaggerated head and eye movements bring a different dimension to dance as they move in exquisite silk costumes.

The native dress of the Indonesian woman presents an elegance and beauty as well. A beauty that is shared by rich and poor women alike. We watch as women carry enormous baskets of rice or fruit and even tall loads of bricks on their heads. Perhaps this accounts for the elegant bearing the women display walking along the roadside. They wear batik design sarongs with a simple blouse.

As we drive north across the middle of Bali, we gaze at the spellbinding beauty of the steep hillsides, magnificently carved into flourishing green rice paddies. It is amazing when we examine the engineering involved to construct the irrigation ditches and dams that provide water to the paddies as they scale the steep slopes. Mountains, sculpted with only a hoe into steppes all supplied with water in this intricate system of canals, are breathtaking in their beauty! As day breaks I stand transfixed to gaze across the mist filled valleys with the sculpted slopes emerging, their emerald, watery fields catching the dawn in scattered shards of fractured mirrors. I can't imagine a man-made vision more lovely. 'Awesome' is the word our grandchildren might use.

Interspersed across this countryside are Hindu temples. With Linda's persuasion we see a majority of these, with their very ornate and intricately carved entrances and walls. Before every temple there is a small sign instructing each visitor to wear a sash upon entering plus a warning to all women against entering at the time of their 'uncleanness' or menstrual period. Don and Paul, after a fair number of temple visits, claim they have fulfilled their 'temple culture quota'.

Almost in the center of this small island eighty-six miles long and forty-eight miles wide, is the mountain Agung, reverently called by the Balinese 'the navel of the world'. With the spirit world dominating every aspect of Balinese life, this mountain represents good. They have assigned to heights, a significance of good fortune and well being that provides spiritual powers for a healthy life. In contrast, the nadir of the surrounding ocean holds sinister implications, their fear of evil gods. Making this one of the few island populations that does not look to the sea for sustenance or good fortune. Usually this mountain is shrouded in clouds, but we are favored today with only a wispy necklace that encircles the paddies scrambling up its slopes.

Our guide, Cebra, is anxious to take us to every corner of his fascinating world. Some of these corners hold enchanting scenes where young boys execute beautifully detailed carvings, or the many layered process of batik dyeing, to the fascinating religious processions with women carrying elaborate baskets of fruit four to five feet tall on their heads. He finds more dances in remote villages, some only performed by men using the dagger, known as the kris with its blade of wavy contours - symbol of a searing flame. These dancers use movements that gradually evolve into a frenzied and hypnotic trance as they press the kris to their glistening bodies. Our heads now swirling with the visions of these last ten days we leave Bali and fly west to the larger island of Java.

Yogjakarta is a bustling city with busy streets swarming with cars, buses and the little becaks with their gaudy designs and harnesses. Linda finds the pleasant, clean loseman she had enjoyed on her previous stay. Complete with a dining room and small pool, we enjoy this spot as our base from which to sightsee.

Again the Ramayana story is the essence of still more discovery for us. A performance of Wayang reveals another descriptive art that permeates the daily life of Indonesia. The term, Wayang, can be translated to mean, shadow. With very intricate design, flat leather puppets are cut into large, mythical shaped heads above small bodies to be manipulated with attached sticks. The long performances, many all night long, use these puppets as shadow images held behind a lit screen to portray the battle of good and evil - the Ramayana legend once more. Since Muslims banned copying the human form, these puppets take on grotesque and ugly proportions, exquisitely designed. There are records from the first century that this art influenced civilizations from Egypt to Java.

As we tour the Water Palace, music drifts across the background, a signature of this culture rich in creating artistic expression. A gamelan orchestra is playing in the palace pavilion. Resting in carved teak racks are varying sized bronze kettle-shaped bowls with a raised nipple on the top - all being struck with sticks or mallets. The sound from this large orchestra resonates with its highly distinctive sonority. The tinkling quality of the smaller ones is underlined with the deep reverberating rumbling and gong-like resonance from the large ones. It drifts as smoke over our heads - nebulous - veiled in mystic antiquity. Gamelan music, with its unfamiliar intervals is a new sound to our ears. There are over fourteen layers of sound that seem to fly away in unpredictable directions, constructing a loose and free structure. The compositions take on a quality of bird songs and ethereal spirits. It seems fitting that such accompaniment surrounds the visual expressions of myth and mystery we are enjoying.

A trip by bus the next day finds us walking toward a Buddhist shrine, the world's largest stupa. As described to us, stupas are shrines built to pay homage to the memory of the Master, Buddha. Dating back to 700 A.D. this man-made mountain, Borobudur, is alone in the world in its depiction of a Buddhist mandala or prayer symbol. It was modeled to represent the universe. Combining squares, denoting the earth, and circles, signifying the heavens, it rises in a symbolic combination for ten terraces to form a huge dome of carved stone built over a hill.

We continue from this stylized Buddhist model of the universe to the Dieng plateau high in the mountains known as the 'Abode of the Gods'. A misty plain atop the twisting incline we've just climbed is centered within the crater rim of the volcano surrounding us. With bubbling hot springs and steaming muddy cauldrons, we keep in mind this volcano is not fully asleep. Along the ride down the mountain we pass vegetable gardens dug into the mountainside. They're not as fragile as the rice paddies we've seen, but the amazing irrigation engineering is still employed.

By the time we reach the foothills, dusk has arrived. The highway is filling with a lot of traffic - cars, buses and the ever-present mob of bikes. By dark, a real nightmare opens before us. Our bus is the only vehicle using this busy highway that has any lights showing . . nothing but darkness surrounds us. Our bus driver continues at breakneck speed through the dark as glimpses of moving objects loom momentarily ahead, then vanish. Bikes suddenly appear in our sphere of meager light then disappear, a car creeps by or people jump to the side of the highway as we explode through the darkness. I wish we hadn't been in such a hurry to get the front seat with such a clear view of this highway madness.

We spend the last few days here on these enchanting islands visiting art shops and batik designers. We add to the collections of silver charms that are representative of the countries we are visiting. Bracelets dangling the charms of this world we've visited will encircle our granddaughters' wrists.

Indonesia adds new items to the menu, 'Tastes of the World' we're acquiring. With the distinctive cuisine of this multi-cultured society, nasi-goreng and mei-goreng, two stir- fried dishes that are popular in all the restaurants, become favorites of ours. Nasi meaning rice and mei, fried noodles act as the base over which the stir-fried veggies with varied meats are ladled. At the airport we bid farewell to Linda and Paul then board our plane for Singapore.

It's early summer. We have thoughts of moving on. Singapore has been a good place to get repairs completed. The anchorage is filling with new friends who always contribute to the knowledge we need for good safe passage ahead. There seems to be a consensus that sailing north through the Malacca Straits should wait until fall. Taking this advice, we sail instead along the East coast of Malaysia to the islands lying off shore. At Aur Island we welcome three young Malaysian fishermen aboard. We take them sailing for the day to show us how they catch fish. We are impressed with the catch that includes squid. The day is complete with their offer to prepare a seafood dinner in our galley. It's a fine meal of squid over a bed of rice. As they leave, they extend an invitation to visit them at their home on the mainland. They still have a two-week obligation to finish on their fishing contract. We'll see them then.

Their home is a surprise. The three young bachelors share a small tidy bungalow of cement block that they have nicely furnished. Borrowing a car from one of their dads they seem more than eager to drive us quite a distance to a large supermarket. We realize this has given them a chance to meet their girlfriends living far from them. We joined all of them at an ice cream shop before returning to their home where they treat us to the new flavor of fresh lychee nuts.

Still waiting for the right weather to sail around Singapore and on to points north, we visit more offshore islands along the east coast of Malaysia. It's at Tiamin Island I write and illustrate three books for our young granddaughters, Amanda, Natasha and Lindsey. Michelle's will emerge later.

It's only September but the weather looks favorable. We are going to grab the opportunity to embark on this Malacca leg. With the clearance paperwork completed in Singapore, we are once again sharing close quarters with those big freighters as we make the passage between buoys. There are times we're at the waterline of one of these giants looking up the sheer wall of a hull, that we wonder if they are even aware of the gnat at their side. We must be a frustration to them as well. There are glimpses of skyscrapers and loading docks as we make our way west around the southern coast of Singapore to steer a heading north.

The Strait opens up by nightfall and we all spread out a bit. In the darkness now it's not the familiar navigation lights of the freighters that is a concern, but the hundreds of small fishing boats with only flickering coal-oil lamps flashing about us. We are not sure if there are nets stretched between these lights. Occasionally there will be a sudden quick flash of light off our bow warning us there is a tiny boat ahead. We cautiously sail our way forward through this maze. Dawn is a welcome sight. The weather is cooperating as we continue up the west coast of Malaysia with a few overnight stops to relieve the fishing fleet anxiety as well as escape boarding by pirates. There had been warnings of piracy in the Straits. However, large freighters seem to be the targets where captured loot is more profitable than that of dumpy little yachts. We felt somewhat safe with our tiny cache of possessions.

It's been a five-day sail from Singapore. We decide to head for Lamut. This small village is situated only a short distance up a river. The chart outlines a place that looks like it will offer good protection. It's not far, but these last twelve miles have taken us fifteen hours. We ram into head winds and contrary currents that are building square seas. My watch stretches endlessly. I hate the wind for its insistence; I hate the boat for giving up to these bully seas; I hate Don for thinking such a trip is exciting; I hate the motor with its feeble attempt to push through these walls of water; I hate myself for hating all of the above and, most of all; I am saddened there have been no prayers that have changed any of the above conditions. A smooth passage, indeed!

With the dawn, we finally see an island ahead where, hopefully, we can tack our way behind it. Perhaps it will hide this wind - not to intimidate us any longer. A good decision - the smooth water allows us to sail by busy fishing villages where the smell of drying fish permeates the air. Continuing around a bend, we follow the river as the village of Lamut soon comes into view. In calm water, we anchor with other sailboats just off the small Perak Yacht Club. We are granted three months stay with permission to enjoy land travel in their country - so hassle free compared to the strict guidelines demanded in Singapore.

What a nice little town is Lamut. The evening is touched with the Muslim call to prayer at sundown. Here there is a special quality to this call. An intricate duet being sung by a pair of muezzin with their modal supplication is haunting in its simplicity - a pleasant contrast to the blaring recordings we have heard in other places. Here, a mystical blessing encircles its beneficence as evening shadows descend.

During the day, we enjoy the small shops that offer tasty food. *Roti canai* is an Indian specialty we enjoy for lunch. It is a large, thin pancake filled with your choice of meat and vegetables neatly tucked into its rolled dimensions. The tree-lined streets are clean pleasant places to walk. On Monday evenings the main street is closed to traffic when booths and stalls offering fresh meat and vegetables, t-shirts and music tapes line the streets. We routinely challenge the butcher to cut the chicken we choose into parts, legs, breasts and wings - instead of their method of using the large cleaver that slashes across the bird in parallel slabs holding myriad bone fragments. This always brings a puzzled glance, a shrug of the shoulder and a shaking of the head as he carefully sections our bird. We trust our smile of appreciation balances their misgivings of those strange Western ideas.

With all this time to explore and rest, we decide to tie *Horizon* to the grid here to paint the bottom once again. Positioned in shallow water, this grid consists of three tall posts deeply driven in a line from the shore. At high tide we motor beside these and tie fast to one side of the boat. At low tide, with the bottom of the boat exposed, we begin the scraping and final painting for a few more years' protection from barnacles. Because low tide lasts about two and a half-hours we make every minute count as we scrape and sand the bottom to accept three coats of paint. With two low tides a day we are back on our anchor after two days of work. With cuts on our hands and feet from the barnacles we decide to rest aboard a few days. Later we enjoy delicious meals at the yacht club.

By taking a bus into Ipoh we arrange for our flight to India and Nepal. We have given up our intention to sail to Bombay; the red tape was just too overwhelming. With round trip air tickets to Bangkok-India-Nepal in our pockets, we still have time to see more of this country before departure on October 10. We always travel light, with a backpack each. With this minimum wardrobe we board the bus to Kuala Lumpur, the capitol of Malaysia.

It's a strikingly beautiful city with its Moorish style architecture. The government buildings stretching along the parade grounds present elaborate, distinctive archways that are embraced with onion domes towered around the perimeter. The domes are all copper clad, each one clasping the sunlight to radiate in a coppery glow. This magical, almost fairy tale building holds our attention as the sun fades into a dusk that shades its beauty until the striking outlines are revealed with tiny, twinkling, white lights in the dark. We stand in an Arabian Night setting. Without forethought or planning, our visit is timed perfectly. We delight in the full moon with its luminescence filtering through the tall trees on couples strolling hand in hand below. It puts us in the mood, too. We join the lovers as we, with our arms around each other, realize we are strolling through a treasured dream come true - happy to be sharing it with each other.

When we return to our hotel, we notice for the first time an arrow painted in one corner of the ceiling. This points towards Mecca. The kneeling direction for the devout worshipper is an essential connection in their worship to Allah. Our bathroom has other unique qualities as well. The wash basin has a drain, as it should, but the first time we wash our hands we jump in dismay as the draining water splashes over our shoes. Looking underneath, we see there is no pipe attached. However, there is a large drain in the center of the floor that accommodates this stream. For bathing, there is a *mandy* built in one corner. Nicely decorated with tiles, this is a large, high, square tub filled with water. A dipper is resting on the edge of the tub. Taking this I splash water over myself as it streams through this drain at my feet. After a good soaping I dipper more water to rinse. It's a very sensible solution; one we have seen in varying dimensions across Pacific countries.

The 'Blue Mosque' is one of the largest in the world. Located in neighboring Shah Alam, it is delicate in the filigree and colored glass grilles designed in traditional Islamic patterns that decorate the enormous walls. A shimmering blue dome blooms 300 feet high above this delicate carved base. The 20,000 male worshippers kneel beneath its magnificent ceiling where four giant chandeliers cast a gentle radiance over their backs. As the sunlight brushes brilliant strokes across this amazing structure, the mosque creates rippling reflections across the adjoining lake. From here we hurry back to Kuala Lumpur to another distinctively Moorish building. Glistening white in the sun, we hurry through the ornate arches of the train station to catch the train that will take us to the Cameron Highlands.

This trip gives us a closer view of the green fields and towns as we rumble along the track, ninety-eight miles toward Tapah at the foot of the Highlands. An Englishman named Cameron took a gamble early in this century and bought a land grant to start a tea plantation on these highlands 5000 feet above sea level. Like many projects of this kind, there were successes and failures. Today among the rolling hills of the Highlands there remain vast stretches of the manicured tea bushes of the Boh Tea Estate. With misty, cool days we visit the estate to learn more about the fermenting process used to make the tea enjoyed around the world. It is a fertile plain high in these clouds. Here strawberry farms abound with the beauty of hundreds of butterflies suspended over the rich vegetation in fluttering pointillism. We return to the low plains as our driver winds along the roads carved into the hillsides. From the mists above we descend through giant bamboo stands, jungle palms and giant tree ferns arching across the road to the warm, dry surroundings of the plain.

Time to get back to Lamut and aboard *Horizon*. We need to make her secure for the month long leave we'll be taking from her. We pick a spot a safe distance from other boats to set two anchors in the soft mud bottom. Mike aboard *Loreley* has consented to keep an eye on our barque while we are gone.

By taking a seven-hour bus ride to Penang Island, we find a cheaper flight to Bangkok than one out of Kuala Lumpur. This gives us a chance to see more of the countryside. Along the passing landscape rubber plantations with their long corridors stretch to a distant horizon. Late in the day we arrive at the island city of Penang and board the plane. As we fly over the coast en route to Bangkok, we look down through scattered clouds at the contours of the sailing journey we will be making when we return. Driving in a taxi from the airport into the city of Bangkok, we realize why this city has attained the epithet, 'The Smoggiest City in the World'. We are bumper to bumper in traffic jams as we move a snail's pace to our hotel. With just a couple days scheduled here in this fascinating city before the next leg of our flight to India, we fill the days with sightseeing.

The Grand Palace is breathtaking as its elegance gleams in the sunlight. These royal residences and temples of exquisite Siamese architecture were walled-in about 1783 by Rama I to shelter the succeeding royal families. The roofs, distinguished by series of peaks, each defined with golden needles, are covered with tiles of rich hues that sparkle in the sunlight. We wander among gilded rooms where walls of tapestries and mosaics glisten with turquoise, purple and gold outlining or highlighting intricate designs. We join the throngs viewing this gem. The Emerald Buddha is carved from one large piece of jade that sits high on a gold throne centered in a bejeweled room. It is venerated as crowds pay respect to the memory of Buddha. This makes it difficult to get a brief glimpse over the many shoulders in front of us. The entire complex, with its many palaces, glistens in the sunlight with colors in rich dimensions defining the architecture. A wall stretching a great length along a colonnade displays the Ramayana story with the characteristic Siamese painting technique that creates a layered panorama of scenes in beautifully executed tiny strokes. Somehow the predominance of peacock colors seems revealed to me in the iridescence unveiled all about us. Words get lost trying to describe its radiant beauty.

We complete the day with a fast, wet boat trip along the Chao Phya River to a large shed. Here is housed the golden Royal Barge with its bow shaped as a golden swan's neck, the upraised beak holding a long gold pendant. Alongside are lesser golden barges that accompany royalty on festive parades along the waterfront, all ornate in their decorations.

In the evening, we discover, just a block from our lodging, the home of Jim Thompson. An American architect who, after spending many years in this part of the world, became fascinated with the homes of this country. This gem of a house he constructed combines rooms and parts of buildings from many Thai structures. This creation has resulted in an enchanting residence. His life ended in mystery. His disappearance in the Cameron Highlands of Malaysia left no clues to solve the riddle.

We finish our last days at the Christian Guest House. Here we enjoy orchids in the courtyard with its quiet surroundings a background for the delicious meals offered more cheaply than the center city hotel. An invitation to dinner at the home of Mark and Jan Seimens, living here in Thailand with several other couples working with the Mennonite Central Committee, our church relief agency, gives us a chance to reminisce about shared friends back home.

The Taj Mahal provides a breath-taking setting to celebrate my 62nd birthday.

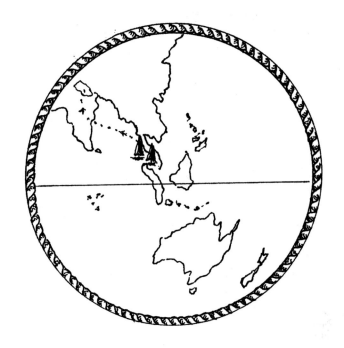

India to Nepal to Thailand

CHAPTER 15
DUSTING OFF CHILDHOOD MEMORIES

By morning of the 15th we are flying once again. This time our destination is Calcutta. To describe this part of our journey, I am turning to the letters Don wrote to the family. This is the country of his birth. And now for the first time, he is returning to recapture childhood memories of those first ten years he spent here.

"Even though I was born here and have heard all my life about India, this remains a place that has to be seen to be believed. We landed in Calcutta and sped through customs and I tried to phone MCC headquarters. I found no phones working, only signs directing one to a certain booth where help was available. On the way to the booth, a charming young Indian who spoke reasonable English approached us. He inquired if he could be of assistance. He gradually became my Executive Assistant ~ mistake number one. I showed him the Mennonite Central Committee address and phone number. My EA conveniently had a taxi, "so why not just go direct," he says. Out we went. Standing beside the cab is his assistant who will help with our luggage, our two knapsacks. There is no meter in the cab, but 'no problem'. We agreed upon a price-$10 (about twice the normal fee, we later learn, but what do I know). We get in while the driver is carefully pouring two liters of gas into the tank. I am suspicious. . . but committed. The engine finally settles down to firing on all four cylinders, and we are off with a running commentary of the passing scenes. We get to a busy part of the city and the engine dies. There is some fiddling under the hood, but finally, everyone agrees the cab is out of fuel. 'No problem'. If I could just advance a 100-rupee note, he will return in five minutes with more fuel. We hand push it to the side of the road. Thirty minutes goes by, I am concerned about getting to MCC before closing time. I get out and flag another cab. The assistant to our Executive Assistant speaks with the driver of this cab who claims not to speak English, plus not a clue to the location of the address we seek. The taxi takes off. By now a sizable crowd has gathered and luckily includes a nice lady who speaks English and offers assistance. She flags down a rickshaw driver and arranges a fee. When I show her the address, she says, 'Oh Mennonite', and then explains the location to the rickshaw driver. We finally settle on a price for the 'invaluable services of the E.A'. Climbing into the rickshaw's diminutive structure, we are off. Immediately there is a hill to negotiate and our gaunt rickshaw 'walla' is sweating, getting pale and hawking big gobs of phlegm (no doubt full of tuberculosis bacteria) as he struggles pulling us up this hill. Mary Lou is overwhelmed with pity and wants to walk, but I explain that we don't know where to go and the man pulling this rickshaw would lose face. The walla ultimately survives to the top of the hill and your Mom and I make it to MCC.

They were expecting us, having received a letter from Dr. Martin about our visit. For $10 a night we enjoyed delicious food and pleasant lodging in the guesthouse. Dr. Glen Miller, an internal medicine physician from Ohio with his wife, had just started as director here and we enjoyed evenings together. The office here made the arrangements for a train to Raipur and for a later flight to Delhi for us. We toured one of the MCC farm projects - two simple pumps of PVC piping manually operated, one for well water, the other for irrigation that affords small villages easy access to this vital resource. We are in Calcutta for 'Dewali' the Hindu festival of lights. But trouble is brewing throughout the country with student immolations carried out as protests rise. Hindus are planning to tear down a Muslim mosque they claim is built on their holy ground.

We leave Calcutta by train giving us a chance to see the countryside. At every station stop the chai sellers rush to sell us tea steaming in small clay cups. We arrive in Raipur and take a taxi to the bus station, an open sided pavilion. There are many women in colorful saris and men garbed in the dhoti all milling about. We are unable to phone Dr. Martin -phones not working here either. Now we are REALLY in India - no English for a while. I go to the ticket window and find an agent who finally understands we want to go to Dhamtari, but he won't sell a ticket until the bus arrives. I'm trying hard to understand this when I am approached by a 'Sadu' or Fakir who is obviously a hebephrenic schizophrenic - looks wild and had his last bath when Gandhi died. His hair, which looks like a dirty carpet, is down to his waist, and his only garment is a tattered orange shawl over one shoulder. He also wears a chain with 1/4-inch links. One end of this is looped around his neck and the other end of the chain is tied around the head of his penis, under the foreskin, as near as I can determine from the distance I am trying to maintain. He begins speaking to me in tongues with an occasional shout to answer his own internal voices. When he shouts, he pulls this chain causing him to bow and to 'salute' simultaneously. All the local Indians have cleared a twenty foot circle around us, while the ticket agent has completely disappeared. Meanwhile, Mary Lou is having her own problems. She is parked on a bench trying to maintain her composure while she is being approached by a wandering sacred cow. The cow, undoubtedly affected by all the excitement, relieves itself, missing Mary Lou by a few inches. It isn't easy to stand in the 'body language of infinite cool' wearing a backpack and being patted on the arm by a dirty Sadu speaking in tongues and yanking his chain, but I am determined. The Sadu finally wanders off leaving a wake about him. The bus arrives and I am able to buy two tickets. We are on our final leg to Dhamtari, my birthplace. . . (to be continued) . . ."

"In looking back with what I remember and what I see now, The India Mission I knew, was part of the British Raj, with the large stately homes and yards, the servants, the schooling in the hills, the trips to Ahdamabad, etc. But I must say it left a good legacy. The good schools, the hospital and nursing school that have developed here are quite impressive, especially in view of the prevailing conditions. The hospital is now 250 beds and soon to add another 75 to the new obstetric wing - a real tribute to my father and mother and their generation whose vision broke ground for much of what I am seeing now.

Our most gracious hosts during this visit are Dr. and Mrs. Martin. He is a physician and the Director of the hospital. They are an outstanding Indian family that has contributed greatly to the welfare of the community. Mrs. Martin is very active in the school system. We are fortunate to share this time with friends from the States, Paul Miller and his wife, Vesta. He is a part of this visionary generation that I mentioned. We enjoy his reservoir of stories and dry wit that help me relive some of those childhood memories. A van and driver are provided and the four of us take long journeys over rough and bumpy roads - picturesque with bullock carts, even elephants, of course herds of cows and goats and the never ending line of people walking and riding bikes.

We visit Dondi where we are surrounded with extraordinarily gracious and friendly folks, who remember my parents. Here we visit Dr. Matthi, an unbelievable man! He bought the mission bungalow and transformed it into a fifty-bed hospital by himself. He does major surgery, C sections, bowel perforations and resections all under spinal or open-drop ether plus all the medical problems, TB etc. with no x-ray, low pay, no time off, and no one to consult on difficult cases. That kind of schedule would bury me.

In Dhamtari the streets are teeming. 10,000 when I left in '37 and 100,000 now. It's hard to see how it all functions. We take walks along the dusty streets in step with the cows wearing garlands that join the crowds. We hope to find the house where I lived those years ago. It is now an insurance office but we are allowed to walk about as I remember Mom's gardens around a fishpond. There is no evidence to that past glory here today in this dusty space.

The day we visited the school Dad was instrumental in starting, a group of hoodlums appeared and demanded the school close, as a demonstration by the party that is responsible for the national upheaval between the Muslims and Hindus. The school closed. This upheaval is being felt everywhere in the country with the leaders fomenting as much unrest as possible. A curfew has been imposed not only here in Dhamtari but throughout the country. We wonder if our plans to fly to Delhi will be a problem. It doesn't stop us, however, from continuing our daily jaunts to Balodgahan, to the dam at Rudri where I swam as a kid, on to a small and old Raja palace, with a final picnic under the stars in the jungle - such a beautiful country. I had forgotten just how beautiful it is- the dusty plains and the distant hazy mountains. My spirit is renewed."

We leave Raipur by plane, thinking the trains were too dangerous with reports of sabotage on some lines. With the good arrangements of Dr. Martin we are met at the airport and dropped at the front door of the YMCA in Delhi. From here we arrange a bus trip to Agra. With the Taj Mahal glistening in the sunlight, it is hard to describe the beauty of this carved marble gem that surpasses every picture I've ever seen. An Edward Lear is quoted as saying, 'Henceforth let the inhabitants of the world be divided into two classes; them as has seen the Taj Mahal and them as hasn't '. It seems too fragile to have withstood over three hundred years of turmoil. The perfect proportions are a testimony to the art of those craftsmen, 20,000 of them taking more than twenty years to complete this memorial to the wife of grief stricken Shahjahan, a great Mughal. With this pearl as a backdrop, its reflection stretching the length of the pool at its base, Don and I have our photo taken to celebrate my 62nd birthday.

The builder of the Taj later moved to Delhi where he was instrumental in the design of the renewed city. The Red Fort with its walls carved from red sandstone still stands today as a reminder of the vital link it played in the survival of the city. A magnificent light show at night captures the atmosphere of those regal times and provides a vivid lesson in Indian history for us. We spend a day shopping in Delhi before our plane departs for Nepal.

We fly over the plains of India and approach the Himalayas as they raise their forbidding boundary ahead. A path opens as we bank away from the mountains to swoop through a pass. A legend declares it was ripped open by a god as he slashed with his saber to allow the lake trapped in this enormous bowl, to flow free. Ahead stretches this golden floored bowl with the mountains carving their intricate designs on all sides. As if the gods had set their most precious vessel here at the pinnacle of the world, it reposes with carefully inscribed designs, a blueprint for bliss from which to drink the elixir of heaven.

We are so fortunate to enjoy the best of all worlds. To be immersed in a new culture is exciting, but to enjoy this experience with those who have some knowledge of the people and their customs, further enriches our visit. Meeting us at the airport are good friends, Ethel and Ed Metzler, two of these knowledgeable folks. As Director of the United Mission of Nepal, Ed is responsible for the management of several church denominations from thirty-seven countries as they coordinate projects in health, education and agriculture here in Nepal. Ethel continues to engage in a family counseling practice, a profession she had established in Elkhart. They share their home and delicious meals with us, taking time from their busy professions to escort us on forays into the foothills.

Again we are immersed in an awesome panorama. The colors gold and purple wash across the landscape before us. Terraced fields of golden rice and maize are once again sculpted along the slopes. Above these a faint fringe of green stretches a line from where the distant purple mountains thrust jagged peaks into cerulean blue skies. The days are so clear, I think they must shatter with the brilliance. A glimpse of distant Mt. Everest presents a spellbinding display as we watch the late afternoon sun walk across the Himalayan peaks, dazzling each peak with an orange glow before moving on, leaving a purple footprint on the shadowed peaks behind.

Ed and Ethel live in Patan across the Bagmati River from Kathmandu with their rooftop view of the surrounding mountain peaks offering a spectacular sunset display. Don and I walk through the narrow streets of Patan to Durbar Square. It is a square surrounded by temples. The distinctive and unique carvings on the eaves and roof struts describe myths and stories, some display erotic themes. Many of the buildings built by the Newari tribes in the 15th and 16th centuries display latticed windows that are characteristic of this architectural period. As we drive through the valley, we recognize the distinctive Newari styled houses. They are built three stories high with the unique carved struts supporting the upper overhanging floors. It is a signature silhouette.

One morning Don and I start an eight-hour trek from Gunivihar Temple outside Kathmandu to follow a path along the narrow dikes surrounding the rice paddies. Along the way we meet Nepalese women in colorful dress with ornaments of many bangles and dangling earrings above bibs of chains and necklaces. We share easy smiles with them. Pausing under the shade of a tree, we watch women tossing grain high in the air from large flat baskets. The chaff blows away like a cloud of dust while the kernels start falling. With flashes of gold, the seeds are caught, then tossed from the baskets onto piles nearby. This harvest ballet with an easy rhythm from the waists of the brightly garbed women, holds our attention with its spellbinding motion.

We struggle up a serpentine path; its rock-strewn way twisting among the evergreens, some tall, some gnarled and stunted. We catch our breath as we quietly stand in the room of a monastery. The saffron robed monks, seated cross-legged on the floor, are centered in meditation with the sonority of their A-U-M echoing through the pines rustling outside the open windows. This is the country of Buddha's birth in 553 B.C.

On many of the roofs, we see sheaves of rice or grain lying in the sun to dry. On lines stretching just below the eaves, corn with the husks pulled back is tied, making golden cornices along the wall. Although we are tired when a bus picks us up high in the foothills, we agree it has been a wonderful view into the daily work of the villages.

The fascinating cobbled streets of Kathmandu with crowded stalls sheltered beneath the overhanging balconies of aged wood defining the Newari architecture, portray a Far Eastern atmosphere. We wander amidst the sights and smells of a market embraced by a timeless culture. Stalls display baskets of fragrant spices crowded

174

beside hanging tapestries of vibrant colors that find a place beside gaudy plastic bowls and pails - hanging fowl in stalls crowd beside bowls of cheese and yogurt all attended by hawking sellers trying to attract your attention and purse - it's noisy - it's dusty - it's crowded with pushing and shoving. We stand mesmerized as this market's fragrance drifts across dust motes caught in shafts of sunlight, transfixed in the dizzying midst of a bazaar straining with ancient rhythms.

The second week of our stay we take the bus for a seven-hour ride along winding mountain roads that creep higher into the foothills to Pokhara. Leaving the valley below, we climb closer to starting points for the famous treks to those highest peaks seen in. the distance. Here in Pokhara the peaks of Macchapucchara dominate the mountain views with the prominent fishtail configuration outlining the distant high horizon.

Our trekking has been modest - day hikes to surrounding foothills and villages. We rent bikes one day. Huffing and puffing as I pedal up a steep path, my passage suddenly seems easier. Glancing over my shoulder, two young boys are grinning as they push on the rear fender of my bike. We have found two good guides for the day. They point to the bloody ground around an altar where daily sacrifices are offered. They declare chickens are the usual sacrifice. By the end of the day we share cool drinks with the two proud and grinning boys at a quiet Tibetan food stand. Many Tibetans fled their homeland when China invaded their country to settle in Nepal.

These refugees have developed the fine art of weaving rugs. On our return to Patan we visit this fascinating process. Under large shade trees stand big iron vats over glowing coals. Here large skeins of wool are being dyed as the loose knot is stirred through rich liquid colors. When the chosen shade is determined the knot is removed then hung on lines to dry in the shade. A live watercolor painting is caught in this beauty.

But it is the long shed behind us with soft melodies floating overhead that piques our curiosity. We walk into a large room where huge looms are suspended from the ceiling, one after the other in a long line. Sitting on the floor before each loom, a woman is singing a counterpoint of eastern modality that blends with the voices of the other weavers. This creates a space of delicate melodic mystery shimmering in this modest shed. The Tibetan puzzle is revealed. They weave these tones with yarns of accompanying colors that follow this auditory weaving directive - each tone represents a stitch of color. The design composed to music becomes an interesting and lovely transition into duplicate designed rugs. We purchase rugs composed of such beauty to send to our children. As we pack our backpacks again, we gaze at the breathtaking beauty of this tiny country, a special memory to pack with our growing collection. It's hard to leave.

We have two days travel back to Lamut after leaving Nepal. As we walk towards the marina from the bus stop, our step is light and our conversation is recalling the places and people that have renewed childhood visions and memories. Can we remember all of these experiences?

Walking towards us is the Australian couple from the boat 'Magoo'. They tell us about a freak storm that passed through the anchorage a few nights ago. About half the boats in the harbor dragged their anchors, they said, and ours had been one. To make matters worse, *Horizon* had taken off on her own in the middle of the night with fifty-knot winds shoving her stern right into the bow of '*Albatross*' owned by Heinz. This Heinz, from Germany, is also known as Heinz the Horrible Hun, possessing a reputation all over SE Asia as a man with irrational behavior. With that disarming news, we hurry back to our boat and climb aboard. There doesn't seem to be any hull damage, but the rear of the cockpit is in shambles. The wind generator is half gone, the two solar panels broke loose and sank, the stainless steel railing around the stern is bent. The hardest to repair is going to be the prop shaft bolt that sheared off, leaving us with no forward or reverse capabilities. This will mean another stint being tied to the grid. Don was able to manage a feeble grin and say, 'all it takes is money'. Many of our friends stopped by to offer their help and condolences on our choice of boats to crash into. It isn't long until Heinz and his Malay girlfriend dinghy over, he with a determined and set jaw. I smile and welcome them aboard saying, 'It looks like we both have our work cut out for us the next few days'. He stares at us a long time, then decides discussion won't hurt. He seems to relax as they come aboard. Don has just come up greasy and sweaty from working on the prop shaft. He continues promoting the idea that both of us have problems we can help each other solve. In fact, during our discussion we determine we have an expensive turnbuckle for his shroud that he can use, which we give him. Keeping our fingers crossed, he continues to be even-tempered, including his offer to help us since our boat has sustained more damage. His bowsprit is cracked. We agree to purchase the new wood post to replace it. He says he can shape it himself. We hope we can continue this good-will policy. He has been reasonable. There's been no evidence of that 'the horrible' factor finding a place in our relationship. We are able, by sharing work, to get both our boats ready for the next leg.

Christmas is in the air and it's time to move on. We drop off gifts of cookie-filled coffee mugs to Heinz and Soo, and a loaf of banana bread to Mr. and Mrs. Chan, the gracious master of the Yacht Club. We raise the anchor and leave Lamut.

It is a nice overnight sail with the strongest winds during Don's watch. The NE monsoon winds of fifteen knots have finally arrived. We are approaching the large island of Lankowie, the northern point of Malaysia on this western coast. We make our way through a labyrinth of small islands reminding us of those Rock Islands of Palau. Finally we sail along the long passage into Bass Harbor. We anchor in this large sweeping bay, well protected by all the surrounding islands. The small village of Kuan on shore offers duty-free shopping. Ahoy! We see *Sunshine* anchored nearby and hurry to join Jimmie and Jim for 'catch up' about the last two years we've been apart. They will be leaving tomorrow for Thailand. We make plans to meet there for more good times together. The post office only presents us with a modest stack of mail - what a disappointment! We had hoped the stack would be overflowing with the Christmas cheer we longed for.

Tomorrow is our third Christmas away from the States. We join *Orion* from Switzerland and *Magoo* from Australia to celebrate at a nearby anchorage with access to an inland lake. We spend the morning swimming and bathing in this fresh water lake followed by a holiday meal aboard *Horizon*. There was no bird of any kind available at the market for the festive table. However there were chicken patties. Using these to create a 'bird shape' stuffed with dressing, I'm hoping this will be 'no turkey' of a bird. It looks okay but tastes strange. However this doesn't dampen the festive mood we're in. We all enjoy the day and continue sharing stories and jokes even late into the evening. Tino of *Orion* keeps us laughing with his great storytelling. After a phone call to Potter next day, he tells us the boat parts we have been waiting for, for weeks, from the States have only just been mailed. We will have to hang around till they arrive. I take this time to create the book for granddaughter Michelle, my fourth this year. I'm happy with the results.

The New Year 1991 comes in with a whimper here in Lankowie. With friends joining us, we walk to town for a celebratory dinner out. We're all disappointed at the expensive poor meal we are served. As we stroll down the deserted road at mid-night, striding arm in arm, we sing 'Should Auld Acquaintance Be Forgot' as one horn toots a lonely welcome to the New Year.

We set sail next day with the charts of Thailand well studied to find our next port of call. A stop on the way, to walk where there is a cascade tumbling over the face of a high, broad boulder, gives us the opportunity to visit Hans on his boat *Tumblehome*. Hans hails from the States, not Germany. Never has there been a more apt description for a disaster afloat. I can't imagine setting sail in such a mess. Nevertheless, we enjoy visiting with this most generous and sociable salty-swab.

We continue along the coast and pass the border into Thailand waters. With these erratic monsoon winds whipping across the Andamann Sea from the Sumatra Mountains, we look for shelter among the Butang group of islands. This is home to a village of sea gypsies - indigenous Thai tribes, somewhat disenfranchised much as our own American Indians. Many of these islands are used as sleeping stops for fishing fleets with surprisingly few protected anchorages. Since we are fighting head winds, we decide to stop for the night. My anxiety level is right up there, with sea gypsy legends making me wary of these anchorages. But we have no problems and set off in the morning only to return once again for another night at anchor. We don't care to bash into the high seas still out there.

Finally we are off with reasonable winds and approach Phi-Phi Island - pronounced pee-pee. It presents a beautiful high profile with its sheer rocky karst cliffs plunging to deep crevices that sets this tourist attraction apart. The island is shaped like an H, with the western stroke shorter than the eastern half. The two are bridged by a narrow and gorgeous sandy stretch that cradles the hotels and a small village full of shops selling exquisite batik. We enjoy watching the intricate process of wax resist used to design the colorful batik patterns being created. We sailed by the high karst (crevice riven) cliffs on the west that shelters the nests of the tern. Men who climb these sheer faced cliffs on rickety bamboo scaffolds harvest the small nests in springtime. It is the expensive ingredient in the birds' nest soups we have been seeing on the menus from Hong Kong to here. The price reflects the danger involved to bring them to the soup bowl. We did dinghy to one of these cliffs and try a partial climb up the terrifying face. After looking straight down at the rocks and swirling water below, I make a hasty and shaky retreat down the bamboo ladder.

We anchor in the northern bay of the H. Anchored beside us, we recognize Gene and Mel, friends we last saw in Palau. She is now displaying a certain freedom enjoyed on this offshore island. Mel waves to us attired only in a sarong. She is gorgeous in her topless array. Don looks like he might choke. He immediately dives into the crystal clear water, no doubt to clear his head or whatever. It's not long before he manages to bring back to the boat two nice grouper for dinner. It has been over a year that 'diver Don' has been able to plunge into clear water. Not since Palau, a year ago, has the water been clear enough to see fish. No doubt he thinks he's died and is now in heaven!

After a week here we sail west with just a day sail to arrive on the east coast of the large island of Phuket. It is about the same size as Singapore. There are many protected bays and harbors cradled around its perimeter. We fill the diesel tanks and jugs at the fuel barge then sail around the southern tip to anchor at Ao Chalong, a large bay offering protection from every quarter but west. This gives us access to the tuk-tuk that drives us to town - about a half-hour ride for fifty cents. These tuk-tuks look like the jeepneys of the Philippines, although less colorful. One of the first tasks we rush to complete after the arrival formalities, is to find the post office. Ah, we are rewarded for our lean Christmas bundle last month. Poste Restante has been holding a fat bundle of mail that includes some packages. Hurrying back to the peace and quiet of the cockpit, lemonade close by, the rest of the day is leisurely spent enjoying this correspondence. Much to our chagrin, a letter from dear Thelma informed us that the $2500 check we thought we had sent her for our taxes was written for $25. She and Weyburn scrambled around with their own funds to cover our faulty synapse gap. Yet they still sent us gifts contributing still more to our bundle of Christmas packages from family back home.

We are surrounded with the friends of earlier anchorages. There is a lot of boat- hopping to share the varied experiences since we parted paths. For some it's months and from others it's years since we've shared anchorages. We chuckle as, repeatedly, we listen to a couple telling stories of the places and experiences they've shared aboard their sailboat. The stories each mate tells differ so much that we declare they have each taken separate journeys. It's quite possible the story Don might tell of our circumnavigation would, no doubt, hold impressions and details so different from mine that readers might well declare we shared not a day together. To each his own dream, this voyage becomes uniquely mine.

It's agreed that our new TV center Don built in Hong Kong, will accommodate a "Super Bowl' party. Three couples quietly dinghy to Horizon at 5 a.m. that last Sunday of January to muffle our cheers for the Denver Broncos. The English, of course, has all been dubbed to the Thai language, but who needs words for football anyway?

Phuket town is emerging to satisfy the voracious appetites of worldwide tourists beating a path to these shores. The ingenious craftsmen of this country are skilled at copying toney brand names for sale on the street corners. A Rolex watch can be had for $50. Some of the classier French designer labels are displayed on clothes that hang on racks in booths stretching along the streets. And along the beach, music tapes, movies and medicines, all copied, are for sale. It 's a booming economy for Thailand.

Without any quality control or thought for copyright infringement, you can't be sure how accurate the watch may be or just what is in that medicine. But it's selling and it's cheap.

We enjoy the new taste of Thailand and find some wonderful restaurants that acquaint us with new spices and the use of ginger and lemon grass in soups and sauces. A special dish we enjoy several times is a succulent lemon chicken on a bed of deep fried seaweed with its crispy, crunchy texture. Tucked in dusty corners of antique shops, treasures defining old customs give us more history to this nation of fine craftspeople. The tidy market fairly blooms with the stalks of bright green asparagus, thick orange carrots, shining purple eggplant nestling beside a curly fringe of fresh leafy lettuce all outlined with brilliant red strawberries in delicate baskets. There are clean meat markets with cheese and dairy products nicely laid out beside the fish and meat. Such tantalizing displays have us enjoying flavors almost forgotten.

In response to our letter inviting them to join us on *Horizon* for two weeks, Ed and Ethel fly to Phuket from Nepal. We sail just offshore from the airport and drop the anchor. With a short walk, the four of us soon are enjoying refreshing drinks in the cockpit as the sun is setting to the West. This anchorage looks across a seamless sea that becomes a platform for the dramatic green flash we rarely see. We watch as a brilliant sun dips a final emerald curtsy on the stage of that distant horizon. With lazy days we sail north along the Thai coast finding protected little harbors to drop the anchor where we swim and snorkel in turquoise water with coral beds flourishing below. We walk through villages and hike along beaches. And always with these two friends, there is stimulating conversation by candlelight after dinner in the cockpit. We sail to the Surin Islands thirty miles from the Burma border and feel it's not safe to move closer to that country now in conflict with its neighbors. The two weeks go so fast. Since our visa will expire in a few days, we make our way back to Phuket and drop them off at a motel for their remaining two weeks of vacation.

The last minute stocking of supplies is a carefully carried out task this time. Our next port is a secluded spot in the world where no shops are seen and where no one lives. We are making ready for several months' stay in the Chagos Archipelago, an unheralded Shang-ri-la.

Squalls cause havoc en route to Chagos.

Don harvesting heart-of-palm.

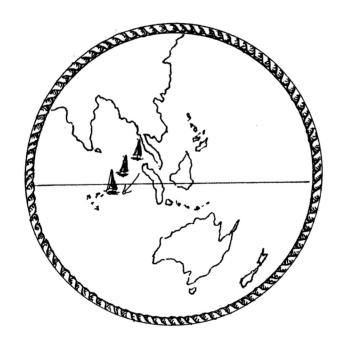

Chagos Archipeligo

CHAPTER 16
TOWARDS SHANGRI - LA

Six days after exchanging valentines, we sail out of Ao Chalong towards the sun as it makes that daily dash for the western horizon. It always takes special energy to compose my thoughts and use the knowledge I know to be true. The earth is spinning along its path to bask in the glory of that stationary glorious glowing globe. However, we continue to tell each other the sun is rising and then at day's end . . . there it goes setting once more.

The sails are filled, the Aries wind-vane is set. We sit back and enjoy the wind across the beam as Horizon heeds our directives for the course to Chagos. I raise the binoculars to take a last look at the outline of Phuket as it diminishes to a hazy patch where earth meets sky. When I scan north I am surprised to see another sail skimming the horizon. With a call on the radio to identify ourselves, '*Horizon* calling'. I ask about this other boat we see leaving the coast of Phuket, 'would you please identify?' In a moment the familiar voice of Jimmie is returning our inquiry. She says the good ship *Sunshine* is on her way to Chagos as well. This hasn't been planned. We both are delighted for this bit of karma. Our stay in Thailand revealed that karma plays a vital connection in the lives of every Thai person. It is not to be dismissed lightly with our western ideas. So here we are, four good friends sharing a 2000-mile journey to what will become one of the most outstanding experiences of this global adventure. It just might be karma.

As we set a course SW that takes us through the Nicobar Islands, we play leapfrog with *Sunshine* as we make one hundred thirty to one hundred forty-two miles daily for most of the first two weeks. The wind stays steady from the NE and finds us both using our colorful spinnakers to catch this wind abaft. The two of us keep daily radio checks and discover there are other boats out here on this same track, however over the horizon and out of view.

The decisions that were discussed last month at Kanda Bakery back there in Phuket, centered mainly about the courses that we were all thinking to make West. The big news worldwide has been the impending war in Iraq. We were unsure just what this will do to the passage through the Red Sea that many of us have been contemplating. Our own decision-making seesaws back and forth - whether to take the Red Sea track or make the longer trip around South Africa. With information at our fingertips when we scan the dial on the ham radio, we decide to wait to make that decision while we relax in Chagos.

Now we are beginning to be hit with squalls more often as the third week stretches into constant sail changes and reefing. *Sunshine* is the only other boat we've found that shares our watch-keeping schedule. So Jimmie and I, sharing the 7 p.m. to 1 a.m. watch, keep in touch about the weather we're experiencing. We describe the ferocity of the squall we're in, so the boat behind can make preparations for a more comfortable passage. *Sunshine* has torn her spinnaker to shreds in one of these blasts. Adding to their misery, a gust of wind blew the whole thing overboard in its sail bag. A glowing sun decorating that magnificent sail that many times heralded their arrival into an anchorage was now sinking to unimaginable depths.

There are only one hundred fifty miles to go. Another day and we should be seeing those low-lying atolls ahead. However, it's being denied us. Instead we battle days of doldrums snarled with thirty-five knot squalls. One of these blasts tears a rip in our jib sail. This mix of weather is killing our progress. But worst of all, we discover we have water in the fuel. Evidently when we filled the tank at the fuel barge in Phuket, we failed to tightly close the cap. With these squalls throwing green water across the top of the boat, this negligence finally takes its toll. We have been routinely limiting the time we run the engine in order to save fuel because we're planning a long stay in Chagos. Now this carelessness adds a new dimension to our dilemma. However, that's a problem to be solved at another time.

Right now we are sitting with *Sunshine* ahead, both of us turning erratic patterns as the wind has disappeared once more. With the sails aloft waiting for some response, we are banging about with the noise of halyards (lines used to haul the sails) and blocks creating an irritating annoyance. Meanwhile we contemplate how long we'll be sitting in this purgatory. It has to be the latitude 0 approaching that is making this weather so cranky. The equator, as we have moved across it north and south on our voyage, has proven to be irascible as it dishes out weather conditions.

With just two days of doldrums, the winds return once again. We're back to sailing and the chart shows we've moved south of the Maldives Islands. *Sunshine* has disappeared over the horizon and soon radios back they have our destination in sight. We've both been sailing on cobalt blue water, indicating it's amazing depth. *Sunshine* reports they are now crossing a shallow turquoise bank just twelve feet deep as they approach the Chagos atoll called Salomon Island. With more squalls being defined on the weather fax, Don decides to make a dash for this island. We will use the engine by attaching a hose to it from one of the jerry jugs of fuel that should be water free. We carry it below, connect the hose and we're off heading 'for the barn'. Wednesday, March 13, three weeks from Phuket, we motor through the passage into an oblong lagoon and drop the hook beside *Sunshine*.

Looking down the lagoon we see, in the distance, a small congregation of masts bobbing on the diamond studded bay. Don jumps into this clear water to check the anchor and comes up with a big grin on his face - there are grouper and snapper everywhere he looks. For the next several months the choice he has to make for the evening meal is determined by the menu we enjoyed last evening. The selection is as varied as any fish market. The rest of the menu after the first three weeks, however, becomes more limited as the fresh veggies are gone and the canned varieties come out of the bins. A few weeks later we are moving to an all white dinner array, white fish, white rice, and white heart of palm salad. This latter is harvested by the guys as they forage through the jungley island to cut down small coconut trees that grow in great abundance. At the base of an eight-inch trunk, at its core, there are tender pale green overlapping sheaves of thin leaves that compose the trunk. When these are cut loose and chopped fine, it makes a crunchy salad or slaw.

There are twenty sailboats that have managed to find this spot about a 1000 miles south of India in the middle of the Indian Ocean. We move down the lagoon to join this group of sailors. We hail from Australia, Germany, France, Sweden, Tasmania, Canada and South Africa. There are eight boats from the States. When making hikes into the center of Salomon Island we find the remains of a few buildings, a large cistern, the walls of a church and baking ovens. There is one house along a narrow path that now carries the logo, 'Chagos Yacht Club', painted on a gray weathered board nailed above the door. Walking inside, we examine the walls decorated with the names of yachts that have discovered this paradise.

This archipelago originally had natives living here. The English claim title to this 1000 square mile patch of islands. After WW II the Americans arranged with Britain, for a price, to use Diego Garcia as a military supply base, insisting that all the natives be moved away. This base is on an island in the southeast corner of the large archipelago. The remaining hundreds of small atolls were left isolated and abandoned. Many natives were sent to Mauritius and Union, two islands off the coast of Madagascar.

There are cisterns that we use to do our laundry, there are lemon trees and lemon grass growing that take care of 'scurvy' and there's a lovely beach that nicely accommodates our beach parties. Our Swedish solo sailor, Steve, has displayed his prowess at capturing the large coconut crabs. These crabs become a highlight of our barbecue feasts. Since we are here over Easter, a group gets busy to give a fresh coat of paint to the large cement cross that stands at the derelict dock. Later in the day, a festive spirit flourishes with an Easter parade. All the gals are modeling the original chapeau's they've created. The winner of a bottle of rum is Jane from Tasmanian 'Jasmine'. She tore apart her pillow to make two bunny ears and a fluffy tail that appropriately decorated her saucy bikini. No wonder she won. The judges, wearing their captain's hats, were all gaga. The rest of the gals wondered that bunny ears are considered a hat!

We still have two big problems to solve - watery fuel and a torn sail. A German boat, *Monte Cristo,* has a fifty-gallon plastic tank available that we can use to transfer and filter the water from the fuel. Our good friend, Mike, from *Loreley* of Lamut history, has volunteered to help us. His head is upside down in the fuel tank for hours as he cleans out the empty space. Finally with decanting back and forth through filters, the fuel looks useable once more. Steve, our Swedish friend, sews the sail.

Here-in lies a tale. With his sewing machine set up in his cockpit, Steve mended our large jib. Don went over to pick it up. The workmanship was top-notch so Don asked him if he would go over the seams on some of our other sails.

"Vell," he says "ve haven't talked aboot price yet."

"That's right," said Don, "How much do I owe you?".

"Vell, how does $175 sound?"

"Good."

Steve worked on the rest and we had our sails in good shape once again. When Don picked up the remaining sails and paid for them, Steve asked Don to remove a wen on his back. Don examined the spot. It looked like a sebaceous cyst about the size of a large grape. He suggested that Steve wait till Kenya to have it removed.

"No, I vant it out now." Don explained some of his medical equipment wasn't that sharp anymore and he wasn't sure about the effectiveness of his old anesthetics either.

"Not to worry, Don, I can stand it and I voon't sue you, I'm not from America."

"Okay, come over to our boat tomorrow and we'll do some surgery."

Don got busy boiling instruments, noted the anesthetic is out dated, laid out bandages and said he required my services to hand him equipment. Steve arrived and lay on his stomach in the cockpit. Don proceeded with shots to the area, warning Steve of his doubts about the effectiveness. The incision was made with some bleeding but Steve didn't seem in much pain. Don removed the wen and began stitching the wound together. He asked Steve how he's doing as blood trickled across his shoulder. "It's not too bad, keep going." Don said, with a twinkle in his eye, "Now Steve, I'm ready to stitch it together, but you know, we haven't discussed price yet." Ol' Steve's head popped up, "That's right, vee haven't, have vee," he said, looking concerned. Don chuckled and said, "That's okay, you teach me how to catch those giant coconut crabs you so successfully grab and we'll call it a deal." Steve grinned, "It's a deal." Steve healed nicely and Don learned the complicated process of catching these one-foot wide coconut crabs. He declares "catching fish is much simpler."

Don's services are called on for coral sores and infected ears as well. There is one call, as well, to *Loreley* to treat their cat for a paw smashed by a slamming hatch cover.

I start painting more seriously here and complete a dozen watercolors, 'Shades of Chagos'. I change my approach to painting. Usually I sit at a location to paint, but found the results discouraging. Here, I stay 'down below' on the boat. After sketching the scene, I use my mind's eye and color memory of scenes to complete the picture. The images floating across the paper give me more satisfaction with this simple change. I enjoy a new realization of both shape and color.

It's about a month now that we've enjoyed Salomon Island and its lagoon. We decide to explore an adjacent atoll, ten miles west, Peros Banhos. We anchor beside *Loreley* and *Delanie* with Bob, a solo sailor from St. Louis, aboard. While the fellows are diving and fishing, Gwen, from Loreley and I find papaya trees on the island with small fruits to harvest making a nice addition to our diets. Mike on *Loreley* is an outstanding fisherman. Whether spear fishing or trolling, he always returns to his boat well supplied and shares with less capable providers. Gwen started canning and pickling the abundance of fish. After four days here we move west inside this large reef that outlines the atoll.

While we're anchored in the NW corner, we receive a message on the radio that a large U.S. tanker is on it's way from Diego Garcia to bring British officers to our flotilla. They will stamp our passports. **AND** they have agreed to take any mail we want sent. So Don and I are busy writing as many letters as we can, especially from this most special place. Soon we hear the motor of a large military dinghy making its way through the pass. We are the only boat in this corner. They approach and ask permission to come a board. Dressed in their crisp white uniforms, they present a spit and polish aboard our modest vessel, an honor new to our yacht. Our passports are stamped. They relax with the lemonade we serve, while we enjoy sharing our voyage experiences. When they learn Don is a physician, they hurry back to the tanker and return with replacements for a lot of the outdated medical supplies we have. Oh, Steve, if only - The crowd still at Salomon were privileged to receive steaks and ice cream when the ship arrived in their midst. . Lucky guys!

As we continue moving around the atoll following the line of islands, each offers a surprise. At one, *Sunshine* joins us to hunt for orange trees that we've been told are somewhere in the jungley forest. It takes us two days following donkey trails to finally find them. We spied a couple sway-backed wild donkeys eyeing us from a distance. With supplies getting low it's worth the hunt; the tart juice making a refreshing drink. Another small island displays the deep holes dug along the beach where giant sea turtles have laid their eggs. The last isle we anchor beside has the most beautiful sandy beaches with a garden of coral heads and sponges flourishing in the clear turquoise water. Don, Jim and Jimmie from *Sunshine* are diving everyday. Don has to chuckle at an experience Jim has under water.

Both of these guys are good marksmen and bring nice catches back for dinner. Usually hovering in the background may be a shark or two, and maybe a barracuda, to watch the strange behavior. Since these giants are well fed here the fellows don't pay much attention to them. However, they will come and snatch your catch if you don't get it out of the water and in the dinghy right away. This day, Jim wants to practice his shots and has decided taking aim, underwater, at a spot on a soft coral. Each time he shoots, a shark, hearing the ping of the gun, dashes in to grab the fish, turns and looks about, then swims away. Jim continues three more times. Each time the shark comes in for the kill, there is no fish. On Jim's 4th shot the shark hovers in the background, shakes his body, as if to say 'what's with this guy, he can't hit anything,' and peels off to richer pastures.

Our supplies are getting low. I begin painting small watercolors as barter. These are exchanged for flour and sugar, and best of all, Bob's great sourdough starter and bread recipe. We share anchorages here with our special friends and enjoy new ones.

Fred and Nan on *Winsome* become good sailing buddies here and beyond.

The last week we spend at the tiny Isle de Fouquet by ourselves. Everyone else has sailed on. On my daily beach walks I discover exquisite sponges dried and littering the beach. I've never seen any like this before. The sponges mimic the shapes of shells and coral. They're about the size of a man's fist. I fill a garbage bag with their beauty, and could have filled ten bags. There's no room on the boat for excess. This one bag will even take some accommodating. Snorkeling over the lagoon, we can see the live sponges scattered across the bottom.

Don makes one more trip to find some heart of palm for the next leg of our journey. We must get going. He finds a nice sized trunk right at the beach edge. He misjudges his swing with the machete, however, and slashes his knee. He missed the tree trunk completely. I immediately dash down the beach to get the dinghy and take him back aboard *Horizon*. His knee is bleeding profusely. He manages to get aboard to sit in the cockpit. Instructing me which instruments to get ready, I sterilize them in boiling water. He declares he can stitch the wound himself. Thankfully, we now have fresh xylocaine. Without a flinch, he proceeds to make six nice neat stitches across his knee, thankful the cut hasn't severed any nerves or tendons. After closing the wound he has a sip of Madagascar rum to reward this job well-done. That rum, a gift from *Monte Cristo* would take the chrome off a car bumper - purely high octane. We remain here, alone.

As the wound heals, we take this opportunity to look about us to appreciate fully the gift of this very special paradise. It's hard to leave this unspoiled spot with its beautiful colors; turquoise waters, golden sand beaches with green waving palm fronds that beckon coolness. We have enjoyed the freshest fish each day. There has been some food available, breadfruit, papayas, fern fiddles and coconut crab. The absence of any official hassle or language problems has all contributed to the most laid-back place we'll ever experience.

We have treasured every day. At night, there is a depth of color to that deep blue sky overhead that gives a special meaning to eternity. It seems pierced with millions of pinholes that allow a spatial radiance to shimmer light to our small boat below . . . starshine. With no city lights to dim their brilliance, this royal robe stretches over us with its embroidery of twinkling stars that challenges us to know more about these heavens. By gazing north, we see the Big Dipper as it stands steady on its handle at the horizon. Turning our gaze South, we enjoy another signature gem on the night's tapestry. The Southern Cross is hanging there with its familiar tilt a thumb's height above that southern rim. We can grasp them both here at five degrees south of the equator to hold in our hearts an experience few realize.

Regretfully, on Wednesday, June the 12th, after almost three months cradled in these beautiful anchorages, we work our way between the coral reef that releases us to continue our journey of discovery.

As we make our way West the winds favor us with their eastern component. We revel in this auspicious beginning. However, after only one day, we are abruptly faced with the fickle ways of the wind. It veers to the SSW, frustrating our progress towards our waypoint. With the help of the engine we motor-sail for a day. Then, once more, these unpredictable winds back. Now we are off and running for successive days of glorious sailing. We are averaging seven knots an hour - day after glorious day. There are times, as we rush down the face of a huge swell, the knot meter reads ten and eleven knots. The wind persists at a steady twenty knots and continues to fill the jib as it pulls us along in its exuberance. There are some breaking waves that rattle along the gunwales, but we stay dry in the cockpit as we hold on for this exhilarating ride. The days are as sunny as our dispositions. We add the music of Mozart, Debussy and other favorite composers to accompany us while the waves add their own resonant background. The nights are gloriously clear with moonlight blessing us. Luminescence glows a trail behind us as plankton lights its fiery display of brilliant streaks through the waves in our wake. We leave a comet trail glowing behind us. The Aries wind vane is a real blessing on this tack, as it maintains the heading. If we'd be standing back there at the helm, we would be wet. The waves rise steep behind us, then slide under us to curl over the taff-rail, the low rail around the cockpit stern, with their foamy remnant. one hundred sixty-two to one hundred seventy miles a day define the distance log as we become a part of this Indian Ocean Odyssey.

It's June 26, just fourteen days since Chagos bid us farewell. The coast of Kenya is fast approaching. The sat-nav continues to be erratic in the information we receive. Sometimes it's eight hours between fixes. We can see the lights of Mombasa at midnight. Now we need to be careful as we are swept north along the coast with the Mozambique Current. It could push us beyond the small harbor of Kilifi we are seeking. We down the jib to continue with only the staysail flying. Hopefully, this will slow our progress in anticipation of a dawn arrival.

It is daybreak. We decide to take the chance that this is the entrance we're looking for. By reconciling the dead reckoning we're using and the instructions for landmarks we've received from other boats, we can see range markers in line with a red roof ashore that declare an entrance through the reef. With a reassuring call on the ham radio to 'Kiore', Tony Britchford assures us we've found the right spot. He instructs us to 'carry-on' following the buoys then make a sharp turn to port where the Mtwapa Creek will open before us. This will take us under a bridge to the anchorage at the Swynford Boatyard. 'Jambo, Welcome!' He greets us.

The creek opens before us with high cliffs on each side. Passing the splendid homes built along the cliffs, we see bougainvillea of every hue, bursting in bloom to gracefully outline the arches of the distinctive architecture. The baobab tree, with its most unusual profile, stands majestically in a few places along the creek. When it is dressed with a leafy top, it reminds me of a child's drawing with its sturdy trunk supporting a ball of green for its crowning shape. Later, when the leaves are gone, you think surely its growing upside down with the bare branches looking like a root system exposed to the sky - a strange looking tree.

Kilifi is a quiet, dusty little village that offers a lot of amenities for the sailing visitor. The main street, about a block long, supports a bank, two grocery stores, a meat market and a nice fresh vegetable market. There are also vendors that offer fresh shrimp and a variety of fresh fruits along the way. We are delighted to discover a tiny Indian cafe serving delicious samosas, the delicate filled pastry that we have been enjoying since Hong Kong. With a bit more searching we find a laundry that offers sun-dried clothes on the many lines stretched across their yard. After months at Chagos hand washing our laundry, I thought a machine might brighten some of our clothes. This was a good decision, but we chuckled when we picked up our clean laundry pile. Pinned to the top is a note, *'Please, Please and Please, we remind you to know that we don't wash ladies under wares. Thank you.'* That's fine, we are pleased with the bright colors restored to our T-shirts and who sees my underwares anyway.

The generous hospitality of the Britchfords, Tony and Daphne, continues throughout our three month stay. They have lived in Kenya over thirty years. He was born in England and spent years as a pilot with an African Airway, servicing countries along the east coast of Africa. Daphne, with her gracious ways, was born in South Africa and balances nicely the sometimes brusque manner of Tony. They serve us delicious teas and dinners and taxi us to town to meet buses or to ferry fuel in jugs from town to the dock. We enjoy many comfortable, casual conversations in their lovely home high on the bluff along the creek.

In order to complete our customs clearance we need to take the bus south about thirty-five miles to Mombasa. This bustling, dusty city built centuries ago on an island still bears a mystic quality along the cobblestone streets. Evidence of Portuguese influence is defined in the architecture of the old city. Its ancient Fort Jesus reminds the visitor of ancient battles fought here. The city, rich with history, stretches along the ocean where waves dash themselves to pieces on the rock-strewn shore. A few sailboats have ventured in to the Yacht Club here, but rumors of theft, noise and shark infested, garbage-strewn waters just don't appeal to us. There are big dhows and small ships unloading along the pungent docks. Here near the equator, the days are hot as the noon sun bears down to draw forth the steamy and spicy features of this seafarers' province. Before returning to Kilifi, we make arrangements to take a safari later in July.

On July 10 we begin our inland excursion. We take the overnight train that climbs slowly west to the interior city of Nairobi, the capitol of Kenya. This railway lumbers along dragging a history of danger that was expensive to men and material, marauding lions killing workers as fast as they were supplied. That's the past, now our concern is several delays along the way that makes the scheduled 9:00 a.m. arrival late by 4 hours. We are a bit anxious because our seats are reserved on the Best Safari Company van that is to leave at noon. Not to worry, the Best Co. stands behind its name and meets us at the train station with a sign directing us to our noisy group. The van is full of boisterous and happy Dutchmen, our fellow passengers. We're on our way to Amboseli National Park. After eight hours of driving through golden plains, across dry riverbeds and, at one point, a sudden reverse to stay clear of an angry female elephant, we drive into camp. Each couple is assigned a pup tent where we spread out our own sleeping bags. As we meet fellow travelers, we head for the chow line to enjoy a really delicious meal being prepared over an open fire. We sit on logs around the campfire to savor plates of beef stew and biscuits. Overhead, a tree stretches branches decorated with the nests of the golden weaverbird. The small globe-shaped hanging baskets of woven twigs gently swing with the evening breeze catching smoke curling from the fire. We share this campground with six vanloads of visitors. The park is located along the southern boundary of Kenya and offers a spectacular view of Mt. Kilamanjaro, 'The Mountain of Cold Devils'. This shy mountain rarely shows its full beauty. Usually a mantle of clouds drifts over its head to rest on the steep shoulders. A response to those Cold Devils? This magnificence rises from hills in Tanzania, a less prosperous country to the south.

We are up early to be ready for the six a.m. schedule. We climb aboard the van and track through the Reserve to view the array of wildlife. With the rising sun hi-lighting the unsuspecting prey, they move about to forage. There will be a second excursion planned for later in the day, about four p.m. During the heat of the day nothing is moving, including us. We take advantage of this time to visit with some of the Masai tribesmen and women who come to the camp to sell trinkets and share stories. The women come with babies cradled on their backs, comfortable in the hammock affair supporting the tiny body. The tall women are adorned with bangles and bracelets. Their necks display collars of beaded strands that create a tower of design from their clavicle to earlobes. These earlobes are stretched as they hang in loops that swing with more beaded or heavy, designed rings of stones and feathers. Taking the beauty they see around them, they are fulfilling some inner longing to make it a portion of their lives.

By four o'clock we are bundled into the van. Its pop-top open allows all of us to stand for photo taking while in the protection of its chassis. Our driver moves cautiously as he makes way along the dirt roads under the afternoon sun. Suddenly he wanders off through the tall grass. Before us is a front row view of a pride of lions, stretching and lounging under thorny bushes. Moving across a dry and dusty lakebed, we stop to watch a large herd of elephants shuffling through the cloud of dust they're creating. Amboseli protects large herds of elephants. They move across the bare dusty plain with the young ones sheltered in their midst. The vegetation is meager. The few trees, mostly the thorny acacia trees, look forlorn, stripped of much of their foliage. Over some scrubby shrubs, the tall necks of a large herd of giraffes appear. With their bodies concealed behind the scrub and the long necks swaying as they survey their surroundings, my imagination fancies a strange garden of waving blossoms on sturdy, decorated stems growing in the midst of swirling dust. The reason for the taller trees looking bare and desolate, is easily understood. The van moves for a better view. Here we can we see giraffes stretching those long necks between their forelegs spread wide, to reach the grasses tufted over the dry ground at their feet. The optical illusion of a moving field of grain reveals the graceful stride of a large herd of zebras, their lined coats challenging our eyes to try and focus on this optical illusion in motion. Briefly, and only briefly, we catch a glimpse of a tiger in search of prey with its stealthy prowl through the tall grass. They are rarely seen anymore.

When we return to camp, we are granted a view of Kilamanjaro with its mantle of clouds lifted, to reveal its majesty in the hazy afternoon glow. By the time I dash to get the camera set up, the mountain is hiding again under the clouds. After two days traveling across this dry lakebed of Amboseli, seeing the free range of these magnificent beasts, we are on the road back to Nairobi.

Another van is now taking us along the rim of the Rift Valley, until we descend the steep walls of this awesome crack in the African tectonic plate to the Valley below. We are en route to Lake Nakuru where blue-green algae flourishes in an alkaline composition, attracting the thousands of flamingoes feeding on this richness. A pink cloud hovers over the whole area, as these flocks in constant movement, search for a spot at this bountiful buffet. This lake is one of seven that stretch across the floor of the Great Rift Valley. Eons ago they all flowed into the Nile River until changes in the topography, with the shifting plates closed this access. The result was accumulations of minerals and salts that have rendered the waters undrinkable, but provide the right formula for preserving bones along the shores. This area has been the source of discoveries by the Leakey family to mankind's early development.

It is along the high rim with its fertile soil that the vast expanses of gardens and fields proclaim the country's greatest source of vegetables. While down on the floor of this long valley, extending more than five thousand miles, there is a mix of arable land with livestock and grazing fields covering the vast territory.

The road we are taking is mostly potholes held together with a bit of macadam. We are off the road more than we are on it. We have punctured the gas tank as we careened into one of these holes. This gives us a chance to visit with some of the Masai tribesmen who are standing here at the gas station while we wait for repairs. They carry themselves with such pride and dignity. This becomes even more striking because of their height, sometimes seven feet. The favorite stance assumed by this tall warrior, attired in the red cloak thrown across his chest, reminds me of a stork. Standing erect on one leg, he rests that hip against the walking stick he always carries. Then, bending the other leg to rest the foot on the weight-bearing knee, he catches the pose of that statuesque bird in repose. An ornate headdress of feathers, usually black, sometimes is worn, contributing still more to the silhouette of the large bird. They can be seen standing for hours in this pose. At later breaks during safari, we view this striking profile as they tend their herd of cattle, a herd that denotes wealth. Because of our delay, it is after dark when we drive through the gate into the Masai Mara Preserve. Here we enjoy our dinner in an open pavilion before finding our assigned pup tent once more.

It is early rising once more. We're in the van and on our way across the vast and rolling grass covered plains with the distant outline of low escarpments just visible in the purple morning haze. We stand in the van parked only ten feet away from lions preening and licking their paws after a recent feed. The van radio announces the location of a pair of white Rhino. We move cross the veldt to join a half dozen other vans to view this seldom seen giant. Second only to the elephant in size, our driver remains cautious. They are known to charge, even though their eyesight is poor. Continuing across the grassy space we enjoy the exuberance of graceful gazelles. As if on springs or pogo sticks, they are a herd in motion, flashing their white rumps as they make leaping strides across the savanna. We see small herds of wildebeest. Our guide tells us that later this month, stampeding herds, under enormous clouds of dust, will move north from Tanzania. They are a comical combination of parts. A head, with its mandarin-like mask, is far too big for the spindly legs supporting it over massive shoulders that disappear to a meager haunch. Their movements make you wonder if their brains are engaged. They lower this whimsical head, arch the back, and while bucking up and down in place, they stumble and fall over themselves. Others can be seen just charging around in circles like a dog chasing its tail, all the while grunting Gnu- gnu. Ah-ha . . this is the source of my favorite word when winning at Scrabble.

A last stop at a placid river has us staring at the smooth water as it begins roiling with shiny black hides emerging from the muddy swirls. The place is teeming with Hippos, some with only two small eyes that periscope at the surface. Surrounding them nearby, others display huge pink mouths as they yawn to the heavens. On the banks are alligators basking in the sun, with which they share this watery acreage. Surrounded by all these animals, we've also been privileged to find birds we've never seen before. The secretary bird and the marabou stork especially strike unusual profiles. We've enjoyed the springbok and topi, a leopard and a dik-dik all in a setting that reminds us of the variety of landscapes, seascapes and inhabitants that share presence with us on this small oasis in the universe.

We are granted permission to visit a Masai krall, or village, that is within the boundaries of the Reserve. Earlier, I had arranged to have sent to me several bags of kids' T-shirts from the States. I plan to take these along to give to the children in the kraal. We walk through soft mud mixed with manure as we enter the gate between the woven brush barricade that encircles this small village of about a dozen mud huts. At night the cattle are driven into the kraal and contribute to this muddy morass we are tiptoeing through. We meet the chief and I explain that I have clothes to share. Almost immediately I am lost in the center of a swarm of tall women grabbing into the bags I carry. The chief comes to my rescue and gets some kind of order restored. In return, each woman gives me a beaded bracelet for the gift she takes. Don, meanwhile, has been invited into one of the mud huts, circular in shape with a thatch-covered cone-shaped roof. With only the door to provide light, the interior is dark and smoky contributing to a strong pungency from the dung-mud floor.

The next morning as we are squatting by our pup-tent and brushing our teeth, we see a golden globe rising from the western horizon. We are confused. It makes no sense. The sun is rising from the west this morning? We stand to stare, along with the other campers. Slowly the mystery is solved as a giant hot air balloon glides over head, its golden globe shimmering. Its dragon-like breath, as the burner comes to life, offers the only sound across the quiet dawn. We sit back on our haunches and watch it pass over our heads. Those guests up there with ample budgets, are enjoying a champagne breakfast while scanning from aloft these vast plains as the beautiful beasts are brushed with a radiant sunrise. We pack our belongings, leave the tent behind and gather together new pictures etched upon our memories as we ponder the potholes on the road back to Nairobi.

After checking into the hotel, we make a phone call home and learn that our first grandson has been born while we were watching the lions. Charles Donald Bruer has captured the name, Donald, of both his grandpas, thus fixing their presence for another generation. Our steps are light as we walk down the busy street in Nairobi. Adding to the joy of the day, we are looking forward to visiting with Dr. Mary Oyer, my favored fine-arts Professor in college who helped shape many of my ideas about creativity. She has spent many summers here studying the tribal music with its intricate rhythm patterns. She has taught at the University in Nairobi as well. When we knew she would be here during our stay, we arranged to meet for dinner and good conversation. Ready to return to Mombasa we found no train available. This gives us a chance to survey this unique landscape from the air on the flight east. Then a bus ride to Kilifi has us aboard *Horizon* once more. Now I make preparations to fly home in a week.

This month spent getting acquainted with new grandchildren and renewing ties with the family after a long absence revives the sap of a family tree that continues to nurture a healthy relationship among the branches. The grandchildren are certainly the blossoms on our tree. I enjoyed every minute.

The return trip has me loaded with new gadgets that give the Heathrow airport security officers fits. I try to explain to confused agents the GPS navigating instrument plus two large spools of electric wire that I'm carrying. This GPS (Global Positioning System) is a satellite-based navigation system developed by the U.S. Dept of Defense that provides an accurate and simplified method of navigation. It's been recently released by the military for use by the general public. After much discussion they finally decide I'm not the mad bomber. They let me pass. Dashing around with my bags banging my shins, I barely make the final connection at Nairobi for Mombasa. It's a feeling of relief to see Don waiting to ease me back to our singular lifestyle at the end of the bumpy bus ride to Kilifi.

He had arranged to have a carved bas-relief molding in ironwood completed in time to celebrate my birthday. This simple and elegantly designed strip of wood completed by a local carver depicts Kenyan native profiles beautifully carved beside the flowers and trees of their surroundings. It's beautiful. We use it as a 'fiddle' that holds our shelf of books in place. Each time as I pass it, with strokes along its smooth contours, I'm reminded of the splendor we have enjoyed as each culture strives to express in distinctive ways, a common desire to depict this beauty that surrounds us all.

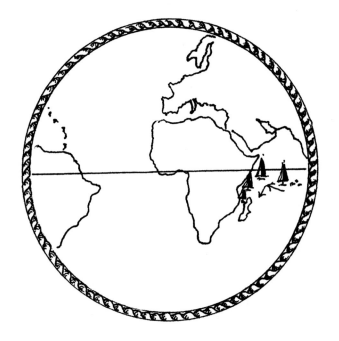

Kenya to Madagascar to Durban

CHAPTER 17
THE RED SEA OR THE CAPE?

Although it's not November, the Britchfords invite several of the boat crews to enjoy a Thanksgiving dinner at their home this cool September evening. The weather is nudging all of us to study our charts and make plans for the next leg of this water safari. The decision has been made. *Horizon* will make the path south around the tip of this magnificent continent, instead of a thrust thru the Red Sea. Now with the Iraq armed conflict begun we don't care to dodge the warships in that area. We stock up on the good veggies here and the inexpensive but delicious beef fillets. We fill the fuel and water tanks before bidding these gracious hosts farewell.

We leave Kilifi at sunset Thursday, September 19, for an overnight sail north along the coast to Lamu. This is a side trip to a fascinating town with a Portuguese atmosphere that has retained an Old World culture. It's a swift kick to our hull as the current pushes us to move even faster than the six knots showing on the meter. By morning we are easing our way along the passage into the harbor of this ancient Arabian looking village. The harbor presents a picturesque setting with the distinctive dhows scattered around its fringe. The streets boast no cars to frighten the small donkeys. Their small hooves clip-clop over the cobblestones as they smartly trot along the narrow streets. They carry bundles of firewood or gunnysacks of leafy vegetables on their backs. Walking along the shaded streets, Arab Muslims garbed in their long white gowns and white skullcaps define a subtlety to this landscape. The whole atmosphere, with sun motes filtering through the lacy branches of the trees onto filigreed shadowy paths below, has a rather dusty, even dirty, appearance. There's an ambiance of mystery emerging from dark doorways. Old buildings that held slaves in squalid, crowded, windowless rooms for endless weeks as they waited to be shipped across the sea are vivid reminders of this heartless saga in man's history.

We join *Vida Nueva* to take our dinghies through a grassy marsh to visit the ruins of an old Arab village, that centuries ago in early Oman Sultan history, bustled as a vibrant trading center. Now only low ruins remain where goats wander among the stones. Last preparations are made to leave for points south and beyond Kenya. We check out of Lamu at the easily accessible customs office located here.

This trip south is slow going. Where the current pushed us almost too fast a week ago, that same current is pushing just as hard against our progress as we retrace those miles going south. We spend three days tacking back and forth across this current to finally pull into Wasin Island, the last offshore island at the southern boundary of Kenya. We are granted permission to visit an underwater park just offshore. The snorkeling here is a disappointment after the vibrant beauty of Palau and Chagos. This coral suffers from its proximity to the mainland. As a result, it lacks the variety and beauty of those earlier stops.

Just a day sail finds us in Tanzanian waters and sailing into the well-protected harbor at Tanga. Doing the required paperwork, we are scolded for not having the proper papers indicating our stop at Wasin. We shrug our shoulders as if we aren't aware there is a problem. I get the impression from this black official that he really questions the intelligence of the white race. The whole immigration process here has been long, confusing and frustrating, with excessive charges demanded. But the Yacht Club here has been most friendly. When they learned we had just enjoyed the hospitality of Daphne and Tony, the floodgates of generosity poured forth. A tour of the island and a bountiful BBQ send us on our way with good feelings.

Pemba Island belongs to Tanzania. It boasts more of an allegiance, however to Zanzibar, that other offshore island that proclaims itself a separate territory from Tanzania. It's a muddled political arrangement that raises occasional mayhem. Nan and Fred aboard *Winsome* are keeping radio contact with us from Pemba. They exclaim about the beautiful coral and the unspoiled beauty of the place. We are on our way, and by nightfall have dropped our anchor beside them. The beds of coral surrounding the island are huge and demand a close watch as we find the path through their jumble. But it does look quiet and lovely. We explore the coral beds with snorkels the next day. Since *Winsome* plans to leave for the Comoros Islands, we decide to take care of customs and spend a couple of days here. The customs process is again a hassle, but with patience it all resolves itself to their satisfaction - but still more scolding. They wonder why we can't seem to understand their convoluted customs process. This 'Isle of Cloves' holds mysteries of its own. Finally cleared, we sail back to the spot we had enjoyed earlier that day to drop the anchor. We're now completely alone in this bay.

The sun is just setting. I start cooking the evening meal when Don announces a big native wooden skiff is roaring down upon us. Before we can scramble topsides, six men are aboard, three of them carrying machine guns. They announce they are the Pemba Navy. 'Do you question that?' 'No' Don declares 'have seats in the cockpit'! They are dressed in shaggy jeans and torn T-shirts. Immediately, they take seats in the cockpit, guns across their laps. Their spokesman, Mr. Buss, his red eyes poorly focused and his speech slurred, inquires about our landing permits and immigration papers. Thank goodness we can hand them the required papers. Mr. Buss is small in stature but big in cockiness. He proceeds to show us just how much he knows about any subject that is discussed. After a half-hour of this showmanship, the rest of the guys having remained quiet, Mr. Buss demands to use the VHF radio to call the Navy office. He insists on going below and makes quite a show of calling headquarters. There is no response from them; "they must be busy," he says. We assume he's checking to see if our radio works. All the while, he's looking around the boat. Then he asks for booze. We tell him we never carry any. 'Well, do you have cigarettes?' We recently purchased a carton, realizing barter is almost impossible without 'a smoke' to offer, and gave him several packs. His response is, 'You expect these few packs to satisfy my whole crew?' So we give him the entire carton. 'Well, do you have cola?' Don said 'Sure,' and moved to the storage bin under the berth to retrieve some cans. This gives Buss a chance to push against me. As he shoves me hard against the stove, he mumbles something sounding like, 'I could sure use a woman like you.' I shove back just as Don walks to the galley - Buss stands clear. After gathering the cans, he returns to the cockpit with his men. He continues to preen and boast his many talents. After what seems an eternity, they leave, assuring us of their protection. It was hard to tell if Buss was on drugs or drunk - our guess is drugs.

Needless to say, the night passes slowly. We raise the stairs at the companionway that block entry there, lock all the hatches and carry to bed a 2x4 board that might fend off an intruder. We have no tacks to throw on the deck as Joshua Slocum did to thwart invaders. There's no way we can leave in the dark because of that treacherous reef. We hunker down and keep a close watch to wait for the dawn.

At first light we are out of there. We make our way around the south coast of Pemba heading for Mayotte. Knowing that Tanzania has been trying to improve its image to the tourist, Don has written a letter to their tourist board describing the confusing customs procedures with bribes expected and the disturbing experience with the Pemba Navy. He suggests some kind of identifying papers or badges might be used to ascertain the identity of official personnel, as a step in assuring the tourist a safe visit while in Tanzania. There were several letters posted from many boats to this office complaining of the procedures faced upon entry.

Never has a coast hung on to us as tenaciously as this Pemba Island is doing. There is a vicious current streaming against us that keeps that same rock on shore fixed in my vision as the hours trudge by. The island isn't that large but continues to hover on our horizon all day. It only reluctantly releases its grip, sliding past us as darkness falls. I've never been so glad to be rid of a place as I am of this dark port.

Mayotte is only 500 miles to the southeast and should offer its protection in a week. But here at the north end of Madagascar there are many currents swirling and curving that continue to cause havoc for sailors. We are not to be denied their provocation. After ten days of bashing into head seas, with uncooperative currents adding their measure as well, we manage to find the pass into the large lagoon surrounding the islands of Mayotte.

This French protected atoll is one of the Comoros group of islands. The remaining islands had elected to be independent of French administration, but Mayotte stands alone and offers a military base for the French in this part of the world. With the good help of *Monte Cristo* as our translator, we easily accomplish the customs formalities with 'Charlie Tango'. He is the local official with a reputation for fast and easy clearance. There are quite a few of our sailing buddies here that we haven't seen since Chagos. *Winsome* is anchored close by as well. We join Nan and Fred to take the ferry from the anchorage to the main island. Here on this crowded ferry we see the startling adornment worn by the local women. Using face paint, some of their black faces are covered with stark white paint, while others use a yellow ochre pigment. Either one creates a mask-like appearance. The eyes stare out from this startling mask in dark shadows. To add to the effect, some eyes are outlined in black kohl with details that make each face unique in its display. There are a few women that punctuate their faces with large spots and dots using this paint. Beauty certainly is in the eye of the beholder, and here beauty is defined with a new, or perhaps, very old tradition. To complete this dramatic presence, they wear a pile of cloth on their heads. A length of brightly colored cloth is deftly dropped on their crown. The result is quite attractive. If I were to try this, it would look exactly like a pile of cloth dumped on my head. Yet, somehow, they wear this millinery construction with assured *haute couture*. To be in an unfamiliar land whose habit of mind is framed in another dimension forces me to challenge my stereotypes.

We are delighted to find a small market place with a nice variety of fresh vegetables and fruit. We purchase modest amounts to replenish our dwindling stores. It's a pleasant village with a few cars moving about on the hardtop roads. As we explore the streets we find the yachties together on the porch of a grocery store enjoying cool drinks. We join them and listen to the stories of passage making that bear out the contrary water challenges we faced. Taking a look inside the small grocery, we see the shelves are stacked full - money won't go far here. The French pates and cheeses plus just plain staples all hold a high price tag, reminiscent of that Tahiti shopping experience. So it's back to the crispy baguettes that will be our 'local food' while we tarry here. We do splurge a bit to enjoy some cheese and pate with a bottle of French wine and crusty bread - one of the world's finest repasts.

Sharing departure decisions with *Winsome*, the two of us explore the surrounding lagoon then stop at a lacy waterfall cascading over a cliff rising high above the shoreline. We can stand below the misty spray and frolic as we bathe in the fresh water just a stone's throw from our boats - a good opportunity to haul out the laundry and finish that long overdue task as well. Meanwhile, Don and Fred are working on the tappets on our engine that have been causing problems. We decide to follow their lead to Madagascar. Three days later, with a lot of squalls demanding constant sail changes, we drop the anchor beside Winsome at Mitsio Island just off the NW coast of Madagascar.

We are in a deep bay that offers great protection. A few grass huts seek shelter under the trees at the water's edge. There are cattle grazing on the grassy hill across the bay. It's not long until a small dugout canoe, with two boys about ten years old, comes paddling to our side. Words are not going to help here. Madagascar has developed a difficult language that few of us ever comprehend. But smiles and hand signals do wonders towards understanding. Floating around in the water in the bottom of their dugout canoe are several very splendid murex shells. They hold two of them up for us to examine and pantomime eating movements. I find the cans of corned beef we had purchased especially for barter and give them four cans and hand them each cookies. They smile and the exchange is made. They wave as they paddle back to the huts. The next day the boys are back with bananas to barter. This time I give them empty mayonnaise jars and cookies once more. We had been told the natives are anxious to get containers of any size to store rice and flour. I'd been saving jars for just such an occasion. Later in the evening an old man paddled out to visit. Proceeding in this sign language mode, he begins to rub his body, arms, face and bare belly. Don and I try to understand what he is asking for as he patiently continues scrubbing away, when it dawns on us, perhaps he is asking for soap. We give him a half-dozen bars of soap and several towels. He nods with a big grin - we have established communication. The next morning as we are raising the anchor, he brings three large papayas to us and lays them in the gunwale, shaking his head when I offer more jars. I believe he meant this as payment for the soap.

Winsome is already heading around the head of the bay as we follow. It is sunny with light breezes that promise pleasant sailing the short leg to another island nearby. We overtake them. Later, we look behind and see they are not moving. Their sails are down. A call on the radio brings no response. We turn back to get close. Both of them are on the foredeck struggling with an enormous fish. They had been dragging a line out of the bay and soon after we passed them, they hooked a six-foot sailfish. The freeboard on their boat is quite high. Nan almost gave up trying to haul the huge fish aboard, while Fred had it gaffed to hold it close to the hull. Finally, with the fish aboard and photos taken, we both sail on to BeJesus Island. It has been christened this name by the yachties because none of us can pronounce its Madagascar name. We anchor in a small lagoon surrounded with coral that just accommodates our two boats. It's a pretty place, with large sand carved rocks looking like dramatic pieces of sculpture standing tall along the beach. The local fishermen use the island as a stopover between fishing trips. No one lives here. We enjoy several days here, with beautiful clear water once again and now familiar colors splashed across our canvas.

Don jumps in the water with his facemask to watch the mating rite of a pair of large turtles. The water stays churned as the two paddle in circles with the female submerged for long periods. We have seen this watery dance in other lagoons. From our perspective, it always looks like the female struggles for air to breathe. No doubt the process is successful, as the large nests dug ashore are testimony to her fertility. At one village in Micronesia, the men used this occurrence as an appropriate time to hunt turtles. We cheered when the turtles were able to elude the hunters' noose.

The evenings here at anchor, however, have us tossing and bouncing about with a chop that seems to aggravate this particular patch of water. We decide to leave in the morning and make our way to Hellsville, the port of entry for Madagascar.

We follow our charts to sail between islands and around the corner to Nosi Bei, a spot favored by tourists. Along the way, we hear Fred talking to *Sunshine* on the radio. We are shocked to hear the tragic news that Steve had been found murdered on his boat - our Norwegian friend, Steve, who mended our sails. We are stunned. Fred likewise, with grief sounding in his voice, soon ended the contact. We were unable to find the exact details of the tragedy, but pieces of the story just made the puzzle even more of a mystery. Steve was a solo sailor who had always warned anyone listening about the dangers of taking crew, a stranger crew, aboard. Weeks before we arrived, there was quite a gathering of our sailing group from Chagos here in Nosi Bei with him. He had had a rough crossing from Chagos. It was a slow trip for him. His food ran low so that he looked pretty haggard when he finally dropped his hook beside his friends here. They all stayed together for a week or so while they moved around the area to different anchorages. Unknown to him and to those anchored around him, it is thought, a native stole aboard, and lying concealed, forced him to sail down the coast of Madagascar. He left after the other boats and no one was aware he was in trouble. His boat, anchor down, was found at a village south of Nosi Bei with the motor still running. The native evidently went ashore telling the authorities the owner would be in later. When he didn't come ashore a skiff was dispatched and his bloody body was found aboard. He was a quiet, gentle man of modest means and truly missed by all of us who had shared his generous and warm ways. Norway sent investigators here to question the local community but the culprit disappeared into the jungle and the mystery remains. This news keeps us cautious as we visit this place. The government, in disarray at this time and financially bankrupt, is unable to pay any of its civil servants - always a recipe for trouble.

We go ashore at Hellsville and find an interesting village flaunting old-world charm. Decrepit, pillared houses with mold etched in patterns on the plastered walls, line a shady boulevard that speak of a onetime grandeur now reclining as gracefully as possible in its golden years. There is a feeling of the New Orleans

French Quarter, a breathing of similar ancestors here so many miles apart. It's pleasant walking the tree lined streets. We pass great piles of rice displayed on sheets spread on the sidewalk. Along the way we are directed to the large shed that is the marketplace. Where the streets have been pleasant, the market turns into a dark and dank place of swarming flies over bloody meat stalls and rotted vegetable refuse laying un-swept along the aisles. The spice stalls are an interesting contrast, however. We purchase vanilla beans, peppercorns and coffee beans that, if you bend very close, reward you with their rich fragrance. We find the source of the robust rum that Monte Cristo had shared with us there in Chagos. The bottles we take to the distillery are filled with its golden distillation. It makes a wonderful essence of vanilla. With a few vanilla beans submerged in its dense ambrosia, it continues to flavor many delicate dishes in my kitchen these many years.

With *Winsome* we visit surrounding bays, barter for some of their embroidered tablecloths and enjoy meals at local restaurants. One evening, a comic episode unfolds offshore the restaurant porch where we are supping. We watch a canoe being paddled just off the beach with two large women shouldering the paddles through the water. The comedy of this drama is that the canoe is floating, but submerged a few inches below the surface of the water. Why it doesn't sink, we can't understand. Is it a 'deadhead log' like those of the Brunei coast? These paddlers, waist-deep in water, continue their voyage as if buoyancy is no problem.

Nearby, a small refuge for lemurs is sanctuary for these monkey-like gentle creatures. While softly resting on our shoulder, the long striped bushy tail dangling behind, they gently take a banana from our grip with their long furry fingers, peel it and eat it. Their big soft eyes make them much more appealing than the nasty monkeys we encountered in Java and India.

Time to check out and head south for Durban, South Africa. Again we discuss the pros and cons with the customs official about the bribe he is asking. We finally pay the fee realizing, perhaps this is his only source of income. It's November 22, we are sailing down the coast of Madagascar, inside the reef, along the track that Steve most likely struggled in fear his last days . . . . a sail of sorrow.

We estimate the trip to Durban is about two thousand miles. We enjoy a port tack with the wind urging us on day after sunny day. Staying in contact with several of our friends who are en route on this same path, we try to determine the course of the Mozambique Current that streams south. According to our friends, the current seems to be coursing closer to the African coast. Our waypoints are along the coast of Madagascar in a line to Juan de

Nova, a small French island at the middle of the hourglass configuration of these two landmasses - Madagascar and Africa. From here, we are swept along with the current as it makes a path in our direction.

There are two periods of three days each when the Navy douses the GPS navigation in order that routine updates and maintenance to the satellite system can be carried out. This puts us back to the old sextant drills when, once again, we question the accuracy of our bearings to determine our Line Of Position. At each return of the GPS we are satisfied when our dead reckoning and sextant skills have been close to confirming the latitudes and longitudes the GPS provides.

We are now closing on Durban - only two hundred more miles to go. It is a sunny day and sailing is going well when over the radio, a message is relayed that a '**buster**' is heading our way. We've heard of these dramatic wind shifts that will, in an instant, reverse their direction and become a major headache to a well-planned trip. We are about to face this new test of the sailing skills of *Horizon* and her crew. The sunny day with moderate winds suddenly, within a half-hour, has lost its blue sky to pull across that space overhead, heavy blankets of clouds harnessing formidable powers of forty-knot winds. These winds from the SW are provoking the Mozambique Current coming from the North creating steep, raucous seas that raise a formidable wall ahead of us. By nightfall we are well into storms with winds of forty to forty-five knots with dizzying seas slowing our progress. These last months there had been a lot of discussion over coffee cups as we sat in protected harbors, about the best procedures to follow when faced with these contrary conditions. Now is the time to make use of this information.

With the shore of Africa offering refuge from SW winds, we sail towards the coast, not only to get its protection, but also to be released from this current producing these high, square seas. With the help of radar to monitor our position, we decide to 'heave to' just offshore. With the smaller trysail raised that spills gusts of wind in combination with the helm tied down, we stay relatively stationary in this water, free of the current. Although the chilly wind coming from Antarctica continues to howl, the water here does offer less ferocity. We continue to be deluged with cold blinding sheets of rain that allow only minimal visibility. With the radar working, we can see the coastline outlined ten miles ahead of us.

It is surprising how calm and quiet the cabin remains when we close ourselves in its fragile protection. I often marvel at this phenomenon of feeling safe in this cocoon, when my better judgment tells me we are sitting ducks out here in a storm. The sounds of the storm become muffled and the tossing about we experience topsides somehow seems diminished as we huddle below. Nevertheless, we realize if we close the boat tightly, it essentially becomes a bottle that will float around in tossing seas and remains relatively safe if we stay away from solid objects like land.

The wind is blowing us away from this coast and eventually we are blown into the rough water of the current again. Then we are topsides once more as Don goes to the helm, releases it and steers, as I work the sail. We try, with the help of the engine running, but with great difficulty, to pull the bow of the boat through the wind and back towards shore again. There are times we just can't get the boat to do this, to 'come about', and have to give in to gybing. This action slaps the sail across the bow with alarming ferocity as the wind sweeps across the stern. About every two hours all night long, we struggle out of our cocoon to the turbulence topsides to repeat the process. It's cold exhausting work. Our foul weather gear isn't keeping us dry or warm in all this storm and fury.

For eighteen hours the wind and waves continue to add to the bluster of this Buster. It's then we decide not to fight the elements any longer. We'll let the storm push us back north to a bay in Mozambique we had noticed on our charts. We'll wait out the remnants of the storm in its protected water. The waves are huge as we surf down their faces. We maneuver with heightened tension as we try to keep the stern quarter addressing these breaking waves. The bay now opens to the West. With a great deal of caution and constant looking over our shoulders, we swing the helm to make a move into the bay, timing our turn so we won't be broached as the boat presents the full length of her hull to these waves and wind. With crests breaking on our port stern quarter, we surf ahead into the bay and float ahead over flat water. As soon as we feel we are out of the path of shipping, we drop the anchor and immediately drop ourselves exhausted, onto the bunks to sleep. Next morning the storm has passed and favorable winds once more beckon us to continue towards Durban.

We are making good time with sunny skies once again. We can't believe it when again the radio warns of another buster forming as we are approaching Richards Bay. We are not slow learners or gluttons for punishment. We plot the shortest course and make a beeline for this harbor instead of Durban. It is dark when we make out the large breakwater that protects this harbor. The lights are confusing. After several wrong approaches, we finally figure out the channel lights and scoot through the entrance between the high walls. It's midnight by the time we follow the channel to tie up along the dock wall. We're in South Africa and we are safe.

The only way to accommodate all the offices required to complete the customs/immigration/agriculture/health pratique is by expensive taxi. No two offices are located close to each other. Finally, spending the entire day at this, Don returns to the boat thinking all is fine. We visit some of our friends docked at the marina nearby and enjoy lunch aboard *Winsome*. We make plans to get together in Durban at Christmas. Now Don has to reverse the paper work to leave the harbor. More taxi rides and he is back. As we loosen the dock lines to leave, an official is running down the dock waving his arms, papers in hand. 'You can't leave, your papers are not in order.' The *right* tax stamp in the *right* corner of the *right* paper has not been duly carried out. Don is growling under his breath, 'Not in order. What does the guy mean?' Evidently the order in which the papers are stamped holds a certain significance - gr-r-r. So the rest of the day is spent with Don again going through the offices in the prescribed order. Finally, with no regrets, we shake their dust from our shoes the next morning and hurry on to Durban. This confusing and complex procedure tends to dog us at every port we enter here in South Africa. With all the extreme weather patterns this coast dish up, the officialdom here does little to make departure an easy, swift or safe process. I guess we expected more efficiency in this country instead of the confusion that has been the hallmark of less organized countries.

We see the prominent stone jetties marking the entrance to Durban and proceed towards them in choppy, uncomfortable water. Out of nowhere a siren sounds with lights blinking ahead. We repeat our call to the harbormaster and are told to wait until they give us the green light. This is the first harbor we've seen that has a stop light at the entrance. It has a narrow entrance with a lot of shipping traffic passing through that evidently warrants such a light; it's a one-ship passage. We douse the sails and motor in circles until we see the green light, then pass into the waterway. Following the channel markers we make our way to the small international dock where sailboats are rafted together - six deep. It is free dockage for a month but we choose, after one day, to settle into an assigned slip, here called a 'walk-on'. Crawling over lifelines of six yachts to get ashore is not fun. Neither is it safe from pilfering. Sometime during the only day we are tied here, someone has stolen from our deck two strong lines we had removed from our jib sail. Inquiries just brought blank stares. Point Yacht Club has a walk-on available. We feel fortunate. The Yacht Club, with its great dining room serving fine cuisine, available showers and hauling out facilities, stretches its amenities along a main thoroughfare of this bustling city of Durban.

Jimmie is running down the dock to greet us. She is *Sunshine*. Her good information about the glories awaiting this salty bunch here in the bustling city of Durban - supermarkets, laundries, restaurants and malls, all within walking distances is welcome news to yachts long-at-sea. Hardware and marine stores also are within reasonable proximity to supply the mechanical and technical support our captains surely need after these months of duct tape and wire being the only available maintenance supplies.

A lot of these friends followed our radio transmissions describing the buster experience. They now inquire if the knowledge that had been shared as common conversation among all of us, was useful. We made use of all we remembered, we tell them.

When we complete, once again, the whole complicated customs process and sign in at the yacht club, there is a message waiting at the desk. Joao and Ligia are waiting to show us around their country. These two kids have captured our hearts. Perhaps it grows from all the great times we have shared in anchorages over the past few years, or perhaps it is their youthful exuberance that reminds us of our own four kids, about the age of Joao and Ligia. Whatever the reason, we continue sharing in their generosity and friendship. They returned to South Africa, completing their own circumnavigation, setting a record for the youngest couple to do so from South Africa. They returned to Johannesburg to continue their professions - Joao an engineer and Ligia doing well in Real Estate. *Solmar*, their steel boat, sits high and dry at a near-by marina with a 'for sale' sign swinging from its lifelines.

They show us around this large city where modern shopping centers and luxurious hotels cater to the tourist trade with vacation packages at the beautiful beaches nearby. Continuing north away from the bustle of Durban, we drive through the green, rolling 'thousand hills' countryside that is home to the Zulus. We are passing picturesque settings, many homes built in the traditional and distinctive Colonial Dutch style with landscapes of lovely gardens and trees. Scattered a bit apart are the shantytowns with hovels crowded together in squalid conditions, displaying the contradiction that is such a part of this country's troubled history.

We are witnessing a part of current history as the Codessa Congress is in session now. We watch on TV, these sessions that have opened dialogue among the many tribes and the ruling whites. There seems to be an effort for resolving a century of repression, to find accommodation for a better life for everyone. It doesn't sound easy, but we are impressed with the intelligent and well-spoken representatives of the majority black population. Our prayers are that this will be a beginning to not only better understanding but also to changes in the way these multi-racial and tribal forces can come together in tolerance and respect.

Christmas is approaching. It's Friday the 20th. We have a date to haul *Horizon* out of the water. It's a tight little corner where the ramp with a hoist is located. We are lifted high and dry on the lot by the yacht club. Braces are adjusted to support us in place. Sitting here with tree tops close by and cars driving under us, we look over the wall protecting the marina, to see the city of Durban busy at work, offering us a different perspective of the world. No sooner are the supports in place than a hand full of black men have gathered underneath asking for food or money. Only James asks if he can work for us. He is hired. A quiet man who appears anxious to please us, he helps us scrub and scrape the bottom in preparation for another paint job. For two weeks he worked, sanding teak for $1 an hour. I felt cheap offering this wage. I heard via a grapevine that I was overpaying him, making it hard for other 'employers'. There is always a group of men lying about below the boat that pose a formidable flank each time we leave the boat. I become known as 'the good lady' because peanut butter sandwiches are often lowered from above. Don meanwhile, has been busy installing new parts and repairing old ones. The electric autopilot has been taken in for repairs after many miles of steering us through storms and across smooth seas. The erratic sat-nav also went to the shop to correct its confusing habits. When it's repaired, it will be a back-up to the GPS. With a high tide required to float away from this ramp, it will be a two-week stay aboard here, high and dry, with air the only buoyancy quotient offered.

It's Christmas once again. This is our fifth Christmas celebration cradled in the sanctuary of another land, far from home. New Zealand, Marshall Islands, Palau and Malaysia have each shown to us the ecumenicity of this celebration. With our Christmas decorations on Horizon sometimes gracing a lovely piece of coral or glittering on a bouquet of beach blossoms, it has continued, all these years, to be festive. Here in Durban, a group of six couples have been invited to celebrate at the home of a local sailor and his family. These South Africans are great cooks. We enjoy a heavy-laden table of turkey and ham with all the trimmings. There is no snow to be seen here at 30 degrees south of the equator - only snowy blossoms crowning the trees with summer elegance just emerging.

Another occasion that calls for camaraderie is the outdoor BBQ that is a weekly feature in most households. Here, however it is called a 'braii.' The grill will be covered, not only with steak, but chicken and bratwurst as well, filling the air with all their tantalizing aromas. We are invited regularly to join in these friendly braiis. We discover, when we arrive around the Cape,

211

there will be more of the same with new friends waiting on the West Coast.

Celebrating the New Year on *Quicksticks* with Sharon and Peter, South African friends, we watch flares and fireworks decorating the skies. Resolutions made, we make plans to drop once more into the water from our perch in the boatyard on the 3rd of January. *Horizon* revels, as she is immersed into this natural environment once again. The feel of gentle rocking becomes her favorite companion in a more familiar setting.

Joao and Ligia are back in a week to continue as our personal travel guides to the Blyde River Canyon. This is a deep, rocky gorge with surrounding cliffs overlooking miles of forests and green hills. From rocky outcroppings, we see spectacular vistas across the canyons to distant hills of the Transvaal area. They have arranged our stay at a lovely cottage in a park nearby. Since we had done a safari in Kenya we choose not to visit the Kruger National game park close by. Instead, we drive inland four hundred miles to Johannesburg to see their new home and become acquainted with each of their families. Both families were forced to flee Mozambique with only the clothes on their backs when the civil war erupted there, confirming their unceasing affection for this country they now call home. South Africa offered them shelter when life looked pretty bleak. We leave them to take a bus back through this fascinating country to Durban. It's time to plan our sail around the Cape.

A nearby marine store close to Point Yacht Club is offering to the international sailing community here, free lectures designed to aid in decisions that have to made when contemplating the Cape sail. We take notes on weather patterns, the position of the Agulhas Current, plus the waypoints for easy harbors that offer refuge. The history of challenging sailing conditions this Cape produces gives an opportunity for the lectures to be laced with a number of horror stories that continue to circulate through our group. Hidden amidst the scare tactics we think we can find valuable information. However, we still feel a new apprehension about this trip we haven't felt before - a feeling of 'waiting for the other shoe to drop' - as the many stories of this treacherous coast linger in our thoughts.

In preparation, Don has raised the storm sail on its track so it's available, with a quick hoist, to use in place of the mainsail, if the high winds start pounding us. We also take down the wind generator and the solar panels that would take a beating in high winds. There are twelve gerry jugs, eight gallons each, of extra fuel tied to the lifelines. We finish the last grocery shopping as we wait for favorable conditions to leave the harbor.

The complicated checking-out system employed here allows us thirty-six hours of waiting time after completing the process, but then you must be gone. The weather forecasts delivered daily by radio are very good, we keep touch with these as departure approaches. When the barometer starts rising from a low, Don makes the rounds to carry out the required paperwork so that, as the barometer is reaching a high, we will loose the dock lines, wave a farewell to good friends and leave the harbor. It's Tuesday Jan.28, about noon, and it looks right. We're going.

Memories penned in Mary Lou's journal.

The navigation station keeps us on track with its GPS, weather fax, ham radio and chart table to occupy Don's hours.

South Africa Capes

CHAPTER 18
TO CAPTURE THE CAPE

The moderate wind from the southwest is frustrating our progress as we try to sail into it. With the help of the engine we are able to make about four knots. By nightfall, as the wind gains strength, we bear off the wind so that the staysail will add its muscle to the motor. We begin tacking across the wind, back and forth, as we try to stay within a ten-mile margin along the coast. We plan to stay away from the threatening current conditions further offshore. It looks like this 800-mile junket is going to be a long journey. Several hours after departing Durban, the electric autopilot starts erratic movements that have the boat wandering a drunken path along the coast. It isn't long until it whirr-rrs and gr-r-rinds. It is refusing to hold a course and stops working all together. This is the autopilot we just had repaired in Durban. When comparing notes with other sailors later in Hout Bay, there is a general consensus that the repairs made in this country are less than satisfactory. That sat-nav we had repaired here has, likewise, failed to perform. The quality of South African expertise in repairs gets a low score in our book.

Our course calls for 180 degrees, directly into the wind, so the Aries that uses the wind for steering is useless in this direction. With no automatic steering working, we will now be standing or sitting at the helm the entire eight hundred miles; the first time we have had to suffer this wearying procedure since leaving the States five years ago. With some experimentation we decide four-hour shifts on and off a watch will allow us time to rest and not get too tired. Our slow progress back and forth across the heading towards Cape Elizabeth at the southeastern tip of Africa seems to insure a tortuous passage.

We are sailing just offshore as slowly the winds sag to mere whispers. We drop the sail. The engine now serves its monotonous background presence to the voyage. No need to tack, our path unfolds as we steer a direct line between waypoints. The voyage has become a sightseers' cruise as we watch the flickering night lights of the coastal towns float by us. In contrast to the crash-um bash-um predictions of this coast's history, we are not about to complain of such placid conditions.

We pass Cape Elizabeth, a haven port some three hundred and fifty miles south of Durban and decide to keep going, since this weather formula is better then we could have hoped for. As the days stretch into each other, we are reminded of the legend of the goddess Alcyone. Her grieving father decreed days of calm and unruffled seas to shelter the birds, *halcyon*. Angry gods had transformed his daughter who had married a mortal into these birds, symbolized as kingfishers. Eventually legends surrounding this story associate the peaceful sound of this word, halcyon, to signify windless days of calm serenity. So we are motor-sailing halcyon days along this coast that holds a frightening maritime history.

The landscape that flows by is so varied. At times we see green fields stretching inland. Then in contrast, further along the coast, there are high escarpments with their flat tops dropping suddenly to waves crashing ashore. Late one evening as we look towards land with the afterglow of a sunset reaching brilliant fingers overhead, there is stitched along the fringe where water meets sand, hundreds of pelicans flowing in one uninterrupted line. With a smooth flowing wave that undulates for at least a mile, they stitch a fascinating embroidery that outlines the shoreline with a perfect ballet of synchronized flight.

Next morning with fair weather continuing to prevail, we turn southwest to skirt the southern coast of Africa. As we look over the flat water there seem to be logs ahead. We cautiously navigate to miss them. There seems to be movement. Approaching we recognize a raised flipper with its wrist flopping about and a small tail flipper just poking out of the water at the opposite end. A shiny head with beautiful brown and watery eyes, slowly raises out of the water to peer and study us a bit before lazily rolling over - it disappears. The water is alive with sea otters frolicking in childlike abandon, splashing and diving around us.

During my watch, one night, with the sky clear and stars thrown across the heavens, suddenly, off the port beam, I see a torpedo shape at least eight feet long. With blazing brilliance it is streaking towards our mid-ship. This huge shape is glowing with the plankton phosphorescence we have witnessed on many night watches. As I stare, there seems to be no way I can steer to avoid this missile. It's coming with such speed - aimed for the side of our hull. I watch, horrified, as this glowing shape reaches the boat. I freeze in dismay, then gasp in wonder when the boat continues its path with nary a quiver. Looking on the starboard side, there, leaving with just as much speed, are three dolphins spinning through the water to outline our wake, weaving luminous paths. It's amazing. Dressed in this cloak of neon, they continue to play with the bow wave. This is the first time such beauty of nature has displayed its brilliance in such a spectacular yet alarming array. There are episodes during the day when a hundred or more dolphin will be leaping across the water as others turn somersaults in the air. One evening Don saw a long line of them surfing together down the slope of a huge swell. Surfers without surfboards moving in concert along the crest. They always make our day. True or not, we think of them as harbingers of good luck. As they play with the bow wave, it's almost as if we have harnessed a team of prancing horses to guide us safely to a new harbor.

The weather fax confirms the excellent reports we have been receiving from a land based ham operator. Alistair makes available not only this good weather information, but with a daily radio check, he maintains a log for each boat making the passage around the Cape. As darkness is approaching, we see noted on the chart a protected bay ahead. It offers an easy entrance that can shelter us for a catch-up night of rest. St. Francis Bay is visible on the radar. We use that information in conjunction with the chart depths to guide us around the headland where we drop the anchor in 15 feet of water, a steep hill in front for protection. The rest feels great. We are refreshed to continue next morning with the wind still bashful. Those gerry jugs of fuel, tied along the lifelines, hold the key to success, as we continue motoring. We follow this path along the southern coast of this huge continent and decide to pull into Mossel Bay. We are about half way between Cape Elizabeth to the East and The Cape of Good Hope to the West. It's a large open bay with a town along its shore where smokestacks belch billowing smoke across the water. We move deep into the bay near an outcrop of large rocks that seem to have a motion of their own in the afternoon sun. As we approach, we see a twisting mass revealing hundreds of seals either basking or pushing each other to a game of slide and dunk into the water - alive with their antics. Since we are not at all anxious to do the South African Customs dance again, we just stay aboard and relax from the steering marathon this trip has become. With soot from those smokestacks blanketing the decks, we are more than ready to push on after a two-day rest.

As the globe has revolved under us these five years, we recognize we are about to pass our southernmost sailing point on this circumnavigation. Cape Agulhas at thirty-four degrees South has us tipping our hats to this prominent rocky headland, a salute to its presence on our chart homewards.

Now we can turn to the northwest. Recalling my grade school geography lessons when I read about the Cape of Good Hope, I look in awe as we sail past this more modest signature Cape rising from Africa's rocky coast. Geography books come alive. It is here we make that definitive turn North.

We will now begin the final leg to that point of origin where this journal had its beginning. As we glide past, we are sailing once more with winds from the East filling the sails. This puts us on a fast track, between squalls, to dash a path into the spectacular setting of Hout Bay just south of Cape Town. Mountainsides rising in sheer cliffs on both sides of the bay, harbor a school of otters guiding us ahead with their flippers waving us on. It is almost a nostalgic feel that we could be sailing in Colorado with Rocky Mountains beckoning a familiar memory. There just ahead we see the unique silhouette of Table Mountain etched against the sky. Today it's wearing a lacy tablecloth of faint clouds spilling over the table edge. Tree filled valleys swoop down from its dramatic height to the long sandy beach before us. Hidden to the left side of Hout Bay, is the protected marina and fishing wharves. And reminiscent of PagoPago is the aroma of fish canneries huddled in one corner of the bay. Their distinctive pungency in the air changes with each wind shift.

Directing us via the ham radio, Lyle from *Cookie Cutter*, talked us into the assigned slip. There, Peter and Ann Elise on *Nori* welcome us. They know us, they say, from conversations with Joao and Ligia with whom they had sailed across the Atlantic many years ago. Like vines spreading across the continents, the world becomes intertwined with these friendships. As they grow we are tied together with new and lasting acquaintances. These new friends help us adjust the lines at the dock and warn of the williwaws, strong winds that dash down the mountainsides at speeds up to fifty knots. They encourage us to add chaffing gear to the dock lines that can strain to the breaking point. They thoughtfully leave us so that we might rest and make things ship shape once more.

It's Friday. We decide to just lay low and tackle the checking-in process on Monday. This has to be carried out in Cape Town, a forty-five minute bus ride away. We venture forth and pay our marina dues here that give us access to hot showers close by. By Saturday morning we are anxious to get some exercise. With backpacks strapped over our shoulders, we wander the tidy streets of Hout Bay, looking for the markets. After many wrong turns and growing frustration, a lady watering flowers in her front yard corrects our misguided ways and points us in the right direction. With the small shopping center now in view, we stop to drop off rolls of film for developing, then walk on to the large supermarket. Standing at the doorway is the lady who had just given us good directions. She had gotten in her car to pick us up, but couldn't find us. Our stop in the photo shop, no doubt, caused us to miss each other. Again, we are touched by the courteous gestures offered us many times. I remember standing on a busy street corner in Durban, waiting for the light to change. While conversing with the lady waiting beside me, I found an invitation for dinner at her home being offered. To the wanderers of the sailing community they offer their hands, smiles and homes with such ease. We continue to be welcomed to braiis and tours whenever we drop our anchors in their midst.

As we wait at the bus stop Monday morning, a car stops to offer us a ride to Cape Town. Steve and Cheryl with their two small sons, Sean and Ross, are going to the same offices we seek. However, they are checking out of South Africa, their home, to sail to the States aboard their small catamaran, *Ruffian*. The drive along the craggy coastline presents a spectacular view at each turn of the road. The water of the Atlantic is a vivid blue-green. I don't remember seeing such brilliance before. The word 'aquamarine' is defined for me with this new color splashed on our palette. With the waves dashing their frothing spume to catch rainbows against the rocky shore, I am reminded of the seascape off Carmel, California all those years ago, when Don did his internship in San Francisco. As we descend from the coastline hills to the city of Cape Town ahead, we drive through an area of elegant seaside homes. The skyscrapers of the city outlining the undulating hills behind them. With the help of Steve, the checking-in process runs so much smoother than we've endured to date. A quick tour of the downtown stores and location of marine repair shops we might need, makes this a profitable day. We share with this family excited about their new adventure, a delightful meal at a fascinating dockside promenade. Subsequent bus trips to Cape Town never fail to thrill us with the spectacular views the coastline trail offers.

Since we had done the major provisioning chore at Durban, we plan to spend our time here on the Atlantic Coast playing and touring. I'm glad we had this task completed, because hauling and storing the quantities of groceries required for a long ocean passage present more problems here.

On a sunny, clear day we take a cable car that climbs up the side of Table Mountain, to spend the day hiking the level top. Surrounding us along the perimeter of this unique formation are outstanding views of the ocean stretching endlessly to the West. As we walk further along the tabletop, the bustling city of Cape Town nestled around its base to the North and East glistens with light colored buildings. There in the distance, amidst eucalyptus groves are the villages stretching to Hout Bay on the South. Rocky and barren, with the wind sweeping across this rather forlorn expanse, we find refuge as we tarry for tea at the lovely restaurant nestled among the rocks on this tabletop.

There is a knock on the hull a few days later. The smiling faces of Ligia and Joao have tracked us down once more. They have driven over twenty-four hours from Jo'burg, to offer us still more views of the outstanding scenery at the base of this magnificent continent. With the benefit of the use of their friend's condo for lodging, we drive south along the coast we had recently sailed along, to climb the rocks that mark the Cape of Good Hope. I marvel many times the different perspective the views from land reveals, compared to those from the deck of Horizon. Up here, the view of the gull lends distance to my gaze, while cradled close to the waves, eight miles is as far as I can see. Up here, I see generalities of shapes and shades; at ship level distinctions become clear, however limited in scope. To us this is a special spot on the globe. A sense of accomplishment is stirring in our bones. There is a feeling that we may just complete this voyage. My continuing course in adult education has attained a new level.

Were there doubts in my mind five years ago? Did I doubt my will to accomplish such an undertaking? A step at a time, I remind myself. With each step trying the ground - in this case, the water - ahead, I uncovered strengths unknown that filled my days with courage to continue. Had Don not pushed, no doubt, these discovered strengths might still be searching for definition. However, I still lack the same enthusiasm he has for this lifestyle. I yearn for space, long for my piano, and miss the proximity to family that have all been points on my compass. But our sharing this place with Joao and Ligia who have experienced the exhilaration and the terror of sailing the many oceans, is a special bond that will remain a treasured gift. We finish the day enjoying a quiet little German restaurant. Here we are served bowls of huge, green mussels that we dip into a creamy sauce accompanied with crusty bread - delicious.

The next morning we are off to the east of Cape Town towards rolling hills where geometric patterns create three dimensional depths with vineyards stretching diagonal rows across the slopes. Driving through the town of Paarl, we pass carts moving in long lines to the family wineries. Almost overflowing the slatted sides, the glistening green and white grapes, their translucence shimmering like jewels where the morning sun touches their dewy cascades, promise a fine vintage. Names like Neethlinghof, Delheim and Simonsig are some of the estates we visit. Tours of their winemaking capabilities with invitations to taste their wine before we leave do persuade us to purchase fine vintages.

The landscapes are so beautiful and tranquil, it's hard to realize there simmers distrust and anger among these hills and valleys. So many of the white population are finding ways to leave. We have been aware of those planning to use boats as means for this flight. Joao and Ligia, however, plan to stay and work. They are such an engaging couple, full of enthusiasm - just the kind of folks needed to help rebuild a nation. Sadly, we will be parting tomorrow. When our paths will cross again may depend entirely upon that karma we once found blessing our days. So many memories! South Africa has surprised us with its natural beauty and the hospitality of its folks. It is shared with such spontaneity and generosity. Vistas opened - never close.

Some days at the marina in Hout Bay, we are almost crawling on all fours to get to our boat. They haven't exaggerated about these winds dashing down the slopes that play havoc with dock lines. Later in the week as we continue checking the forecasts, the weather has taken a favorable turn. It prompts us to make the rounds to finish that cursed paper work. Fortunate or not, we're not sure, we find an inexperienced official who, with a nod, sends us on our way. We hope it's sufficient to get us into the next country. We understand there are some customs offices that will not accept a clearance from South Africa, especially small countries with a predominately black population. So we'll see. In fact, when we check our passports, there has not been a stamp for South Africa entered anywhere.

We share smiles with a zulu lass.

Joao and Ligia join us at the lookout over the Cape of Good Hope.

South Atlantic to North Atlantic

CHAPTER 19
ONE MORE OCEAN

It's March 3rd. We leave these mountainous confines of Hout Bay into the wind that promises, when we proceed around the headland, to put us on a broad reach. We continue putting distance between us and the rocky South African coast. With a heading that takes us West for sixty miles, we then turn NNW and push ahead towards St. Helena Island, two thousand miles ahead. For most of this voyage these past five years our waypoints have stretched across the longitudes of the globe; now on this new heading it will be latitudes crossed that will carve a path North to home. With the ham radio once again functioning as information center, we discover about a half dozen other boats are making this slide homeward. None are in sight, but it's nice to travel with other voices sharing the morning radio patch.

This southwest wind pushes us on a broad reach as we make five to six knots. It's a comfortable point of sail. The days begin to stretch one into the other with distance made good in the range of one hundred twenty to one hundred thirty-five miles each twenty-four hour period. The sky is sunny during the day and the starry nights continue to stretch over us in opulent splendor. It has always astonished me that this mantle of jewels stretching overhead continues to hold me in its spell after all these years of abiding beneath its magnificence. One never tires of its inspiration. I ponder why this *starshine* holds such a fascination for me compared to my routine acceptance of *sunshine*. The mystery of space has chapters added when I look overhead into the Milky Way and realize I am just one small spot in its vast wheel. The sun, on the other hand, envelops me in a blanket of brilliance that shelters my cocoon and holds my small place in the world . . . my feet are grounded.

As the days stretch one into the other, we find the books we traded in South Africa are a blessing, helping to distract from that sameness of the horizon with its persistent hazy presence. Conversations on the ham radio each morning with other sailboats straining to race to St. Helena, keeps a competitive edge to the voyage. Our logs register distances which challenge the choice of sails we hoist, offering another quotient to stimulate strategy and consequently excite the gray matter.

When I turn to gaze behind us, I see a wavering remnant from the wake streaming behind *Horizon* as it courses across this watery surface. In such a short distance, the face of the sea tosses aside our ripples to parade her own complexion once more, as if to boast no hull can permanently crease a wrinkle in her skin. Looking towards that point from where we've come, it's as if we have ceased to exist. The following waves roll on behind us as if our presence never disturbed their direction or movement. But then, glancing forward, our bow wave is displaying, with exuberance, outlines of spray breaking in ruffles along the hull, bubbling with enjoyment as it cuts a definite course across the latitudes, unaware that behind us, no remnant remains. The remains of our day are only momentary. This fickle sea cares not a whit that we have enjoyed its buoyancy. We've left no trail across this sea that it considers significant. But the sea cannot remove the trails across our minds this journey has inscribed for a lifetime.

Perhaps to shake us out of the daydreaming this pleasant sailing is fostering, we are now faced with sail changes to accommodate the squalls pouncing on us. Some push us down with sudden blasts of thirty or more knots. The sunny skies are off to other places and have left behind a blanket of lumpy clouds. Although this grayness persists, the wind settles down after two days, to push us ahead with its steady energy. We aren't about to complain about the ride this offers. We are sailing downwind with the staysail poled out on the starboard side and the big ol' jib poled on the port side, 'wing on wing', just like some big albatross skimming across the waves. The feel however, is more like a waddling duck, as we tick off minutes on the GPS towards the waypoint. Swaying back and forth, this sailing apparatus, called a sailboat, never seems able to manage with any finesse the wind coming from behind. With the slightest variance of the wind to one side, the boat thinks it will start a new tack only to be pulled smartly back by the sail and across the wind to duplicate the delusion on the other tack. With this wind direction, waddling a path towards a compass point seems to be the only course of action it can muster.

Four of our friends hail us on the morning ham session to inform those listening they are planning to stop for a visit at St. Helena, the cloistered prison island of Napoleonic history. We are beyond this point and had decided, when we were fifty miles away, to continue taking advantage of these winds that are showing such a favorable face.

Today is Don's birthday, March 24. He welcomes sixty-five as if it is just another page in a book. But what a book he's written. The equator approaches once again. This great circle on this grand sphere equidistant from either pole reminds me of a Walt Whitman page from his 'Leaves of Grass' that profiles for me Don's passage along the equator. 'Inquiring, tireless, seeking what is yet unfound, I . . . look off the shores of the sea, the circle almost circled. Long having wandered since, round the earth having wandered, Now I face home again very pleased and joyous.' And the insight of Joseph Campbell also defines Don's journey, 'Where we had thought to have traveled outward - we will come to the center of our being.' With plenty of time for contemplation as the winds die and we twist on a flat sea, the focus of just such a journey makes us realize how fortunate we have been. 'Gladness of heart *is* life to man, Joy is what gives him length of days,' sings Solomon in the Old Testament. This is our fortune. And Don gets a lemon sponge pie, 'just like Mom used to make,' to celebrate this new year.

The sails have been our only source of energy for twenty days so we feel we can use the engine to bolster the meager winds around us. In fact, the winds are dying with the threat of that 0 latitude approaching once again. We are now on a definite westerly course just south of the equator, heading towards the coast of Brazil and the tiny island of San Fernando five hundred miles away. A measly two knots of wind is barely filling the sails. Once again this imaginary belt around the belly of the globe lies loose with pitiful winds. We are not surprised when it gives a shrug as if to say, 'It's not my problem, you handle it.' We handle it for a week, using the engine to assist the less than robust sails.

During watches on these long nights, I remember the tales of the *sirens* and their hypnotic appeal with seductive songs to lonely sailors. The noise of wind and water can tease the imagination to lose sight or reason in answer to this temptress and wander with her forever. Yesterday, the month of March ended truly as a lamb. Today, April Fools Day grins at us with cruel delight. We don't seem to be getting the benefit of the current at this latitude that's indicated on the chart. The current's direction should push us on our way. It has surely taunted us . . . we are April's fools.

We've been a month at sea. The ham radio relays a message from the States that we owe $3000 in taxes. Boy, they can find you anywhere in the world. There goes the money we didn't spend this month. It could have, no doubt, gotten us through a second month as well. Easy come - easier go . . . with hardly any effort on our part!

Ten days into April and we are off the mouth of the Amazon River. The wind has returned again. We've shut down the engine to enjoy the quiet peace of hearing the wind in the sails with a background murmur of water rushing along the hull. It never ceases to be an exquisite moment when the rumble of the engine is cut and a magnitude of quiet envelopes me as the wind carries us with determined transport. These butterfly wings of our sails are filled and strain to overcome the encumbrance of the sea. We do seem to fly.

Our chart is inscribed with each day's noon position and the miles traveled. Just curious one day, I retrieve the charts outlining our passage these five years that began at the West door of the Panama Canal to this spot here on the Eastern ocean of the Canal. The spool of thread that unwinds across these charts, noting each days noon latitude and longitude seems to weave into this tapestry of mine, the colors and hues of people, places and moments that are mine alone to treasure. Charts . . places . . people . . happenings . . . penciled on my chart.

Where we were making one hundred miles with the engine, we are now enjoying at least one hundred-fifty miles a day with sails as our generator. A grand total of one hundred-eighty miles covered one day has us shouting for joy. There are squalls accompanying this feast. While we celebrate another one hundred-eighty miles on April 12, we suffer a torn jib in the middle of the night. This has immediately changed the feast to a big bowl of a soggy sea. With only the main and the staysail to do their best, we wallow along at one hundred twenty-five miles each day. Compared to the days we have coursed across the longitudes these last five years, this would have been reason to celebrate a good day's job was accomplished, had we not experienced the delight of streaming across the waves at those magnificent speeds last week.

After six days of this, we decide to hoist the spinnaker. As the sock is released, the full, glorious balloon spreads before the wind once more. With a resounding explosion, it crashes into the sea in tatters. It has succumbed to years of strain and sun. Since it has tried nobly to carry us along the course for twelve years, we think it fitting that a burial at sea be performed. Stuffing it into a similarly tattered sail bag, we tie a rusty anchor around its girth and push its sunset colors overboard to find repose on the ocean bed.

Two days later and forty-six days from Hout Bay, we cross a line that we had sailed once before aboard Horizon - a new line in the sand. From this point off the coast of St. Vincent in the Windward Islands of the Caribbean, our waypoints will be tracing familiar territory once again. Can I consider this the complete circumnavigation? It is Easter, 1 a.m. My watch is just over as we cross this line. I gaze up to the heavens and say a prayer of thanks as this amazing journey overwhelms me with its gifts of discovery. Again the words of Joseph Campbell sum the parts, 'When you're addressing yourself to the horizon, to the world you're in, Then you're in your place in the world . . . It's a different way to live'. We have stripped away the trappings of a productive life to one more attuned to contemplation. Life has taken on the equation of simple denominators that stimulates a new awareness of simple pleasures. To be comfortable in these small quarters, to share this domain with Don, invites a different approach to who I am and a search for some pattern to shape my thoughts and actions. To have spent time with Tavita, Uromo, Carolina, Joao and Ligia and so many more friends sharing space on this fragile globe and feel the bond we share, a commonality of ideas that take shape in culturally varied expressions, reassures me of man's basic goodwill.

The Aries is steering a course to pass east of St. Croix. A feeling surging through our 'numb bums' that a reprieve from the confines of this cocoon we so eagerly began this journey in, is now upon us. With the poor distressed sails doing their best and the engine coughing and sputtering as it feels the sludge of fungus coursing along its fuel line, we realize a port is becoming a necessity. Losing our focus we almost run aground as the long arm of a shallow bank extends from the east coast of St. Croix. Where the depth sounder has been dealing with depths beyond its capabilities, suddenly we see ten feet registering on the dial. We make a hasty course change that saves what can be a frustrating job to free the boat from the clutches of a seabed.

By noon Tuesday, the 21st of April, 1992 we are tied to the customs dock at St. Thomas. Forty-eight days at sea . "Too many days at sea," Don says. His efforts to convince me to stop along the way went unheeded. He patiently put up with my determination to put this journey behind us. 'And the Captain has to take his orders from the Admiral, you know,' is the litany I will have to live with my remaining days. Customs cleared, we move the boat to the large anchorage and dinghy to shore, barely crawling to a nearby Wendy's fast food where we take advantage of the fresh salad bar, refilling our plates with these green vitamins - almost heaven. Regaining strength in our leg muscles and returning to normal sleeping patterns have us back to paying attention to the boat's demands. With sail repairs scheduled, cleaning the infected fuel tanks and installing new filters, our sources of energy are taken care of. Now, while I make grocery stocking my priority, Don dons snorkel and fins to remove the barnacles clinging to the new paint job we had carefully added while in Durban just five months ago. All of the above glitches have considerably slowed our progress these last days.

But now, Sunday, after five days of rest, we plan to leave on the final leg to the Bahamas. For two days we are sailing with reasonably good conditions, when a gale from the northeast roars down on us. We are forced to tack across our path to gain any progress. The thirty-knot winds are churning intimidating, frothing seas that allow us to chart only thirty-six miles in twenty-four hours. What I had envisioned as a coast downhill has turned into a discouraging mountain climb. But we persevere and claw our way across these cliffs.

Just as suddenly, conditions change. Saturday is arriving. Now we need to slow our speed to arrive at San Salvador in daylight. Not only are the winds pushing us, there is a current adding its measure. Slowing this wind machine is like reigning in a team of wild horses. Where was all this help when I needed it? Don somehow manages frustrating sea conditions better than I do. He chuckles at my attempts to curse Poseidon.

Anchored off the village of Cockburntown on San Salvador, we finish the customs procedure and become aware that this island is in a party mood. They are celebrating the voyage of another sailor who, they claim, five hundred years ago first set foot on their small island in the New World. Our voyage, by comparison, has been achieved with new technologies of navigation, with easy resources for making fresh water from seawater, with refrigeration and with a small boat that can maneuver around shallow banks and complex coasts. These luxuries make us aware of the difficulties these early mariners faced, and validate what extraordinary men they were to fulfill their passion for discovery using the latest tools they possessed to accomplish their daring dreams. We realize a certain humility in our own achievement as we contemplate this place. We have reached *beyond the realms of morning* and have discovered a new daylight offering possibilities.

A week is spent returning to favorite haunts in the Bahamas that still please us with the clarity and beauty of the waters, as beautiful as any we have seen these last five years. Remembering waving farewell five and a half years ago to Bob and Marilyn as we left the dock at Ft Lauderdale, the circle is complete when we share hugs and congratulations with these two as they greet us at a favorite anchorage on Highbourne Cay in the Bahamas.

Just a phone call and we have our custom clearance into Miami, May 28, 1992, the fastest and easiest clearance in years. We are trying to realize we have done it, we have completed this journey of our lifetime. A journey of thirty thousand miles that has registered a new awareness about my place on this planet. Misgivings that filled those beginning views stretching West from Panama gradually were missing from my logs and journals, supplanted each day with new views of the world replacing old stereotypes. It is an emotional experience not clearly defined with words. Our small barque content to claim the speed of a butterfly, seemed satisfied to drift across the oceans until the land came home to us once more.

" We shall not cease from exploration and the end of all our exploring will be to arrive where we started and know the place for the first time." So said T.S. Eliot.

Then the moment of ecstatic freedom came.
The peace, the end of the quest, the last harbor,
the joy of belonging to a fulfillment
beyond greedy fears and hopes and dreams.
I became the sun, the hot sand,
green seaweed anchored to a rock,
swaying in the tide.
Like a saint's vision of beatitude.
I dissolved in the sea
-became white sails and flying spray
- became beauty and rhythm
- became moonlight and the ship
- and the high dim-starred sky.
I belong
- without past or future,
-within peace and unity and a wild joy,
-within something greater than my own life.

from 'A Long Day's Journey into Night'
by Eugene O'Neill

ACKNOWLEDGMENTS

Friendships arrive 'out of the blue'. Such a friendship is one I treasure. Jim and Hazel (we call her Jimmie) Conant sailed into our lives early in this voyage. The many anchorages we shared around the world gave not a clue to the editorial expertise I would eventually realize and profit by. My appreciation to both of you for your gentle guidance, encouraging me to write a sentence worth reading.

Companionship is another ship I boarded. Don nudged me to join him on this journey of a lifetime. The passage I've written here cannot fully describe the love and encouragement he has enfolded about me. I'm glad to have shared the years with you.

Order Form

To order additional copies, fill out this form and send it along with your check or money order to: Mary L. Miller, 2328 Caracara Dr., New Bern, NC 28560.

Cost per copy $15.00 plus $3.00 P&H.

Ship _____ copies of *Beyond The Realms of Morning* to:

Name_____

Address:_____

Address:_____

Address:_____

❑   **Check box for signed copy**